NATIONAL ACADEMIES *Sciences Engineering Medicine*  NATIONAL ACADEMIES PRESS Washington, DC

Behavioral Economics
Policy Impact and Future Directions

Alison Buttenheim, Robert Moffitt, and Alexandra Beatty, *Editors*

Committee on Future Directions for Applying Behavioral Economics to Policy

Board on Behavioral, Cognitive, and Sensory Sciences

Division of Behavioral and Social Sciences and Education

Consensus Study Report

NATIONAL ACADEMIES PRESS 500 Fifth Street, NW Washington, DC 20001

This activity was supported by contracts between the National Academy of Sciences and Alfred P. Sloan Foundation (G-2020-12645) and the National Institutes of Health (HHSN263201800029I/75N98021F00015), as well as the National Academy of Sciences W.K. Kellogg Foundation Fund. Any opinions, findings, conclusions, or recommendations expressed in this publication do not necessarily reflect the views of any organization or agency that provided support for the project.

International Standard Book Number-13: 978-0-309-69983-9
International Standard Book Number-10: 0-309-69983-5
Digital Object Identifier: https://doi.org/10.17226/26874
Library of Congress Control Number: 2023938915

This publication is available from the National Academies Press, 500 Fifth Street, NW, Keck 360, Washington, DC 20001; (800) 624-6242 or (202) 334-3313; http://www.nap.edu.

Copyright 2023 by the National Academy of Sciences. National Academies of Sciences, Engineering, and Medicine and National Academies Press and the graphical logos for each are all trademarks of the National Academy of Sciences. All rights reserved.

Printed in the United States of America.

Suggested citation: National Academies of Sciences, Engineering, and Medicine. 2023. *Behavioral Economics: Policy Impact and Future Directions*. Washington, DC: The National Academies Press. https://doi.org/10.17226/26874.

The **National Academy of Sciences** was established in 1863 by an Act of Congress, signed by President Lincoln, as a private, nongovernmental institution to advise the nation on issues related to science and technology. Members are elected by their peers for outstanding contributions to research. Dr. Marcia McNutt is president.

The **National Academy of Engineering** was established in 1964 under the charter of the National Academy of Sciences to bring the practices of engineering to advising the nation. Members are elected by their peers for extraordinary contributions to engineering. Dr. John L. Anderson is president.

The **National Academy of Medicine** (formerly the Institute of Medicine) was established in 1970 under the charter of the National Academy of Sciences to advise the nation on medical and health issues. Members are elected by their peers for distinguished contributions to medicine and health. Dr. Victor J. Dzau is president.

The three Academies work together as the **National Academies of Sciences, Engineering, and Medicine** to provide independent, objective analysis and advice to the nation and conduct other activities to solve complex problems and inform public policy decisions. The National Academies also encourage education and research, recognize outstanding contributions to knowledge, and increase public understanding in matters of science, engineering, and medicine.

Learn more about the National Academies of Sciences, Engineering, and Medicine at **www.nationalacademies.org**.

Consensus Study Reports published by the National Academies of Sciences, Engineering, and Medicine document the evidence-based consensus on the study's statement of task by an authoring committee of experts. Reports typically include findings, conclusions, and recommendations based on information gathered by the committee and the committee's deliberations. Each report has been subjected to a rigorous and independent peer-review process and it represents the position of the National Academies on the statement of task.

Proceedings published by the National Academies of Sciences, Engineering, and Medicine chronicle the presentations and discussions at a workshop, symposium, or other event convened by the National Academies. The statements and opinions contained in proceedings are those of the participants and are not endorsed by other participants, the planning committee, or the National Academies.

Rapid Expert Consultations published by the National Academies of Sciences, Engineering, and Medicine are authored by subject-matter experts on narrowly focused topics that can be supported by a body of evidence. The discussions contained in rapid expert consultations are considered those of the authors and do not contain policy recommendations. Rapid expert consultations are reviewed by the institution before release.

For information about other products and activities of the National Academies, please visit www.nationalacademies.org/about/whatwedo.

COMMITTEE ON FUTURE DIRECTIONS FOR APPLYING BEHAVIORAL ECONOMICS TO POLICY

ALISON M. BUTTENHEIM (*Cochair*), Department of Family and Community Health, University of Pennsylvania
ROBERT A. MOFFITT* (*Cochair*), Department of Economics, Johns Hopkins University
STEFANO DELLAVIGNA, Department of Economics, University of California, Berkeley
CATHERINE C. ECKEL, Department of Economics, Texas A&M University
ANGELA FONTES, Fontes Research
JOSHUA S. GRAFF ZIVIN, Department of Economics, University of California, San Diego
RACHEL E. KRANTON,* Department of Economics, Duke University
LEONARD M. LOPOO, Public Administration and International Affairs Department, Syracuse University
ELDAR SHAFIR, Department of Psychology, Princeton University
STACEY SINCLAIR,^ Department of Psychology, Princeton University
JENNIFER S. TRUEBLOOD, Department of Psychological and Brain Sciences, Indiana University Bloomington
PETER A. UBEL,^,** The Fuqua School of Business, Duke University
KEVIN G. VOLPP,** Perelman School of Medicine, University of Pennsylvania

Staff

MOLLY CHECKSFIELD DORRIES, *Study Director, Program Officer* (until September 2022)
ALEXANDRA S. BEATTY, *Study Director, Senior Program Officer* (beginning September 2022)
TINA M. WINTERS, *Program Officer*
J. ASHTON RAY, *Senior Program Assistant*

---

*Member, National Academy of Sciences
^Resigned, May 2022
**Member, National Academy of Medicine

BOARD ON BEHAVIORAL, COGNITIVE, AND SENSORY SCIENCES

TERRIE E. MOFFITT (*Chair*),* Duke University
RICHARD N. ASLIN,** Yale University
WILSON S. GEISLER,** University of Texas at Austin
MICHELE GELFAND,** Stanford University
MARA MATHER, University of Southern California
ULRICH MAYR, University of Oregon
KATHERINE L. MILKMAN, University of Pennsylvania
DON OPERARIO, Emory University
ELIZABETH A. PHELPS, Harvard University
DAVID E. POEPPEL, New York University
KARL W. REID, Northeastern University
STACEY SINCLAIR, Princeton University
MO WANG, University of Florida

Staff

DANIEL J. WEISS, *Director*

---

*Member, National Academy of Medicine
**Member, National Academy of Sciences

Reviewers

This Consensus Study Report was reviewed in draft form by individuals chosen for their diverse perspectives and technical expertise. The purpose of this independent review is to provide candid and critical comments that will assist the National Academies of Sciences, Engineering, and Medicine in making each published report as sound as possible and to ensure that it meets the institutional standards for quality, objectivity, evidence, and responsiveness to the study charge. The review comments and draft manuscript remain confidential to protect the integrity of the deliberative process.

We thank the following individuals for their review of this report:

LEVON BARSEGHYAN, Graduate Studies for the Field of Economics, Cornell University
STEVEN BERRY, Department of Economics, Yale University
KEITH CHEN, Anderson School of Management, University of California, Los Angeles
ADELINE DELAVANDE, Economics Discipline Group, University of Technology Sydney
BRIGITTE C. MADRIAN, Marriott School of Business, Brigham Young University
NINA MAZAR, Questrom School of Business, Boston University
DANIEL S. NAGIN, H.J. Heinz School of Public Policy, Carnegie Mellon University
ARIEL PAKES, Department of Economics, Harvard University

MATTHEW RABIN, Department of Economics, Harvard University
RICHARD H. THALER, Booth School of Business, The University of Chicago
DAVID YOKUM, The Policy Lab, Brown University

Although the reviewers listed above provided many constructive comments and suggestions, they were not asked to endorse the conclusions or recommendations of this report nor did they see the final draft before its release. The review of this report was overseen by **CHARLES F. MANSKI**, Department of Economics, Northwestern University, and **ELKE U. WEBER**, Departments of Psychology and Public Affairs, Princeton University. They were responsible for making certain that an independent examination of this report was carried out in accordance with the standards of the National Academies and that all review comments were carefully considered. Responsibility for the final content rests entirely with the authoring committee and the National Academies.

Acknowledgments

This report was made possible by support from the Alfred P. Sloan Foundation, National Institutes of Health (NIH) Office of Behavioral and Social Sciences Research, National Institute on Aging, Eunice Kennedy Shriver National Institute of Child Health and Human Development, National Institute on Drug Abuse, National Institute of Mental Health, National Institute on Minority Health and Health Disparities, NIH Office of Disease Prevention, NIH Office of AIDS Research, and National Academy of Sciences W.K. Kellogg Foundation Fund.

The committee is grateful for the valuable contributions of many individuals to this study. As part of our evidence-gathering process, we commissioned three papers, and we thank the authors for their valuable contributions: Kent D. Messer, Diya Ganguly, and Lusi Xie, all of the University of Delaware, for their paper summarizing work on behavioral economics applications to climate change; Elizabeth Linos, Harvard University, for her paper on issues related to the translation of behavioral economics research into policy; and Andrej Svorenčík, University of Mannheim, and Alexandre Truc, Université Côte d'Azur, for their paper on the history and development of the field.

We also invited a number of other scholars to make presentations and engage with us during a public workshop held in July 2022. We thank the following individuals for their insightful and informative presentations at the public workshop: Saurabh Bhargava, Carnegie Mellon University; Ben Castleman, University of Virginia; Lisa Gennetian, Duke University; Michael Hallsworth, Behavioral Insights Team; Chaning Jang, The Busara

Center for Behavioral Economics; Åsa Löfgren, University of Gothenburg; Aurélie Ouss, University of Pennsylvania; Jolene Pomeroy, Mesa, AZ City Nudge Team; Sally Sadoff, University of California, San Diego; Anisha Singh, The Busara Center for Behavioral Economics; Richard Thaler, University of Chicago; David Yokum, Brown University; and Joe Zhao, Mesa, AZ City Nudge Team.

The committee also appreciates the contributions of the staff members who supported this project, Study Directors (in sequence) Molly Checksfield Dorries and Alix Beatty, Program Officer Tina Winters, and Senior Program Assistant Ashton Ray.

Alison Buttenheim and Robert Moffitt, *Cochairs*,
Committee on Future Directions for
Applying Behavioral Economics to Policy

Contents

Summary   1

1   Introduction   9
    STUDY APPROACH, 11
    GUIDE TO THE REPORT, 13
    REFERENCES, 13

PART I: UNDERSTANDING BEHAVIORAL ECONOMICS

2   Development of Behavioral Economics   17
    ORIGINS OF THE FIELD, 18
    INFLUENTIAL BEHAVIORAL IDEAS, 23
    APPLICATIONS AND INFLUENCE, 32
    CRITIQUES AND CHALLENGES, 33
    REFERENCES, 37

3   Foundational Behavioral and Economic Ideas   43
    ECONOMIC MODELING, 44
    FIVE CORE PRINCIPLES, 46
    CONCLUSION, 63
    REFERENCES, 63

4 The Behavioral Economics Toolkit: Policy Levers
   and Intervention Strategies   69
   ADDRESSING LIMITED ATTENTION AND COGNITION, 73
   ADDRESSING INACCURATE BELIEFS, 75
   ADDRESSING PRESENT BIAS, 76
   ADDRESSING REFERENCE DEPENDENCE AND
       FRAMING, 80
   ADDRESSING SOCIAL PREFERENCES AND SOCIAL
       NORMS, 81
   CONCLUSION, 83
   REFERENCES, 84

   PART II: EVIDENCE FROM SELECTED POLICY DOMAINS

5 Health   95
   CARDIOVASCULAR DISEASE RISK, 95
   PROMOTING PREVENTIVE CARE, 101
   PROVIDER BEHAVIOR, 105
   FINDINGS, 107
   REFERENCES, 110

6 Retirement Benefits   117
   AUTOMATIC ENROLLMENT, 118
   STRATEGIES TO REFINE AUTOMATIC ENROLLMENT, 120
   FINDINGS, 123
   REFERENCES, 124

7 Social Safety Net Benefits   127
   LOW PARTICIPATION, 128
   POSSIBLE EXPLANATIONS FOR LOW PARTICIPATION, 129
   INTERVENTIONS, 132
   FINDINGS, 134
   REFERENCES, 136

8 Climate Change   139
   DIFFICULTIES IN APPLYING BEHAVIORAL PRINCIPLES
       TO CLIMATE GOALS, 140
   ENERGY USE AND EFFICIENCY, 141
   TRANSPORTATION, 145
   LAND USE DECISIONS, 147
   FINDINGS, 148
   REFERENCES, 150

| 9 | Education | 157 |

PARENT-CHILD INTERACTIONS, 158
ACCESS TO POSTSECONDARY EDUCATION, 159
TEACHER PERFORMANCE, 162
FINDINGS, 163
REFERENCES, 164

| 10 | Criminal Justice System | 167 |

INFLUENCE OF BEHAVIORAL FACTORS, 168
APPLICATION OF BEHAVIORAL IDEAS, 170
FINDINGS, 174
REFERENCES, 175

| 11 | Findings Across the Policy Domains | 179 |

FINDINGS, 180
CONCLUSIONS, 184

PART III: LOOKING TO THE FUTURE

| 12 | Conducting and Disseminating Behavioral Economics Research | 189 |

REPLICABILITY, 190
GENERALIZABILITY, 192
PUBLICATION BIAS, 193
RECOMMENDATION, 194
REFERENCES, 199

| 13 | Implementing Behavioral Economics Approaches | 201 |

CONNECTING RESEARCH AND PRACTICE, 202
ACCESSIBILITY OF RESEARCH, 205
TRANSLATING EVIDENCE FOR USE, 207
ADOPTING INTERVENTIONS AT A BROAD SCALE, 208
CONCLUSION AND RECOMMENDATIONS, 209
REFERENCES, 210

| 14 | Advancing the Field of Behavioral Economics | 213 |

CONCLUSIONS, 213
RECOMMENDATIONS, 216
CONCLUDING OBSERVATION, 221
REFERENCES, 222

Appendix: Biographical Sketches of Committee Members   225

Boxes and Tables

BOXES

1-1 Committee Charge, 11

2-1 Traditional Economics—An Evolving Discipline, 18
2-2 Modeling the Dynamics of Decision Making, 26

3-1 One Traditional Mathematical Economic Model of Decision Making, 45
3-2 Modeling Present Bias, 55

14-1 Using Behavioral Knowledge to Combat False and Misleading Information, 215

TABLES

4-1 Intervention Strategies Mapped to the Five Foundational Principles, 72

11-1 Overview of Findings on Behavioral Economics from Six Domains, 181

12-1 Examples of Ways to Strengthen Research, 198

Summary

Behavioral economics has had a growing influence on public policy over the past several decades. The awarding of two Nobel Memorial Prizes in economics for work in the field is a mark of the influence of this interdisciplinary approach. The field, which encompasses and draws on findings from many disciplines, can be loosely described as an approach to understanding human behavior and decision making that integrates knowledge from psychology and other behavioral fields with economic analysis.

The field took shape as a growing number of economists recognized the work of psychologists who demonstrated that people do not behave as traditional economists had assumed: as rational actors who consistently make decisions that will optimize their expected benefits. These scholars observed, for example, that people lack complete self-control, make inconsistent choices over time, show selective attention, and respond unconsciously to an array of influences. People also do not necessarily prioritize, or accurately assess, the benefits and costs of different actions, particularly those that accrue over long time intervals; their decisions are often influenced by the social context in which they are made; they respond unconsciously to the way a choice is framed and presented; and they have limited capacity to overcome logistical obstacles that stand in the way of an objectively optimal choice.

While economists continue to consider behavioral influences in their work, behavioral economics is a narrower field that draws on insights from the behavioral sciences; often builds on those insights; and, most important, incorporates those insights into economic models of human behavior.

Behavioral economists have explored ways to apply knowledge of human behavior in the design of policy interventions to encourage people to make beneficial choices that, for example, promote health, support financial well-being, and encourage actions to protect the environment. The field has accumulated evidence about when, how, and under what circumstances the knowledge and approaches from behavioral economics can support effective policy. Along with its influence have come questions and challenges, such as the possibility that behaviorally based interventions may in some cases be paternalistic, ethical concerns about how knowledge of behavioral principles may be applied outside of research settings, and the risk of unintended negative outcomes for some populations.

Recognizing the growing influence of the field, the Sloan Foundation and the National Institutes of Health requested that the National Academies of Sciences, Engineering, and Medicine assess the contributions of the field to public policy. The Committee on Future Directions for Applying Behavioral Economics to Policy—whose members have expertise in economics, behavioral economics, health policy and behavioral design, psychology, cognitive science (e.g., judgment and decision making), methodology, and public policy—was appointed to carry out the study. The committee was charged to review evidence about the application of behavioral economics to key public policy objectives in a range of domains and synthesize what has been learned from this body of work, to suggest guiding principles for future work and applications, and to offer direction for future research.

To carry out its charge, the committee explored the history and theoretical foundation of the field and the available research in six public policy domains: health, retirement benefits, social safety net benefits, climate change, education, and criminal justice. Recognizing that the charge called for a tradeoff between breadth and depth, the committee chose these six as a varied set of important policy domains in which the ideas of behavioral economics have been tested. Three commissioned papers and a public workshop supplemented the committee's survey of the literature.

Foundational theoretical work that has integrated understanding of cognitive and psychosocial processes with economic analysis shows that decision processes are dynamic, malleable, and context dependent and that insights from this work help to explain how and why people make decisions that seem to run counter to rational analysis. This work points to the importance of five behavioral principles that affect people's decision making: limited attention and cognition, inaccurate beliefs, present bias, reference dependence and framing, and social preferences and social norms.

Limited Attention and Cognition	The extent to which people understand, pay attention to, and process information is crucial in any decision. Yet, individuals are able to pay only limited attention to important aspects of their environment, often have a difficult time processing information, and make cognitive errors even in simple situations.
Inaccurate Beliefs	Individuals often have incorrect perceptions of or information about the situations they are in, the incentives they face, their own abilities, and the beliefs of others, often as a result of limited attention or cognition.
Present Bias	People tend to disproportionately focus on issues that are before them in the present moment, paying less attention to future payoffs and consequences. This bias has important implications for decisions about consumption, payments, and utility.
Reference Dependence and Framing	Individuals tend to evaluate risk decisions by considering how the options relate to a particular reference point. That is, they assess whether an outcome would be a gain or a loss by comparing possible outcomes to a single reference point, such as the current status quo, rather than considering all alternative possibilities. Consequently, people are sensitive to the way decision problems are framed, which affects what possible outcomes come to their attention.
Social Preferences and Social Norms	An important aspect of the context for decision making is perceptions of how one's actions relate to those of others, including the well-being of others: people make comparisons between themselves and others, and they care about their social standing, how they signal their values and preferences to others, and how they conform with social norms.

These five principles do not capture all the relevant behaviors, but they have direct application to the kinds of decision making that behavioral economists study and the choices that policy makers hope to influence. The committee applied these five core principles in our examination of research in the six selected policy domains and reached two conclusions.

Conclusion 11-1: Core principles of behavioral economics have been tested repeatedly across six domains—health, retirement benefits, social safety net benefits, climate change, education, and (to a lesser extent) criminal justice—and the evidence for their importance and value in the design of policy interventions is well established.

Conclusion 14-1: The very strong evidence that complex cognitive, social, behavioral, and contextual factors influence judgment and decision making means that behavioral economics concepts are indispensable for advancing scientific understanding of policy-relevant human behavior and for the design of public policies. Behavioral economics has produced invaluable evidence about why people act in seemingly irrational ways, how they respond to interventions, and how public policy and practice interventions can be designed to modify the habitual and unconscious ways that people act and make decisions.

A large and growing array of tools has been developed based on the evidence about influences on behavior. Findings from research on the design of these interventions are nuanced and mixed. For some strategies, such as the use of default options to guide people to a desired choice—for example, making employer-matched increased retirement savings the default option for employees—and the framing of the available options, there is strong empirical evidence of effectiveness. For others, such as behaviorally informed incentives and interventions that appeal to social norms, the evidence is mixed or less robust.

The strongest effects are apparent where interventions have precisely targeted specific behavioral issues. The strongest results the committee observed across the six domains it studied are for a very specific intervention: making retirement savings a default choice for employees. A substantial body of research has confirmed this finding in diverse contexts and with numerous variations. Across all domains, the evidence points to the high value of targeting an intervention to a particular population and set of circumstances. The evidence also supports the cumulative value of multiple small-scale, low-cost interventions. Interventions that operate on a broader scale, such as efforts to reduce the administrative burden associated with social service programs, and better reach the neediest populations who can benefit from them, can also be effective when carefully targeted.

The research demonstrating positive effects for behavioral economics interventions typically shows modest effect sizes. However, as is particularly evident in the work on climate change—a challenge of unmeasurable magnitude—the application of combinations of individually modest interventions can cumulatively bring important changes and benefits for relatively little cost.

Conclusion 14-2: The field of behavioral economics has made significant advances over the past 20 years, producing evidence about both general principles and specific intervention approaches that address policy challenges in many domains. However, the field has not yet produced generalizable and implementable practice guidance and intervention design strategies for determining what works, when, and for whom. Whether the goal of providing such specific guidance can be achieved, given the importance of context and the unique characteristics of many targets of behavior change, is not clear.

Despite strong evidence across domains and contexts that intervention strategies based on behavioral economics can have significant effects on important policy objectives, it is challenging to apply this evidence beyond the scale and setting of a focused research study. A substantial number of individual studies of interventions have been carried out across the six domains we explored, but far fewer studies have followed up promising results with replication studies and systematic efforts at scale.

The process of translating research findings to effective, broad-scale, real-world applications is complex and, ideally, involves an interactive feedback loop that links theory, experimentation, design, evaluation, and implementation. Even when a solid body of evidence is brought to bear and translation to context has been carefully addressed, there is no guarantee that an intervention will perform as expected when implemented on a broad scale, whether in the public or private sector.

Two ways to strengthen policy makers' and practitioners' capacity to implement evidence-based interventions are to encourage collaboration among those trained in behavioral economics and those trained in implementation science or public management, and to improve training in behavioral economics and public administration to better prepare policy makers to collaborate in translating research ideas for real-world policy development and design. With this perspective, we offer a conclusion and several recommendations.

Conclusion 13-1: Collaboration among researchers and policy makers is invaluable both for the continued development of knowledge about the application of behavioral economics to policy and for the development of effective policies. The development of strong intermediary institutions that can function to bring the two groups together and to assist in the translation between different languages could contribute to such collaborations.

Recommendation 13-1: Government units should consider adopting the example of the Office of Evaluation Sciences, in the General Services Administration, to support and fund in-house capabilities for integrating behavioral specialists into policy development, such as through institutional structures that facilitate learning and collaboration among policy makers and researchers in the design, implementation, and evaluation of behavioral economics–based policies in all relevant domains.

The use of temporary research appointments and consulting organizations could bring expertise and assistance to state and local government entities that cannot afford permanent in-house staff.

Recommendation 13-2: University leaders should ensure that training in the principles of behavioral economics and critical thinking about their translation and application to policy making is a core component of training for students pursuing degrees in public administration.

It is clear from the committee's review that behavioral economics has made a substantial contribution to the understanding of decision making and the design of interventions, and that there are numerous promising directions for future research. We also found that attention to the way research is conducted will help to strengthen the field. The research in the six domains we studied pointed to many important directions for specific research to build on the remarkable body of knowledge already accumulated.

Recommendation 14-1: Researchers and funders of research should balance attention and funding across:
- basic research in intervention design, interdisciplinary investigation, and development of methods;
- research to support applications of behavioral economics concepts in practice, including implementation and scale-up and evaluation; and
- research to explore and support the positive contributions of behavioral economics to society, including attention to equity of impact and attitudes about behavioral interventions.

For the field to continue to flourish it will be important for researchers, funders, and others who support their work to consider ways to strengthen the way research is conducted and ensure that research is rigorous and accessible. Behavioral economics, like other fields, has benefited from growing attention to replication, generalizability, and publication bias. Specific changes in the way behavioral economics research is typically funded and conducted will strengthen the field.

Recommendation 12-1: Researchers, funders of research, university leaders, and journal editors in behavioral economics should take steps to support the replicability and generalizability of behavioral economics research, more fully acknowledge publication bias and take steps to detect its presence, and counter publication bias using a variety of approaches.

Future progress will also depend on continued collaboration across disciplines, with each informing the others. Such interaction is not easy: differences in theoretical perspectives, terminology, research methods and tools, and standards of evidence all bring challenges, so persistent efforts to bridge these gaps will be a critical support for this inherently interdisciplinary field.

Recommendation 14-2: Funders and university leaders should prioritize investments in interdisciplinary research collaborations.

Recommendation 14-3: Researchers and funders of research should prioritize research related to methods and ways of understanding the mechanisms of behavior and behavior change. Specifically, research is needed to:
- advance behavioral design and intervention design methods to better link behavioral principles and insights to specific intervention and policy goals;
- advance methods for conducting pilot and rapid-cycle studies;
- accumulate more evidence on how findings from one setting can be applied to other settings or at broader scales;
- realize the potential for artificial intelligence and machine learning approaches to improve tailoring and targeting;
- bring cutting-edge adaptive trial design approaches to behavioral economics studies; and
- incorporate empirical methods from other disciplines and fields that can enrich behavioral economics research.

Recommendation 14-4: Researchers, funders of research, and entities that support or sponsor behavioral units in organizations should prioritize research and practice initiatives that increase the impact of behavioral economics findings through implementation, scale-up, and evaluation of potentially successful interventions and policies.

Recommendation 14-5: Researchers, funders of research, and entities that support or sponsor behavioral units in organizations should prioritize ongoing investigations into the role of behavioral economics in society, with specific attention to the equity implications of behavioral economics policies and interventions; the implications of public attitudes toward the ethics of behavioral economics research and practice, as well as their acceptance by the general public; and possible public policy interest in commercial applications of behavioral economics findings.

Recommendation 14-6: Funders and university leaders should foster the development and application of behavioral economics by supporting training opportunities for public policy professionals. They should also support learning about practices for research transparency.

The benefits that behaviorally based approaches can bring are clear, regardless of whether they are viewed as primarily the province of economics, behavioral science, or a hybrid of the two. Future application of these ideas, however they are categorized, may reach beyond the context of individual behaviors to help explain what appear to be nonrational responses. In the context of complex regulatory structures, for example, there may be behavioral solutions to challenges that are not primarily the result of individual behavioral biases. Behavioral economists can consider not only a broad range of solutions to behavioral biases but also how to apply behavioral solutions even when there is no clear problem of cognitive bias. It is likely that ideas not explicitly identified as coming from behavioral economics research, but that nevertheless take advantage of behavioral insights, have already influenced the development of policy. All of these are reasons to be optimistic about the future contributions of the field.

1

Introduction

Behavioral economics—loosely defined as an approach to examining human behavior and decision making that integrates research and evidence from psychology and related fields such as sociology, anthropology, and cognitive science with economics analysis—has had a growing influence on research and policy. Since economics was established as a scientific discipline in the 19th century, economists have explored the nature of individual choices. In what is called the traditional, conventional, neoclassical, or standard framework, economists have assumed that people make rational decisions in the sense of maximizing possible benefits that are assessed through logical analysis. In this framework, people are assumed to know their own preferences regarding different choices, and those preferences are assumed to be consistent over time. This approach assumes that people correctly perceive the nature of the world around them, at least roughly and with some uncertainty, and that they systematically choose the best alternatives for themselves without being distracted by factors that are irrelevant to the underlying virtues of the alternatives. Economists have always understood that these assumptions about human behavior are only approximate, but that they are useful approximations for many purposes.

Challenges to this framework have come from many other intellectual frameworks, but the one that has had the greatest effect on economics arose around the middle of the 20th century. The work of psychologists Daniel Kahneman and Amos Tversky was an influential counter influence, though many other scholars played a role (as discussed in Chapter 2). The influence of this work on the discipline of economics has grown and led economists to take seriously the limitations of the traditional model's assumptions about behavior (e.g., Rabin, 1998; Camerer, 2003). Today, behavioral economics is a major subfield within the discipline of economics that has had an influence on the study of individual behavior in the contexts of financial behavior, health, education, and many other domains. Indeed, its influence is so widespread that one observer proposed that "we're all behavioral economists now" (Angner, 2019).

While the discipline of economics has a strong theoretical element, it is increasingly an applied discipline with a focus on analyzing the effects of government policies and the actions of other parties and institutions, such as commercial firms and nongovernmental organizations. The development of behavioral economics and its application in many domains has led to changes in the structure and evaluation of government policies designed to promote health, safety, well-being, and other societal objectives (National Research Council, 2012; National Academies of Sciences, Engineering, and Medicine, 2017). Behavioral economics has been formally integrated into public policy in other countries, starting with the Nudge Unit (now the Behavioral Design Team) in the United Kingdom in 2010.[1] Other countries followed suit, and a growing number of nongovernmental entities, such as the Behavioral Science and Policy Association, are now helping to foster international collaboration among behavioral science researchers and policy makers.

In the United States this influence was evident when the Obama administration established a Social and Behavioral Sciences Team that was charged with looking across agencies for areas where behavioral economics and other ideas from the social and behavioral sciences could be used in tackling urgent policy challenges, such as increasing retirement security for military service members, supporting sound decision making about claiming Social Security benefits, and supporting consumer adoption of renewable energy sources (Office of the Press Secretary, 2016).

Researchers have continued to explore policy applications, accumulating evidence about when, how, and under what circumstances the tools of behavioral economics can help shape policy in desirable ways. Ideas associated with behavioral economics have also become influential beyond academia and policy making: for example, consultants offering to practice it for commercial purposes have proliferated (Hollingworth & Barker, 2017). Given the growing influence of the field, there is a need for an assessment of its contributions.

The Sloan Foundation and the National Institutes of Health requested that the National Academies of Sciences, Engineering, and Medicine conduct a consensus study to review the evidence regarding the application of behavioral economics to public policy objectives. The committee's charge is shown in Box 1-1. The Committee on Future Directions for Applying

---

[1]See Chapters 2 and 4 for definition and discussion of nudges.

INTRODUCTION   11

> **BOX 1-1**
> **Committee Charge**
>
> The committee will review the evidence regarding the application of insights from behavioral economics to key public policy objectives (e.g., related to public health, multiple areas of chronic illness [including mental health and HIV], economic well-being, and responses to global climate change). The committee will examine applications from the past 5 to 10 years (including available evidence on U.S. federal and state policy applications as well as international examples) to identify features of successful applications (including progress in methods for assessing outcomes of behavioral interventions), and also less successful applications that may offer valuable lessons. The committee will also examine main controversies that have arisen as the field has progressed, particularly with regard to intersections with related disciplines including cognitive psychology, social psychology, and the decision sciences.
>
> The committee will provide conclusions and recommendations regarding (1) guiding principles for applying behavioral economics to research and policy; and (2) a research program to support future progress, including possible avenues for collaboration across disciplines that could advance theory and method. The committee will consider ethical issues related to the applications of behavioral economics, for example in health, political influence efforts, or commercial marketing.

Behavioral Economics to Policy—whose members have expertise in economics, behavioral economics, health policy and behavioral design, psychology, cognitive science (e.g., judgment and decision making), methodology, and public policy—was appointed to carry out the study. This report describes the committee's conclusions and recommendations and the evidence on which they are based and presents an agenda for future research.

STUDY APPROACH

The committee reviewed a range of information to develop a clear picture of the current state of the field, its theoretical foundations, its contributions, and the issues behavioral economists may need to address. An early question was how the committee should identify the boundaries of the field. Definitions of behavioral economics vary, along with ideas of what it should encompass, when it really began, and what might be considered its essential features. The boundaries of behavioral economics are not precise because work in the field builds and draws on work in economics, psychology, sociology, and other fields. Because the study charge focused on the application of insights that can guide future progress, the committee chose to consider what can be learned from research, whether conducted by economists or other scientists, influenced by findings from domains in the behavioral sciences. Our focus was on exploring applications that use tools, methods, and approaches with a behavioral economics bent, rather than establishing arbitrary distinctions among fields. We explored key developments in the growth of the field and ways in which behavioral economics has differed from traditional economics as both fields have evolved over the past few decades. We used the term "traditional" when there was a need to address distinctions between the behavioral approach and other economic approaches, but we did not establish a filter for classifying different types of work. These issues are discussed in detail in Chapters 2 and 3.

Reviewing the evidence regarding the application of insights from behavioral economics to key public policy objectives called for an explicit tradeoff between breadth and depth. A systematic review of behavioral economics research across all relevant domains was not feasible. Instead, the committee determined that an overview of a varied subset of fields would best meet the charge of surveying the available research to identify features of clearly successful and less successful applications and assess this body of work, including controversies and questions that have arisen. Thus, the committee focused on the published literature in six domains: health, retirement benefits, social safety net benefits, climate change, education, and criminal justice. Within each of these domains we concentrated on a handful of important topics, recognizing that it would be necessary to leave out other important societal issues in which valuable work has been done (e.g., reducing credit card debt, obesity, behavioral finance). The six domains we selected are all policy domains of prime importance to society in which behavioral ideas have been tested.[2]

We supplemented our own information gathering with additional input through informal consultations with experts, a public workshop,[3] and three commissioned papers:

- Linos, E. (2022). *Translating evidence into policy and practice.*
- Messer, K., Ganguly, D., & Xie, L. (2022). *Applications of behavioral economics to climate change mitigation and adaptation.*
- Svorenčík, A., & Truc, A. (2022). *A history of behavioral economics and its applications: What we know and future directions.*

---

[2] The charge also directed the committee to consider evidence from other countries; however, we were not able to do this systematically with the available time and resources.
[3] See https://www.nationalacademies.org/event/07-18-2022/workshop-on-behavioral-economics-exploring-applications-and-research-methods

GUIDE TO THE REPORT

The report is organized in three parts. The first part functions as a primer on behavioral economics, offering an overview of the development of the field: its origins, influential ideas, and evolving influence (Chapter 2); a discussion of its theoretical foundations and core principles (Chapter 3); and an overview of the principal implementation strategies used in policy and practice and how they relate to the foundational ideas from the theoretical literature (Chapter 4).[4]

Part II presents the committee's findings: the evidence from applications of behavioral economics in the six policy domains we chose. It was not possible for the committee to examine the entire landscape of applications, even confining our attention to developments over the past 10 years, as our charge directed. For each of the six domains (Chapters 5–10), we reviewed the available literature selectively, seeking synthetic reviews and meta-analyses where they were available and attempting to obtain a clear sense of the primary areas in which behavioral economics tools have been studied. These are not comprehensive literature reviews: our objective was to learn how and under what circumstances behavioral economics ideas have been effectively applied and what can be learned from contexts in which that has not yet happened. We looked for themes and patterns that might be apparent across contexts and drew lessons about the factors that appear to influence success and the matching of tools to objectives. Chapters 5–10 each end with a summary of principal findings from the research. The overall themes and the conclusions we drew from this body of work are discussed in Chapter 11.

Part III provides the committee's guidance for the future of the field. Chapter 12 addresses ways to strengthen behavioral economics research methods. Chapter 13 discusses the significant challenges associated with implementing tested ideas from behavioral economics research in real-world policy settings. Chapter 14 presents the committee's general conclusions about the contributions of behavioral economics, offers recommendations for strengthening the field, and suggests directions for future research.

REFERENCES

Angner, E. (2019). We're all behavioral economists now. *Journal of Economic Methodology, 26*(3), 195–207.

Camerer, C. F. (2003). *Behavioral game theory: Experiments in strategic interaction.* Russell Sage Foundation.

---

[4] A number of terms used in this report may be unfamiliar to some readers; they are defined when they first appear.

Hollingworth, C., & Barker, E. (2017). How behavioural economics is shaping our lives. *The behavioral economics guide 2017*. Behavioral Science Solutions Ltd.

Linos, E. (2022). *Translating behavioral economics evidence into policy and practice*. Commissioned paper prepared for the Committee on Future Directions for Applying Behavioral Economics to Policy, National Academies of Sciences, Engineering, and Medicine. https://nap.nationalacademies.org/resource/26874/NASEM_Commissioned_Report_Linos.pdf

Messer, K., Ganguly, D., & Xie, L. (2022). *Applications of behavioral economics to climate change mitigation and adaptation*. Commissioned paper prepared for the Committee on Future Directions for Applying Behavioral Economics to Policy, National Academies of Sciences, Engineering, and Medicine. https://nap.nationalacademies.org/resource/26874/Applying_Behavioral_Economics_to_Climate_Change_Messer_Ganguly_Xie.pdf

National Academies of Sciences, Engineering, and Medicine. (2017). *Lessons learned from diverse efforts to change social norms and opportunities and strategies to promote behavior change in behavioral health: Proceedings of two workshops*. The National Academies Press. https://doi.org/10.17226/24824

National Research Council. (2012). *Using science as evidence in public policy*. The National Academies Press. https://doi.org/10.17226/13460

Office of the Press Secretary. (2016). *Fact sheet: New progress on using behavioral science insights to better serve the American people, September 15, 2016*. The White House. https://obamawhitehouse.archives.gov/the-press-office/2016/09/15/fact-sheet-new-progress-using-behavioral-science-insights-better-serve

Rabin, M. (1998). Psychology and economics. *Journal of Economic Literature*, 36(1), 11–46. http://www.jstor.org/stable/2564950

Svorenčík, A., & Truc, A. (2022). *A history of behavioral economics and its applications: What we know and future research directions*. Commissioned paper prepared for the Committee on Future Directions for Applying Behavioral Economics to Policy, National Academies of Sciences, Engineering, and Medicine. https://nap.nationalacademies.org/resource/26874/BE_history_20221009.pdf

Part I

Understanding Behavioral Economics

2

Development of Behavioral Economics

Economists have long been interested in human behavior, but it was not until the second half of the 20th century that they began to systematically integrate ideas from psychology—particularly growing understanding of cognitive frameworks—into their work. The field that emerged, behavioral economics, challenges some of the assumptions of traditional economics and seeks to use detailed understanding of the social and cognitive aspects of decision making in the design of policy strategies.

The development of behavioral economics as a distinct field is just one of many important developments in economics in recent decades. Rapid gains in computing power and the availability of new kinds of data, along with new methodologies for analyzing data, have contributed to important advances in most social science fields, and economics is no exception.[1] Economists have also increasingly extended the application of their methods beyond traditional areas, such as the analysis of financial markets, to support the development of public policies to address a wide range of issues, including environmental protection, public education, and poverty. Behavioral economics has a complex history, and many different scholars and approaches have contributed to its development. This chapter provides an overview of the history and development of behavioral economics; key ideas, particularly from the domain of psychology, that have been

---

[1]Two examples are applied microeconomics, the study of such decisions as people's choice of one alternative over another, and econometrics, the application of statistical methods to the analysis of economic data.

influential in the field; its growing influence; and critiques and challenges for the future.

ORIGINS OF THE FIELD

Behavioral economics draws on insights from social and cognitive psychology, sociology, and neuroscience to challenge some of the assumptions made in traditional economic analysis (see Box 2-1). The term behavioral economics was first used in the 1940s, though it has never had a precise consensus definition (Svorenčík & Truc, 2022).[2] The name has its roots in early work by psychologists such as B. F. Skinner, who studied the role of conditioning and reinforcement in shaping human behavior. The idea that psychological and sociological factors are crucial for economics can be traced back to the early days of economic thought, with roots in the work of Adam Smith and other early economists who recognized that human behavior often does not follow the path that rational analysis would predict (Ashraf, Camerer, & Loewenstein, 2005).

Among other precursors of behavioral economics was the work of Herbert Simon, a researcher working in the 1950s and 1960s at the intersection of computer science, organizational science, and economics. He

---

BOX 2-1
Traditional Economics—An Evolving Discipline

There is no single definition of traditional economics, but the generally accepted understanding is that it is based on the assumptions that individuals have full information about the world around them (making accurate assessments of the probabilities of uncertain events); know their own preferences and objectives, which are stable over time; and make rational decisions and actions to maximize their own individual well-being, subject to constraints which they accurately perceive. In recent decades, economists have developed models that go far beyond these assumptions. They have incorporated new information into their models, about how people develop subjective expectations about the world and participate in networks and social groups that influence each others' behaviors, for example. However, these models assume that people behave with a certain level of rationality, and it is there that behavioral economists have diverged, arguing that actual human behavior does not demonstrate this degree of consistency. Behavioral economists, thus, attempt to enrich traditional economic models by incorporating additional behavioral insights, derived primarily from research in psychology.

---

[2]The chapter draws on the paper by Andrej Svorenčík and Alexandre Truc that was commissioned for this study, available at https://nap.nationalacademies.org/resource/26874/BE_history_20221009.pdf

advocated for the concept of *satisficing*, accepting an option as acceptable for the circumstances, as an alternative to the concept of *maximizing*, the traditional assumption used by economists. His concept was intended to capture the reality that people's rationality is limited, or bounded (see, e.g., Simon, 1955). But Simon himself noted that a number of prominent economists, some who worked far before his time—including John R. Commons, George Katona, Joseph Schumpeter, and Thorstein Veblen—had already introduced behavioral economics concepts.

Drawing on Psychological Theory

While the concepts associated with behavioral economics have been influenced by many disciplines, including sociology, research in psychology is the source for the primary ideas in the field. Cognitive psychologists, particularly Daniel Kahneman and Amos Tversky, contributed concepts that have been critical to the development of behavioral economics. They systematically documented how heuristics (short-cut problem-solving strategies) and biases influence people's perceptions of probability and their decisions (see, e.g., Tversky & Kahneman, 1973). Equally influential was their concept of prospect theory, which proposed an explanation of individual decision making that takes into account comparative judgments, framing, and reference dependence (Kahneman & Tversky, 1979).[3,4] Indeed, such was the influence of prospect theory that the publication in which it was introduced is one of the most cited articles in economics in the past 50 years (Kim, Morse, & Zingales, 2006).

This work laid the foundation for the collaboration of psychologists with economists that created behavioral economics as a distinct field. Economist Richard Thaler worked with Kahneman, Tversky, and others to incorporate insights from cognitive and social psychology into economics. Among other contributions, Thaler (1981) pointed to the importance of evidence about present bias (the tendency to give greater weight to near-term risks or benefits than to more temporally distant ones) from the field

---

[3]Prospect theory posits that individuals compare the expected outcomes of decisions they have to make with the expected outcomes for an alternative possible decision, called a reference point. Prospect theory assumes that the reference point is the default choice—the one that would seem easiest or most obvious—but reference dependence can refer to any situation where a decision is weighed against a hypothetical alternative choice. The framing of alternative decisions (the way they appear to the decision maker) also plays a role in other areas: framing may determine whether the possible options or outcomes are perceived as an overall loss or gain relative to the reference alternative.

[4]Reference dependence is the tendency to make decisions by comparing the options to a single possible case, such as considering whether an outcome would be better or worse than the current status quo, rather than objectively assessing a range of possible outcomes.

of psychology. A set of articles that stimulated growth in the field examined the impact of people's *taste for fairness* in the setting of prices and wages, and the impact of prospect theory on trading (Kahneman, Knetsch, & Thaler, 1986).[5] The authors suggested the existence of an *endowment effect*, the idea that people place a higher value on something when they have it than when they do not (i.e., sellers value goods at higher rates than buyers; Kahneman, Knetsch, & Thaler, 1986).[6] This early work set the stage for several of the key themes in behavioral economics discussed in Chapter 3.

A growing number of economists drew on work from psychology as they developed new theories to explain how people make decisions under uncertainty and how biases can influence individual decision making. During this period, concepts and findings from psychology were incorporated by economists into formal theoretical models of decision making and tested using observational and experimental methods. Early examples focused on patterns of behavior in individual decision making under uncertainty and over time, and the ways in which the framing of the available options affects decisions.

A later wave of research focused on field data and extended the work on behavioral biases to two main areas: the study of financial markets (by scholars such as Richard Thaler, Robert Shiller, and Andrei Shleifer; see, e.g., Thaler, 1993) and the study of consumption and savings by David Laibson and others (see Ericson & Laibson, 2019). These empirical projects with field data were very important to the success of behavioral economics. Equally important, at a time when behavioral economics was not taught in most universities, was the establishment of training opportunities for economists interested in these ideas, especially a series of behavioral summer camps initiated in 1994 that offered two weeks of training by leading researchers to interested Ph.D. students from across the globe. The Russell Sage Foundation played an important role in supporting this summer school and other initiatives in the area.

Learning from Laboratory Experiments

While one set of insights for behavioral economics came from cognitive psychology, another source for understanding the significance of human

---

[5]Taste for fairness refers to the fact that "a wealth of experimental data corroborates the everyday observation that people care about, and respond to, fair and unfair treatment. Individuals exhibit both an aversion to arbitrary inequality and a preference for inequality based on desert" (Fennell & McAdams, 2013, p. 1).

[6]Other contributors to early work in behavioral economics in the 1980s and early 1990s include, among others, George Akerlof, James Andreoni, Colin Camerer, Catherine Eckel, Ernst Fehr, Robert Frank, Elizabeth Hoffman, George Loewenstein, Kevin McCabe, Matthew Rabin, Tom Schelling, Andrew Schotter, Robert Shiller, and Robert Sugden.

psychology for economic analysis emerged from the work of experimental economists. The insights of Vernon Smith, Charles Plott, and Reinhard Selten, among others, as well as Elinor Ostrom, a political scientist who worked on culturally embedded policy solutions, played a key role in these developments (Grether & Plott, 1979; Isaac, McCue, & Plott, 1985; Smith, 1989, 2003; Ostrom, 1990; Selten, 1998). What distinguished these scholars was their interest in how individual behavior produced outcomes in specific institutional contexts.[7]

Experimental economists examining the behavior of individuals and groups in controlled conditions were confronted by the complexity of human motivation in the course of their attempts to test formal game theory in laboratory experiments. Unexpected findings emerged repeatedly and became well documented (e.g., Güth, Schmittberger, & Schwarze, 1982; Isaac, McCue, & Plott, 1985).[8] That is, subjects' responses systematically diverged from game-theoretic predictions: they were clearly sensitive not only to their own payoffs but also to payoffs for others. Their behavior diverged from the predictions in several ways, showing that people were generous, trusting of, and trustworthy toward other people; cared about relative earnings; and were responsive to the efficiency effects of their choices. A growing body of evidence demonstrated that economic agents responded differently to incentives and information than was usually predicted by traditional economists' models.

The junction between this work and the work in psychological theory discussed above led to the modeling of such phenomena as social preferences (the way in which people take account of the utility of others, such as the taste for fairness or inequity aversion; Fehr & Schmidt, 1999; Bolton & Ockenfels, 2000; Charness & Rabin, 2002). This work fostered the development of behavioral game theory, the study of how people make decisions in strategic situations, such as in business negotiations or political elections,

---

[7]Smith argued that individually "rational" behavior emerged when it was most valuable—for example, when individuals are subject to the discipline of the market and other competitive situations—while cooperation is favored when it can increase the size of the resource pie: that is, the key to understanding behavior is an understanding of the institutional environment. Plott focused on nonmarket decision making and the development of institutions for solving collective action problems. Selten stressed the importance of observing regularities in subject behavior in lab settings, such as whether and how groups achieved equilibrium play, and using those to modify theoretical models. Ostrom documented the ways in which local public goods and commons problems were solved with cultural contexts by the development of local institutions.

[8]Richard Thaler hosted a column in the *Journal of Economic Perspectives* for many years, titled "Anomalies." Written with a variety of cohosts, these columns introduced economists to "behavioral" phenomena. While many of the columns focused on heuristics and biases, a number of them featured the cooperative anomalies arising from experimental studies (Dawes & Thaler, 1988; Thaler, 1988; Camerer & Thaler, 1995).

and how these decisions are influenced by such factors as emotions, biases, and social norms (Camerer, 2011). Behavioral game theory thus incorporates the idea that people often make decisions based on factors other than economic self-interest, such as fairness, trust, and reciprocity. These ideas had roots in sociology and earlier economic theory but had not generally been explicitly factored into economic models (Homans, 1961; Blau, 1964).

This work further made the case that it is important to more explicitly take account of human cognition and behavior in research and, ultimately, policy making. It also led to the investigation of mechanisms to solve public goods problems and other market failures and to the development of new theoretical models of behavior and tests using observational and experimental methods.

Behavioral economics has benefited from the confluence of the research from these two origins: the analysis of heuristics and biases and the experimental analysis of behavior in specific contexts (particularly contexts of interest to policy makers).[9] While these two branches in behavioral economics also continue to work independently, together they have fostered appreciation of the importance of more psychologically accurate models of decision making. Some researchers primarily consider individual-level behavior and policies, using laboratory experiments, formal theory, observational data, and field experiments; others focus on lab experiments to test mechanisms for fundraising, public goods provision, and market design (including kidney exchange and medical-intern matching "markets"). Behavioral economics has achieved considerable success and influence in economics; the awarding of two Nobel Memorial Prizes for behavioral economics research and experimental economics highlighted the field's growing influence.[10]

By taking the utility-maximizing model typically used by traditional economists as a baseline and building related models that incorporate behavioral elements, and by adopting state-of-the-art empirical methods to obtain field evidence (such as natural experiments and randomized controlled trials), behaviorally inclined economists have generated work that

---

[9]The heuristics and biases research has largely been funded by the Sloan and Russell Sage foundations, while the experimental economics agenda has largely been funded by the National Science Foundation. The National Institutes of Health has supported work on applications of behavioral economics to aging and health. In all these cases, key personnel at the relevant organizations were instrumental in supporting and fostering the emergence and growth of behavioral economics.

[10]In 2002, Daniel Kahneman and Vernon Smith were each awarded a Nobel Memorial Prize: Kahneman for his work on behavioral biases, and Smith for his work on how institutions shape behavior. In 2017, Richard Thaler received the prize for his pioneering and wide-ranging contributions to behavioral economics. In addition, Herbert Simon, one of the early contributors to the field, received the prize in 1978.

has become widely accepted. These scholars succeeded in making psychological research a fully established source of economic knowledge.

INFLUENTIAL BEHAVIORAL IDEAS

A wide range of psychological findings have been influential in the development of behavioral economics. That mass of evidence covers human emotions, cognitive processes, and behavior, as well the complexity of social interactions. In particular, cognitive psychologists and neuroscientists have produced an ever more detailed picture of the complex functioning of the human mind, while social psychologists and sociologists have focused on the complex ways that environment and context influence thinking, emotions, and behavior. By providing empirical evidence that people make judgmental errors, exhibit inconsistent preferences, are often overconfident, have a taste for immediate gratification, and are influenced in complex ways by social norms and contexts, among other findings, these fields have been invaluable to the economists seeking to refine their models and methods for understanding and influencing behavior. The field of economics has been influenced by many developments in the behavioral sciences, such as work on learning and new approaches to surveying both individuals and firms about their actions and thinking, but behavioral economists have been particularly focused on several core ideas. An acquaintance with some of these ideas is an important foundation for understanding the core principles of behavioral economics, which are discussed in Chapter 3.

Research in cognitive psychology and neuroscience has shown that human decision making is influenced by fundamental cognitive processes, such as perception, attention, and memory, and their significant limitations. Research in social psychology and sociology has also contributed to understanding that decisions are highly contextual, shaped by multiple aspects of the circumstances in which a decision is made and past experiences that affect how each individual construes the world. These two core sets of ideas—the multiple cognitive influences on decision making and the influence of context on how decisions are represented—have particular relevance for thinking about decision making and public policy. The descriptions below are designed to provide a flavor of the research and ideas that have been influential.

Cognitive Processes That Affect Decision Making

Theoretical and empirical research in cognitive psychology, neuroscience, and the newer field of neuroeconomics has fueled increasingly detailed insights about human cognition and decision making. A thorough review of this vast research landscape would be beyond the scope of this report, but three fundamental classes of cognitive processes stand out as particularly relevant: perception, attention, and memory. This work has demonstrated that these three processes have important influences on decision making across individuals and in a wide range of domains.

The Nature of Perception

The way people perceive the world around them involves input from their senses, but this information is filtered and shaped by past experiences, beliefs, motivation, attention, and other factors. That is, people's day-to-day experiences over the course of a lifetime, along with their attitudes, perspectives, and other factors, shape (or bias) how they respond to information. The word *bias* has a negative connotation in some contexts, but humans naturally take into account past knowledge and experience when processing new information; in the context of cognitive science, the word refers to the fact that the brain necessarily filters information (National Academies of Sciences, Engineering, and Medicine [National Academies], 2018). Indeed, this capacity to filter is the basis for the development of knowledge and expertise. Yet the influence of past experience on both perceptions and preferences can lead to distortions in perception and even in how neurons encode information. These influences may distort even seemingly straightforward perceptions, such as visual interpretations of an image (Sun & Perona, 1998). And these distortions can lead to inaccurate inferences that affect people's decisions.

An example of this distortion comes from neuroscientists who measure the activity of neurons. They have proposed the efficient coding hypothesis, which posits that neural representations adapt to the statistics of sensory input available in the environment so that perception is more precise for stimuli that occur more frequently (Barlow, 1961; Laughlin, 1981). The idea of efficient coding is also relevant for how individuals learn and make decisions. In both learning and decision making, a critical problem is how agents internally represent information. In the domain of learning, there is evidence that individuals adopt a hierarchical scheme for encoding actions, similar to an efficient coding strategy (Botvinick et al., 2015). Researchers have also suggested that efficient coding extends to the domain of risky choice and could explain why risk-taking behavior varies across different environments (Frydman & Jin, 2022).

The key idea is that efficient coding results in a subjective value function (an individual's estimation of the value of possible rewards in a given situation) that is more sensitive to frequently occurring payoffs and less sensitive for infrequent payoffs: that is, the function is steeper for frequently occurring payoffs and flatter for infrequent payoffs. Similar arguments about perceptual biases have been used to explain small-stakes risk aversion (Khaw, Li, & Woodford, 2021). Perceptual biases can be either positive or negative. People must and do learn over time to distinguish what is most important among the many stimuli they encounter. In the context of the kinds of decision making that behavioral economists study, it is important to understand that people's existing knowledge and experience lead them to recognize and process information and apply interpretations to what they perceive in unique ways that may differ from what might be expected in a given circumstance (National Academies, 2018).

The Nature of Attention

In making decisions, people need to process multiple pieces of information. For example, making a binary decision between two options in a gambling situation requires attention to the potential value of each option as well as the probability of each possible outcome. When people are faced with multiple pieces of information, they cannot allocate attention to all of them at the same time. Researchers who study attention—using such methods as tracking the eye movements of participants as they view stimuli—have suggested that people allocate attention to subsets of the available information and develop preferences for the aspects of the information to which they are attending (e.g., Krajbich, Armel, & Rangel, 2010); see Box 2-2. As they deliberate, people shift this "window of attention" to evaluate each of the alternatives they face. In this way, attention acts as a spotlight, enhancing processing within a certain area (similar to a zoom lens; Posner, 1980; Carrasco, 2011; Logan et al., 2021).

In decision making, people tend to choose options that they have looked at longer, a phenomenon known as attention bias (Fiedler & Glöckner, 2012; Gluth et al., 2020). Gaze (a common measure of visual attention) is hypothesized to both reflect and influence preferences (Shimojo et al., 2003). This phenomenon has been demonstrated in varied settings, such as food decisions, risky monetary decisions, and social decisions (e.g., Krajbich, Armel, & Rangel, 2010; Smith & Krajbich, 2018, 2019).

Numerous factors may influence how people allocate their attention. A decision maker may prioritize processing of information that is of highest relevance to particular goals, such as gaining the most reward in the least amount of time. For example, one study has shown that visual fixations and choices in simple choice tasks approximate an optimal information sampling policy to maximize rewards and minimize costs when taking account of environmental constraints (Callaway, Rangel, & Griffiths, 2021). In this study, the researchers assumed that values are uncertain and need to be estimated through a sampling process and that the goal of the decision maker is to select the highest-value item within a reasonable amount of time. This idea is closely related to research on rational inattention in economics, which examines the hypothesis that as people allocate effort to

> **BOX 2-2**
> **Modeling the Dynamics of Decision Making**
>
> A popular way of formalizing and testing theories about decision making in cognitive psychology, neuroscience, and neuroeconomics is by developing models of how decision-relevant information is processed. A commonly used modeling approach, called sequential sampling, assumes that individuals dynamically accumulate preferences for various options while they are deliberating. This specification provides a formalized way of understanding how preference is constructed during deliberation. This modeling approach has been used as a descriptive theory of human behavior, as well as a theory for studying the optimality of human decision making because of its relationship to Bayesian inference (Bogacz et al., 2006).
>
> In these models, the preference state is represented by a variable that increases or decreases over time, based on the quality and strength of the decision-relevant information. Once the preference state reaches a certain threshold, the person makes a decision. This class of models has been used in psychology for over 60 years (Stone, 1960; Link, 1975; Luce, 1986; Ratcliff & Smith, 2004) and provides a mathematical framework for linking choices and response times, and it has received significant support from neuroscience research (Gold & Shadlen, 2007; Shadlen & Shohamy, 2016). These models are also key to understanding the influence of perception, attention, and memory on decision making (e.g., Krajbich, Armel, & Rangel, 2010; Gluth et al., 2015; Frydman & Jin, 2022). Recently, these models have also been used to investigate the effects of various behavioral interventions—including defaults, social norms, and attribute salience—on underlying decision processes (Zhao, Coady, & Bhatia, 2022).

extracting pieces of information they factor in the costs of acquiring that information (Sims, 2003; Caplin & Dean, 2015). If some information is costly (in time or money) to obtain, then people may not consider all available information. This can result in decisions that might appear irrational by some standards but are optimal if the costs of information are taken into account. Rational inattention models are discussed further in Chapter 3.

Contextual factors can also affect attention and, consequently, decision making (Trueblood, 2022). For example, decisions involving multiple options that have different features (e.g., consumer goods that vary in both price and quality) are often sensitive to the context created by the choice set (Tversky, 1972; Huber, Payne, & Puto, 1982; Simonson, 1989). This is best illustrated by the *attraction effect*, which was first discovered in research on marketing (Huber, Payne, & Puto, 1982, 2014) and subsequently studied in marketing and other domains including psychology, neuroscience, and economics (Busemeyer et al., 2019). This effect occurs when a clearly inferior (decoy) option is added to a choice set and boosts preference for a similar, but slightly superior (target) option over other alternatives. Eye-tracking studies have shown that this boost in preference is related to increased visual attention toward the decoy and target options (Marini, Ansani, & Paglieri, 2020; Trueblood, 2022). The attention bias is significant because it reveals how simply attending to particular information can influence a decision.

The Nature of Memory

Memory—the capacity to store and retrieve knowledge and information—also plays an important role in decision making. But memory is a complex process. It is not the case that stable memories are stored and can be retrieved in identical form whenever they are needed. Rather, people reconstruct past experiences each time they are remembered and identify new connections among them and with new experiences (National Academies, 2018). That is, many factors, including a person's emotional state, may influence which memories are recalled in a given moment. In addition, memory has subsequent consequences on decision making.

For example, it is hypothesized that during deliberation, people sample arguments for various alternatives from memory (Johnson, Häubl, & Keinan, 2007; Appelt, Hardisty, & Weber, 2011; Weber & Johnson, 2011). This memory sampling process can be biased so that arguments supporting some options are sampled before thoughts supporting alternative options, thus biasing the deliberation process and ultimately choices. Empirical studies have also shown that decision makers prefer options they can remember better (Kraemer et al., 2022). In some cases, people are willing to accept relatively bad options when they remember them well (Gluth et al., 2015). Thus, the memories that are brought to bear when an individual is making a decision might or might not be the ones that would best support a purely rational decision-making process.

This brief overview of the role of perception, attention, and memory in decision making cannot do justice to the sophistication of ongoing work in psychology, neuroscience, and neuroeconomics, but the research highlighted here is especially relevant for understanding of decision making; see Box 2-2 for a discussion of modeling approaches.

The Relevance of Context

Social psychologists and sociologists have explored the concentric rings of influence on how people think, learn, behave, and feel about their world, from family and friends, to school and work environments, to geographical location, and outward to the sociopolitical context. This work has produced a significant body of evidence that the context in which decisions are made and how people interact is critical. Research on the influence of context and culture on cognition and behavior has spanned decades and disciplines and yielded an increasingly nuanced view of the influence of the physical and social environment on development, cognition, behavior, and even biological systems (National Academies, 2018). Research on learning has demonstrated that an individual's cultural and social contexts interact with cognitive and biological processes throughout the lifespan to shape thinking, memory, and learning—all of which have implications for decision making. This important work from other disciplines has had a major impact on behavioral economics.

For understanding behavioral economics, there are two key points: (1) any time an individual makes a decision, cognitive processes are influenced not only by the cognitive biases discussed above, but also by factors that reflect cultural and other influences from the decision maker's environment; and (2) the specific context in which the decision is made may have a strong influence on the decision maker's choices. The context for a decision includes the specific combination of options in a choice set, whether the context is a lab experiment, a supermarket shelf, a place (a bank, workplace, school, or doctor's office), or another circumstance of daily life. Contexts might also include societal norms and expectations; temporal or financial concerns; the salience of particular personal identities; the structure of relationships among people; and the cultural, linguistic, and institutional setting of the decision maker. It is the incorporation of the interaction of cognitive and noncognitive forces with the surrounding environment, and the attention individuals pay to the detailed context in which they are making decisions (called framing), that make behavioral economics models different from those usually developed in other disciplines.

Myriad Contextual Influences

Behavioral research has shown that humans are deeply influenced by their immediate contexts, including the time and place, the social and economic environment, and the relationships they have with other people at the time. This context can shape many aspects of life, including perceptions, emotions, reasoning, choices, and judgments. For example, preferences are highly malleable and can be shaped by context in ways that people may not even be aware of. As a result, seemingly minor contextual factors can have a significant impact on behavior, even when it does not seem rationally justified. This is often seen in *framing effects*, where small changes in the way options are presented can lead to widely different perceptions, reactions, and choices (see below).

Other contextual factors that affect decisions include culturally transmitted concern about fairness and societal norms, the tendency to defer difficult decisions, and even attitudes toward gains and losses. Fairness and social norms have appeared extensively in the work of economists working in traditional frameworks and in the work of scholars in other disciplines, but the interaction of those factors with difficulty in individual decision making and attitudes toward gains and losses has not been emphasized. All of these considerations may be, at least in part, conscious and intentional. Others, however, like those based on automatic or implicit processing, happen entirely out of awareness. For example, job candidates interviewed on rainy days tend to receive lower ratings than people interviewed on sunny days (Schwarz & Clore, 1983). This bias extends to admission interviews at large medical schools, where the difference in scores accounted for by the weather was equivalent to approximately a 10 percent lower total score on the Medical College Admission Test (Redelmeier & Baxter, 2009).

Personal identity (both one's own and one's perception of others' identities) is another aspect of context that has strong influence. For example, the concept of "mother" evokes strikingly different values and ideals from those evoked by "CEO." Identity salience has been shown to affect various behaviors, including resistance to persuasion, reactions to advertisements, and ratings of consumer products (e.g., Forehand, Deshpandé, & Reed, 2002; Reed, 2004; LeBoeuf, Shafir, & Belyavsky Bayuk, 2010).

Evoked identities are those that are brought to the forefront of a person's thoughts and behavior by a specific context or situation, and these identities often have associated tastes, values, and priorities that can shape decision making. Although people might be expected to make consistent choices, based on well-ordered preferences, evoked identities can influence which concepts and priorities are activated at the time of a specific decision, along with individual tastes and values. The result can be inconsistent, context-dependent preferences associated with the salient identity (e.g., Higgins, Rholes, & Jones, 1977; Bargh, Chen, & Burrows, 1996). One study that illustrates this concept explored the effects of ethnic stereotypes on decisions about saving. The experiment made ethnic identities salient by asking participants to first fill out a background questionnaire that asked which languages were spoken by their family and how many generations their family had lived in the United States. The researchers found that those who filled out the questionnaire before making a decision tended to make choices that aligned with ethnic stereotypes about their own family group (Benjamin, Choi, & Strickland, 2010).

Framing

Psychologists use the concept of *construal* to understand the influence of context: it is the notion that people's perceptions are the product of their mental representation or interpretation of themselves, others, or aspects of the world around them. That is, people react to the world around them in a way that is filtered through their internal representations of the people, situations, and things they observe—and those representations can vary significantly from one person to another. Psychologists describe these different representations as *framing*. For example, one person might look at a situation in terms of losses versus gains, while another looks at it in terms of lives saved versus lives lost. They are looking at the same outcomes but describing and interpreting them differently.

Framing can profoundly affect decisions. For example, people may be more favorably inclined toward actions that prevent disease when their chances of success (i.e., a gain frame) are highlighted, while highlighting the avoidance of a negative outcome (i.e., a loss frame) may be more effective at promoting screening or detection procedures (Rothman et al., 2006). Similarly, in a very different context, ground beef, which can be described as 75 percent lean or 25 percent fat, tends to be evaluated more favorably when the percentage of lean is provided (Levin, 1987; see also Levin, Schnittjer, & Thee, 1988). And a community may allocate more police resources if it is described as having a 3.7 percent crime rate than if it is described as being 96.3 percent crime free (Quattrone & Tversky, 1988).

This phenomenon has clear relevance to decision making. Traditional economic models generally portray individual decision making as a function of probabilities—the likelihood that different future states of the world will occur if they take different actions. Those probabilities are typically assumed to arise from rational evaluations of past events (learning) and from the information available to an individual. The behavioral economics framework views the problem through a different lens, positing that decisions are not directly the product of rational calculations of objective probabilities of states of the world but rather the product of assessment of the world as the person has mentally represented it. That is, individuals choose not between things in the world but between those things as they are mentally represented. These two views of decision making are not inconsistent—behavioral economists do not discount the role of rational analysis—but they portray the behavior in different terms.

Researchers have found that the way a choice is framed can significantly influence the outcome of the decision. This phenomenon, known as a framing effect, has been studied in a variety of settings. For example, in one field experiment, clients of a money lender in South Africa were sent letters offering short-term loans (averaging one-third of borrowers' gross monthly income) at randomly determined interest rates. Not surprisingly, those offered higher rates were less likely to take up a loan than those offered lower rates. In addition, however, various peripheral features of the offer letter also had a large effect on take-up. The picture of a smiling woman randomly placed in the corner of the offer letter had the same positive effect on take-up among male clients as dropping the monthly interest by 4.0 percentage points (Bertrand et al., 2010). Similarly, showing one example of a possible loan (easy to process) rather than four examples (harder to process) had the same positive effect on take-up as dropping the monthly interest by more than two percentage points. In a similar vein, Huberman, Loch, & Önçüler (2004) found that employees' overall participation in 401(k) plans drops as the number of fund options proposed by their employer increases.

Other studies have examined the effects of weighting the various elements of a set of options. Because people are often uncertain about the relative importance of various dimensions of a choice, the weights assigned to those dimensions are often influenced by relatively immaterial changes in the task, the description, and the nature of the options under consideration. For example, changing the weighting of relevant attributes (e.g., emphasizing the payoff of a gamble rather than the risk) will yield changes in people's expressed preferences (Slovic, Griffin, & Tversky, 1990). Similarly, attributes that are difficult to evaluate in isolation get weighted more heavily when they can be directly compared (Hsee, 1996; Hsee et al., 1999).

Behavior is the outcome of a variety of social, cognitive, and affective processes that are partly influenced by their context. But local contexts change, and with them the cues and features that affect people's behaviors also change. As a result of this malleability, people's decisions and behaviors fluctuate and frequently diverge from what might be expected. As this sampling of the large landscape of work on human cognition and behavior suggests, there is a firm empirical base of understanding about the ways humans process and act on information that can be integrated into the work of behavioral economists.

Conclusion 2-1: There is strong evidence that people's decision making is affected by two factors:
- *perception bias, attention bias, and memory bias all significantly influence the way people understand available options and make decisions about them; and*
- *complex aspects of the specific context can influence people's perceptions and the decisions they make.*

The research discussed in Chapters 5–10 highlights insights from research in psychology that have been incorporated in economic models and how they have been applied in a variety of policy domains. This body of work can best be understood in the context of a few additional notes about the field's growing influence and ongoing challenges it faces.

APPLICATIONS AND INFLUENCE

In recent years, behavioral economics has been applied in a variety of fields, including economic development, finance, marketing, and public policy. It is also increasingly represented in university undergraduate and graduate curricula. While only a few colleges and universities taught behavioral economics, experimental economics, or behavioral game theory in the 1980s and 1990s, most major universities now offer such coursework. Behavioral economics approaches have also gained popularity as a tool for policy makers, and the consultants who advise them, to use in designing policies that take account of what is known about human cognition and behavior.

Many people associate behavioral economics with the concept of a "nudge." Though not precise (and possibly overused), the term nudge has come to be a shorthand for many types of interventions based on behavioral economics.[11] One well-known definition comes from a best-selling and widely influential book by Thaler and Sunstein (2008, p. 6):

> Any aspect of the choice architecture [the context in which the choice is made] that alters people's behavior in a predictable way without forbidding any options or significantly changing their economic incentives. To count as a mere nudge, the intervention must be easy and cheap to avoid. Nudges are not mandates. Putting the fruit at eye level counts as a nudge. Banning junk food does not.

This concept has been particularly influential through the proliferation of *nudge units*—centers dedicated to identifying nudges that could help a government agency or institution use behavioral science evidence to meet important policy goals. The United Kingdom's Behavioural Insights Team is widely recognized as the first government-based nudge unit: indeed, the term was coined in reference to the UK group. Since its founding in 2010, many more nudge units have been created around the world at all levels of government, as well as in corporate entities, nongovernmental and multinational organizations, and health systems. Countries that have a nudge unit include Germany, the Netherlands, Qatar, Greece, Australia, Singapore, Peru, Japan, and Canada, as well as the United States. Several nonprofit organizations provide behavioral analysis on a contract basis. Many focus outside of what are characterized as the western, educated, industrialized,

---

[11]One frequently cited example of a nudge comes from the study of participation in retirement savings plans. If the default is "no," so that an employee has to make a change to opt in to an offered benefit, fewer people sign up than if the default is "yes." In traditional economic analysis, there is no difference in the two situations; behavioral economics has shown that this assumption is not correct. The research on this is the subject of Chapter 6.

rich, and democratic (WEIRD) countries: the Busara Center for Behavioral Economics, the Abdul Latif Jameel Poverty Action Lab, Innovations for Poverty Action, and ideas42, among others, pursue research to improve the generalizability of behavioral economics findings (Henrich, Heine, & Norenzayan, 2010; Berge et al., 2020). Questions about the balance of evidence from countries at different stages of economic development are among the challenges for the field as its influence grows.

Despite the influence of nudge-style policies, many policies motivated by behavioral economics are much more than nudges. As we discuss in Chapter 6, for example, the use of automatic enrollment in pension plans clearly addresses behavioral biases but is not a nudge. Rather, it is a redesign that constrains people's choices by making enrollment the default so that people must actively decline if they do not want to enroll. Another non-nudge intervention is the U.S. Department of Agriculture's simplification of application procedures for its food stamp program, which reduced the bureaucratic complexity of the program to make it easier for low-income families to participate. Another example of a non-nudge behaviorally informed intervention is the redesign of tax forms based on findings about salience, which suggests ways to make important elements stand out to individuals (see Chapter 3).

CRITIQUES AND CHALLENGES

The committee was mindful of challenges to and critiques of the field. We kept them in mind as we reviewed the literature and developed our recommendations. We note here the responses behavioral economists have offered to several frequently raised concerns:

- behaviorally based interventions may in some cases reflect an unexamined paternalistic attitude toward the targets of behaviorally based interventions;
- many behavioral economics studies showing positive effects have comparatively small effect sizes;
- interventions that focus on individual-level behavioral change may distract from or undermine policy attention to the need for system-level change;
- behavioral insights may be exploited by nongovernmental private agents, such as in the realms of political influencing and commercial marketing;
- behavioral interventions may have the unintended negative consequence of exacerbating disparities in society; and
- the representativeness in the samples used in behavioral economics research is often lacking.

Paternalism

Critics of behavioral economics have suggested that it is implicitly based on, or conveys, a paternalistic vision of human behavior, in which interactions and choices need to be "corrected" (e.g., Wright & Ginsburg, 2012; Gigerenzer, 2015; McMahon, 2015). They make the point that some behaviors operate below the level of consciousness and that interventions that affect them could have a negative impact on the well-being of people targeted by such interventions.[12] A particular concern for behavioral economics is that decisions based on factors other than reasoning may in many cases be valid and that the idea that people need to be nudged or otherwise induced to make more seemingly rational decisions reflects a narrow understanding of human rationality.

Critics have raised the concern that the use of behavioral economics tools in a public policy context could be regarded as an example of government agencies deciding what people should do instead of letting them decide for themselves. A government agency doing this, it is argued, violates the concept of "consumer sovereignty" in economics, the idea that consumers know what is best for themselves. Moreover, many people, perhaps particularly those who are most vulnerable in terms of education and income level, have a strong trust in government and authority. This circumstance heightens the responsibility of those who develop policies to consider them carefully from an ethical point of view—specifically considering possible outcomes and whether people may be induced to make a choice that does not contribute to their well-being.

Behavioral economists respond in multiple ways to this critique. One frequent response is that all government policies are paternalistic in some sense. Even though traditional economic theory recommends government action only in specified circumstances (monopolies, market failures, pollution), there has always been a rationale for what are called "merit goods," outcomes that society deems to have merit for their own sake. For example, many of the goals that behavioral economists target for interventions, such as high application rates to college, higher take-up of medicines, or higher retirement savings, are broadly supported and generally not controversial. Behavioral economists have suggested that paternalistic actions to improve these outcomes would have a high rate of social approval. Behavioral economists also argue that a core presumption in their approach is that some behavior reflects biased judgments that reduce people's well-being (e.g., Bernheim & Taubinsky, 2018). They acknowledge that identifying when judgments are biased is difficult—and, in fact, the heart of the issue. But some behavioral economists argue that there are many behaviors that are

---

[12]We use "well-being" as equivalent to the term "welfare" that is used in economics.

transparently not the result of intentional behavior, and that the hypothesis that they may have subtle benefits is implausible. For example, individuals who lose tens or hundreds of thousands of dollars by not enrolling in retirement plans offered to them cannot be plausibly understood to be making a rational choice in doing so.

Nonetheless, there are unquestionably grey areas in making these distinctions. It is important that designers of behavioral interventions, particularly ones that might fall uncomfortably close to constraining individuals' autonomy, have strong evidence that the people whose behavior they hope to modify are affected by biases and would consider themselves better off if the intervention had its intended effects.

Small Effect Sizes

A second critique is that many, though certainly not all, behavioral economics studies showing positive effects have comparatively small effect sizes. There are examples where extremely large gains have been documented, such as for automatic pension deductions. But in many cases, researchers expect small effect sizes because the intervention itself is modest. Behavioral economists emphasize that the most relevant benchmark is the ratio of the effect size to the cost, and that the ratio can be large even if the effect size is small. This point is discussed further in Chapter 14.

Individual Focus

Another critique of behavioral economics is that it focuses on changing individual behavior rather than on reforms that regulate firms or change government program designs to pursue the same goals (Chater & Loewenstein, 2022). This criticism is mostly focused on the small interventions represented by many nudges that have low effect sizes and do not radically change behavior. In response, behavioral economists point to the many behaviorally motivated interventions that are much more than nudges and that have major effects. But a more fundamental response is that the behavioral patterns identified by behavioral economists can be used to design governments' regulatory, tax, and transfer policies: that is, for systemic changes. Behavioral economists argue that those policies are more likely to achieve their aims if the behavioral responses of the people targeted are taken into account in the design of the policy. Behavioral scientists argue that most government regulatory efforts to reduce suboptimal behaviors (consumption of sugary cereals, for example) are based on behavioral research even if they address the actions of firms, not individuals. Indeed, behavioral economists would argue that regulations and behaviorally informed interventions are complementary, not in opposition to one other.

Political and Commercial Use

Others have noted that it is easy to observe—perhaps all too difficult to ignore—the many ways behavioral insights are applied in daily life in the service of marketing efforts and efforts to advance political and other ideas. Knowledge of behavioral bias is not restricted to academics and policy makers advised by academics. That knowledge can also be used in an adversarial fashion to influence people's thinking and decision making or to frustrate their efforts to make optimal choices, such as through counter-nudges, or "sludge," that can make it more difficult for people to understand potential advantages, notice hidden costs, or claim benefits. The committee was not able to explore these issues, which concern ways behavioral economics research is used rather than the nature of the research and analysis produced by the field. However, we note that there is a growing body of research that will be of value as policy makers consider ways to address them (see, e.g., Petticrew et al., 2020; Shahab & Lades, 2021; Mills, 2023).

Disparities

It has also been suggested that behavioral economists may not have paid enough attention to the effects of the tools they design on economic and social disparities. One concern is that behavioral biases may tend to affect populations with varying levels of education differently, particularly in the contexts studied by economists, and the result could be that interventions have unintended disparate impacts. A related concern is that interventions designed to bring benefits for certain segments of a population may indirectly disadvantage those not targeted. Some behavioral economists argue that these critiques are refuted in part by the large body of evidence on interventions designed explicitly to close equity gaps (such as unequal distributions of government benefits) and that many behavioral policies are directed to assist disadvantaged groups, at least in the United States (e.g., behavioral redesigns of financial aid forms for low-income college students [see Chapter 9]). Despite this argument, it is important that researchers evaluate the effects of behavioral interventions and nudges on disparities more broadly than they have in the past. Improvements to standard research practices may also help to address this issue, as we discuss in Chapter 14.[13]

---

[13]It is also worth noting concerns about methods used in the conduct of behavioral research (see, e.g., Meyer et al., 2019; Heck et al., 2020; Mislavsky, Dietvorst, & Simonsohn, 2020).

Representativeness

Finally, like researchers in most social science domains, behavioral economists are subject to the critique that they have not paid adequate attention to the importance of ensuring that their research is representative of diverse populations. In the past 20 years a substantial body of behavioral economics research has been conducted in the context of developing countries—including work that has been recognized in Nobel Prize awards—and behavioral development economics is one of the most active areas of the field (see, e.g., Duflo & Kremer, 2004; Banerjee & Duflo, 2009; Banerjee, Duflo, & Kremer, 2020). This work has, thus far, yielded findings in lower-income societies that largely mirror those in the higher-income ones (Kremer, Rao, & Schilbach, 2020). Nevertheless, the bulk of behavioral economics research conducted by U.S. researchers has been carried out in this country, and thus the body of evidence about many behavioral challenges and intervention approaches so far rests primarily on evidence collected in WEIRD contexts; this is a challenge the field will need to continue to address.

REFERENCES

Appelt, K. C., Hardisty, D. J., & Weber, E. U. (2011). Asymmetric discounting of gains and losses: A query theory account. *Journal of Risk and Uncertainty, 43*, 107–126. https://doi.org/10.1007/s11166-011-9125-1

Ashraf, N., Camerer, C. F., & Loewenstein, G. (2005). Adam Smith, behavioral economist. *Journal of Economic Perspectives, 19*(3), 131–145. https://doi.org/10.1257/089533005774357897

Banerjee, A. V., & Duflo, E. (2009). The experimental approach to development economics. *Annual Review of Economics, 1*, 151–178. https://doi.org/10.1146/annurev.economics.050708.143235

Banerjee, A. V., Duflo, E., & Kremer, M. (2020). The influence of randomized controlled trials on development economics research and on development policy. *The state of economics, the state of the world*, 482–488. Massachusetts Institute of Technology Press. https://doi.org/10.7551/mitpress/11130.003.0015

Bargh, J. A., Chen, M., & Burrows, L. (1996). Automaticity of social behavior: Direct effects of trait construct and stereotype activation on action. *Journal of Personality and Social Psychology, 71*(2), 230–244. https://doi.org/10.1037/0022-3514.71.2.230

Barlow, H. B. (1961). Possible principles underlying the transformation of sensory messages. *Sensory communication*, 217–234. Massachusetts Institute of Technology Press. https://doi.org/10.7551/mitpress/9780262518420.003.0013

Benjamin, D. J., Choi, J. J., & Strickland, A. J. (2010). Social identity and preferences. *American Economic Review, 100*(4), 1913–1928. https://doi.org/10.1257/aer.100.4.1913

Berge, L. I. O., Bjorvatn, K., Galle, S., Miguel, E., Posner, D. N., Tungodden, B., & Zhang, K. (2020). Ethnically biased? Experimental evidence from Kenya. *Journal of the European Economic Association, 18*(1), 134–164. https://doi.org/10.1093/jeea/jvz003

Bernheim, B. D., & Taubinsky, D. (2018). Behavioral public economics. *Handbook of behavioral economics: Applications and foundations*, 381–516. North-Holland. https://doi.org/10.1016/bs.hesbe.2018.07.002

Bertrand, M., Karlan, D., Mullainathan, S., Shafir, E., & Zinman, J. (2010). What's advertising content worth? Evidence from a consumer credit marketing field experiment. *The Quarterly Journal of Economics, 125*(1), 263–306. https://doi.org/10.1162/qjec.2010.125.1.263

Blau, P. M. (1964). *Exchange and power in social life*. Wiley.

Bogacz, R., Brown, E., Moehlis, J., Holmes, P., & Cohen, J. D. (2006). The physics of optimal decision making: A formal analysis of models of performance in two-alternative forced-choice tasks. *Psychological Review, 113*(4), 700. https://psycnet.apa.org/doi/10.1037/0033-295X.113.4.700

Bolton, G. E., & Ockenfels, A. (2000). ERC: A theory of equity, reciprocity, and competition. *American Economic Review, 90*(1), 166–193. https://doi.org/10.1257/aer.90.1.166

Botvinick, M., Weinstein, A., Solway, A., & Barto, A. (2015). Reinforcement learning, efficient coding, and the statistics of natural tasks. *Current Opinion in Behavioral Sciences, 5*, 71–77. https://doi.org/10.1016/j.cobeha.2015.08.009

Busemeyer, J. R., Gluth, S., Rieskamp, J., & Turner, B. M. (2019). Cognitive and neural bases of multi-attribute, multi-alternative, value-based decisions. *Trends in Cognitive Sciences, 23*(3), 251–263. https://doi.org/10.1016/j.tics.2018.12.003

Callaway, F., Rangel, A., & Griffiths, T. L. (2021). Fixation patterns in simple choice reflect optimal information sampling. *PLoS Computational Biology, 17*(3), e1008863. https://doi.org/10.1371/journal.pcbi.1008863

Camerer, C. F. (2011). *Behavioral game theory: Experiments in strategic interaction*. Princeton University Press.

Camerer, C. F., & Thaler, R. H. (1995). Anomalies: Ultimatums, dictators and manners. *Journal of Economic Perspectives, 9*(2), 209–219. https://doi.org/10.1257/jep.9.2.209

Caplin, A., & Dean, M. (2015). Revealed preference, rational inattention, and costly information acquisition. *American Economic Review, 105*(7), 2183–2203. https://doi.org/10.1257/aer.20140117

Carrasco, M. (2011). Visual attention: The past 25 years. *Vision Research, 51*(13), 1484–1525. https://doi.org/10.1016/j.visres.2011.04.012

Charness, G., & Rabin, M. (2002). Understanding social preferences with simple tests. *The Quarterly Journal of Economics, 117*(3), 817–869. https://doi.org/10.1162/003355302760193904

Chater, N., & Loewenstein, G. (2022). The i-frame and the s-frame: How focusing on individual-level solutions has led behavioral public policy astray. *Behavioral and Brain Sciences*, 1–60. https://doi.org/10.1017/S0140525X22002023

Dawes, R. M., & Thaler, R. H. (1988). Anomalies: Cooperation. *Journal of Economic Perspectives, 2*(3), 187–197. https://doi.org/10.1257/jep.2.3.187

Duflo. E., & Kremer, M. (2004). Use of randomization in the evaluation of development effectiveness. *Evaluating development effectiveness, World Bank series on evaluation & development, 7*, 205–232. Routledge.

Ericson, K. M., & Laibson, D. (2019). Intertemporal choice. *Handbook of behavioral economics: Applications and foundations 1, 2*, 1–67. North-Holland. https://doi.org/10.1016/bs.hesbe.2018.12.001

Fehr, E., & Schmidt, K. M. (1999). A theory of fairness, competition, and cooperation. *The Quarterly Journal of Economics, 114*(3), 817–868. https://doi.org/10.1162/003355399556151

Fennell, L. A., & McAdams, R. H. (2013). *Fairness in law and economics*. Edward Elgar. https://chicagounbound.uchicago.edu/cgi/viewcontent.cgi?article=2381&context=law_and_economics

Fiedler, S., & Glöckner, A. (2012). The dynamics of decision making in risky choice: An eyetracking analysis. *Frontiers in Psychology, 3*(335), 1–18. https://doi.org/10.3389/fpsyg.2012.00335

Forehand, M. R., Deshpandé, R., & Reed II, A. (2002). Identity salience and the influence of differential activation of the social self-schema on advertising response. *Journal of Applied Psychology, 87*(6), 1086. https://doi.org/10.1037/0021-9010.87.6.1086

Frydman, C., & Jin, L. J. (2022). Efficient coding and risky choice. *The Quarterly Journal of Economics, 137*(1), 161–213. https://doi.org/10.1093/qje/qjab031

Gigerenzer, G. (2015). On the supposed evidence for libertarian paternalism. *Review of Philosophy and Psychology, 6*, 361–383. https://doi.org/10.1007/s13164-015-0248-1

Gluth, S., Sommer, T., Rieskamp, J., & Buchel, C. (2015). Effective connectivity between hippocampus and ventromedial prefrontal cortex controls preferential choices from memory. *Neuron, 86*(4), 1078–1090. https://doi.org/10.1016/j.neuron.2015.04.023

Gluth, S., Kern, N., Kortmann, M., & Vitali, C. L. (2020). Value-based attention but not divisive normalization influences decisions with multiple alternatives. *Nature Human Behavior, 4*(6), 634–645. https://doi.org/10.1038/s41562-020-0822-0

Gold, J. I., & Shadlen, M. N. (2007). The neural basis of decision making. *Annual Review of Neuroscience, 30*(1), 535–574. https://doi.org/10.1146/annurev.neuro.29.051605.113038

Grether, D. M., & Plott, C. R. (1979). Economic theory of choice and the preference reversal phenomenon. *The American Economic Review, 69*(4), 623–638. https://www.jstor.org/stable/1808708

Güth, W., Schmittberger, R., & Schwarze, B. (1982). An experimental analysis of ultimatum bargaining. *Journal of Economic Behavior & Organization, 3*(4), 367–388. https://doi.org/10.1016/0167-2681(82)90011-7

Heck, P. R., Chabris, C. F., Watts, D. J., & Meyer, M. N. (2020). Objecting to experiments even while approving of the policies or treatments they compare. *Proceedings of the National Academy of Sciences of the United States of America, 117*(32), 18948–18950. https://doi.org/10.1073/pnas.2009030117

Henrich, J., Heine, S. J., & Norenzayan, A. (2010). The weirdest people in the world? *Behavioral and Brain Sciences, 33*(2–3), 61–83. https://doi.org/10.1017/S0140525X0999152X

Higgins, E. T., Rholes, W. S., & Jones, C. R. (1977). Category accessibility and impression formation. *Journal of Experimental Social Psychology, 13*(2), 141–154. https://doi.org/10.1016/S0022-1031(77)80007-3

Homans, G. C. (1961). *Social behavior: Its elementary forms*. Harcourt, Brace.

Hsee, C. K. (1996). Elastic justification. How unjustifiable factors influence judgments. *Organizational Behavior and Human Decision Processes, 66*(1), 122–129. https://doi.org/10.1006/obhd.1996.0077

Hsee, C. K., Loewenstein, G. F., Blount, S., & Bazerman, M. H. (1999). Preference reversals between joint and separate evaluations of options: A review and theoretical analysis. *Psychological Bulletin, 125*(5), 576–590. https://doi.org/10.1037/0033-2909.125.5.576

Huber, J., Payne, J. W., & Puto, C. (1982). Adding asymmetrically dominated alternatives: Violations of regularity and the similarity hypothesis. *Journal of Consumer Research, 9*(1), 90–98. https://doi.org/10.1086/208899

———. (2014). Let's be honest about the attraction effect. *Journal of Marketing Research, 51*(4), 520–525. https://doi.org/10.1509/jmr.14.0208

Huberman, B. A., Loch, C. H., & Önçüler, A. (2004). Status as a valued resource. *Social Psychology Quarterly, 67*(1), 103–114. https://doi.org/10.1177/019027250406700109

Isaac, R. M., McCue, K. F., & Plott, C. R. (1985). Public goods provision in an experimental environment. *Journal of Public Economics, 26*(1), 51–74. https://doi.org/10.1016/0047-2727(85)90038-6

Johnson, E. J., Häubl, G., & Keinan, A. (2007). Aspects of endowment: A query theory of value construction. *Journal of Experimental Psychology: Learning, Memory, and Cognition, 33*(3), 461. https://psycnet.apa.org/doi/10.1037/0278-7393.33.3.461

Kahneman, D., & Tversky, A. (1979). Prospect theory: An analysis of decision under risk. *Econometrica, 47*(2), 263–291. https://doi.org/10.2307/1914185

Kahneman, D., Knetsch, J. L., & Thaler, R. (1986). Fairness as a constraint on profit seeking: Entitlements in the market. *The American Economic Review*, 76(4), 728–741. https://www.jstor.org/stable/1806070

Khaw, M. W., Li, Z., & Woodford, M. (2021). Cognitive imprecision and small-stakes risk aversion. *The Review of Economic Studies*, 88(4), 1979–2013. https://doi.org/10.1093/restud/rdaa044

Kim, E. H., Morse, A., & Zingales, L. (2006). What has mattered to economics since 1970. *Journal of Economic Perspectives*, 20(4), 189–202. https://doi.org/10.1257/jep.20.4.189

Kraemer, P. M., Weilbacher, R. A., Mechera-Ostrovsky, T., & Gluth, S. (2022). Cognitive and neural principles of a memory bias on preferential choices. *Current Research in Neurobiology*, 3, 100029. https://doi.org/10.1016/j.crneur.2022.100029

Krajbich, I., Armel, C., & Rangel, A. (2010). Visual fixations and the computation and comparison of value in simple choice. *Nature Neuroscience*, 13(10), 1292–1298. https://doi.org/10.1038/nn.2635

Kremer, M., Rao, G., & Schilbach, R. F. (2020). Behavioral development economics. *Handbook of behavioral economics: Foundations and applications*, 2, 345–458. https://doi.org/10.1016/bs.hesbe.2018.12.002

Laughlin, S. (1981). A simple coding procedure enhances a neuron's information capacity. *Zeitschrift für Naturforschung C*, 36(9–10), 910–912. https://doi.org/10.1515/znc-1981-9-1040

LeBoeuf, R. A., Shafir, E., & Belyavsky Bayuk, J. (2010). The conflicting choices of alternating selves. *Organizational Behavior and Human Decision Processes*, 111(1), 48–61. https://doi.org/10.1016/j.obhdp.2009.08.004

Levin, I. P. (1987). Associative effects of information framing. *Bulletin of the Psychonomic Society*, 25(2), 85–86. https://doi.org/10.3758/BF03330291

Levin, I. P., Schnittjer, S. K., & Thee, S. L. (1988). Information framing effects in social and personal decisions. *Journal of Experimental Social Psychology*, 24(6), 520–529. https://doi.org/10.1016/0022-1031(88)90050-9

Link, S. W. (1975). The relative judgment theory of two choice response time. *Journal of Mathematical Psychology*, 12(1), 114–135. https://doi.org/10.1016/0022-2496(75)90053-X

Logan, G. D., Cox, G. E., Annis, J., & Lindsey, D. R. (2021). The episodic Flanker effect: Memory retrieval as attention turned inward. *Psychological Review*, 128(3), 397. https://doi.org/10.1037/rev0000272

Luce, R. D. (1986). *Response times*. Oxford University Press.

Marini, M., Ansani, A., & Paglieri, F. (2020). Attraction comes from many sources: Attentional and comparative processes in decoy effects. *Judgment and Decision Making*, 15(5), 704–726. https://journal.sjdm.org/19/191024a/jdm191024a.pdf

McMahon, J. (2015). Behavioral economics as neoliberalism: Producing and governing homo economicus. *Contemporary Political Theory*, 14(2), 137–158. https://doi.org/10.1057/cpt.2014.14

Meyer, M. N., Heck, P. R., Holtzman, G. S., Anderson, S. M., Cai, W., Watts, D. J., & Chabris, C. F. (2019). Objecting to experiments that compare two unobjectionable policies or treatments. *Proceedings of the National Academy of Sciences of the United States of America*, 116(22), 10723–10728. https://doi.org/10.1073/pnas.1820701116

Mills, S. (2023). Nudge/sludge symmetry: On the relationship between nudge and sludge and the resulting ontological, normative and transparency implications. *Behavioural Public Policy*, 7(2), 309–332. https://doi.org/10.1017/bpp.2020.61

Mislavsky, R., Dietvorst, B., & Simonsohn, U. (2020). Critical condition: People don't dislike a corporate experiment more than they dislike its worst condition. *Marketing Science*, 39(6), 1033–1201. https://doi.org/10.1287/mksc.2019.1166

National Academies of Sciences, Engineering, and Medicine (National Academies). (2018). Implications for learning in school. *How people learn II: Learners, contexts, and cultures*, 135–162. The National Academies Press. https://nap.nationalacademies.org/login.php?record_id=24783

Ostrom, E. (1990). *Governing the commons: The evolution of institutions for collective action.* Cambridge University Press.

Petticrew, M., Maani, N., Pettigrew, L., Rutter, H., & Van Schalkwyk, M.C. (2020). Dark nudges and sludge in big alcohol: Behavioral economics, cognitive biases, and alcohol industry corporate social responsibility. *The Milbank Quarterly, 98*, 1290–1328. https://doi.org/10.1111/1468-0009.12475

Posner, M. I. (1980). Orienting of attention. *Quarterly Journal of Experimental Psychology, 32*(1), 3–25. https://doi.org/10.1080/00335558008248231

Quattrone, G. A., & Tversky, A. (1988). Contrasting rational and psychological analyses of political choice. *American Political Science Review, 82*(3), 719–736. https://doi.org/10.2307/1962487

Ratcliff, R., & Smith, P. L. (2004). A comparison of sequential sampling models for two-choice reaction time. *Psychological Review, 111*(2), 333. https://doi.org/10.1037/0033-295X.111.2.333

Redelmeier, D. A., & Baxter, S. D. (2009). Rainy weather and medical school admission interviews. *Canadian Medical Association Journal, 181*(12), 933. https://doi.org/10.1503/cmaj.091546

Reed, A. (2004). Activating the self-importance of consumer selves: Exploring identity salience effects on judgments. *Journal of Consumer Research, 31*(2), 286–295. https://doi.org/10.1086/422108

Rothman, A. J., Bartels, R. D., Wlaschin, J., & Salovey, P. (2006). The strategic use of gain- and loss-framed messages to promote healthy behavior: How theory can inform practice. *Journal of Communication, 56*(Suppl 1), S202–S220. https://doi.org/10.1111/j.1460-2466.2006.00290.x

Schwarz, N., & Clore, G. L. (1983). Mood, misattribution, and judgments of well-being: Informative and directive functions of affective states. *Journal of Personality and Social Psychology, 45*(3), 513. https://psycnet.apa.org/doi/10.1037/0022-3514.45.3.513

Selten, R. (1998). Multistage game models and delay supergames. *Theory and Decision, 44*(1), 1–36. https://doi.org/10.1023/A:1005099909043

Shadlen, M. N., and Shohamy, D. (2016). Decision making and sequential sampling from memory. *Neuron, 90*(5), 927–939. https://doi.org/10.1016/j.neuron.2016.04.036

Shahab, S., & Lades, L. (2021). Sludge and transaction costs. *Behavioural Public Policy*, 1–22. https://doi.org/10.1017/bpp.2021.12

Shimojo, S., Simion, C., Shimojo, E., & Scheier, C. (2003). Gaze bias both reflects and influences preference. *Nature Neuroscience, 6*(12), 1317–1322. https://doi.org/10.1038/nn1150

Simon, H. A. (1955). A behavioral model of rational choice. *The Quarterly Journal of Economics, 69*(1), 99–118. https://doi.org/10.2307/1884852

Simonson, I. (1989). Choice based on reasons: The case of attraction and compromise effects. *Journal of Consumer Research, 16*(2), 158–174. https://doi.org/10.1086/209205

Sims, C. A. (2003). Implications of rational inattention. *Journal of Monetary Economics, 50*(3), 665–690. https://doi.org/10.1016/S0304-3932(03)00029-1

Slovic, P., Griffin, D., & Tversky, A. (1990). Compatibility effects in judgment and choice. *Insights in decision making: A tribute to Hillel J. Einhorn*, 5–27. University of Chicago Press.

Smith, S. M., & Krajbich, I. (2018). Attention and choice across domains. *Journal of Experimental Psychology: General, 147*(12), 1810. https://psycnet.apa.org/doi/10.1037/xge0000482

———. (2019). Gaze amplifies value in decision making. *Psychological Science*, *30*(1), 116–128. https://doi.org/10.1177/0956797618810521

Smith, V. L. (1989). Theory, experiment and economics. *Journal of Economic Perspectives*, *3*(1), 151–169. https://doi.org/10.1257/jep.3.1.151

———. (2003). Constructivist and ecological rationality in economics. *American Economic Review*, *93*(3), 465–508. https://doi.org/10.1257/000282803322156954

Stone, M. (1960). Models for choice-reaction time. *Psychometrika*, *25*(3), 251–260.

Sun, J., & Perona, P. (1998). Where is the sun? *Nature Neuroscience*, *1*(3), 183–184. https://doi.org/10.1038/630

Svornenčík, A., & Truc, A. (2022). *A history of behavioral economics and its applications: What we know and future research directions*. Commissioned paper prepared for the Committee on Future Directions for Applying Behavioral Economics to Policy, National Academies of Sciences, Engineering, and Medicine. https://nap.nationalacademies.org/resource/26874/BE_history_20221009.pdf

Thaler, R. H. (1981). Some empirical evidence on dynamic inconsistency. *Economics Letters*, *8*(3), 201–207. https://doi.org/10.1016/0165-1765(81)90067-7

———. (1988). Anomalies: The ultimatum game. *Journal of Economic Perspectives*, *2*(4), 195–206. https://doi.org/10.1257/jep.2.4.195

———. (Ed.). (1993). *Advances in behavioral finance*. Russell Sage Foundation.

Thaler, R. H., & Sunstein, C. (2008). *Nudge: Improving decisions about health, wealth, and happiness*. Penguin Books.

Trueblood, J. S. (2022). Theories of context effects in multi-alternative, multi-attribute choice. *Current Directions in Psychological Science*, *31*(5). https://doi.org/10.1177/09637214221109587

Tversky, A. (1972). Elimination by aspects: A theory of choice. *Psychological Review*, *79*(4), 281. https://doi.org/10.1037/h0032955

Tversky, A., & Kahneman, D. (1973). Availability: A heuristic for judging frequency and probability. *Cognitive Psychology*, *5*(2), 207–232. https://doi.org/10.1016/0010-0285(73)90033-9

Weber, E. U., & Johnson, E. J. (2011). Query theory: Knowing what we want by arguing with ourselves. *Behavior and Brain Sciences*, *34*(2), 91. https://ssrn.com/abstract=1957335

Wright, J. D., & Ginsburg, D. H. (2012). The goals of antitrust: Welfare trumps choice. *Fordham Law Review*, *81*, 2405. https://ir.lawnet.fordham.edu/flr/vol81/iss5/9

Zhao, W. J., Coady, A., & Bhatia, S. (2022). Computational mechanisms for context-based behavioral interventions: A large-scale analysis. *Proceedings of the National Academy of Sciences*, *119*(15), e2114914119.

3

Foundational Behavioral and Economic Ideas

In the words of Richard Thaler, people behave as *humans*, not as *econs*. Individuals' choices are highly malleable, often shaped by what would otherwise be considered irrelevant factors, particularly the behavioral phenomena discussed in Chapter 2. Behavioral economics is a response to the fact that the traditional economic model, which assumes that rational individuals behave in predictable ways, is incomplete and fails to account for important aspects of human behavior. Evidence from the behavioral sciences has demonstrated the critical role of phenomena such as biased perception, attention bias, memory bias, and complex influences of context in decision making that are not considered in traditional economic models. Behavioral economists have integrated understanding of these phenomena with tools and methods from traditional economic analysis. In this chapter we look first at traditional economic modeling and its role in economic analysis and then discuss the behavioral phenomena that have been particularly important for behavioral economics.

We emphasize that behavioral economics is only a subset of the larger field of behavioral science, which encompasses numerous disciplines that explore human behavior, including psychology, sociology, anthropology, and cognitive science. It is a vast field that has developed many insights into human behavior. Behavioral economics is a narrower field that draws on insights from behavioral science; often builds on those insights; and, most important, incorporates those insights into economic models of human behavior.

Modeling, a key tool of economic analysis, is the development of simplified representations of reality that can be used to test hypotheses.

Behavioral economists have incorporated behavioral insights into such models. In this chapter and in our discussion of findings from the six policy areas (Part II), we show how insights from behavioral disciplines have been used by economists to develop new economic models, often yielding important new policy implications.

ECONOMIC MODELING

As noted above, modeling is a fundamental tool in economic analysis. Economists use formal mathematics to portray the world in a set of equations intended to illustrate the key mechanisms in a given scenario they wish to analyze, taking into account many kinds of behavior. Behavioral economics models are not radically different from traditional economic models and do not constitute a complete rejection of those models. Instead, they build on, extend, modify—and, indeed, enrich—those models by adding behavioral features to them. Formally modeling behavior allows economists to make quantitative forecasts of the effects a particular intervention might have that can be more precise than qualitative or intuitive predictions. Quantification using mathematical models can also serve as a guide to empirical estimates of key parameters of those models; this, in turn, allows economists to make quantifiable policy recommendations, which are the main subject of this report. But not everything can be captured in formal models, and many behavioral features are captured only in simplified versions.

There is no single traditional economic model; different designs capture different behaviors. However, most traditional models share common features, such as representation of individuals (or firms) who know their own objectives or preferences, who always act to maximize those objectives to the extent possible, who accurately perceive the world around them (at least in terms of probabilities of uncertain events), and whose preferences and objectives are stable over time. Most economists understand these assumptions to be only approximations of reality but regard them as close enough to reality to support policy predictions. The types of policies most commonly addressed in traditional models are those based on incentives, such as taxes, transfers, and subsidies, and the usual assumption of traditional economists is that individuals respond to the incentives roughly in the way the model predicts. A chief difference between traditional economic models and behavioral economic models is the nature of the policy prescriptions they support, as we discuss throughout this report (also see Madrian, 2014).

Box 3-1 describes a stylized version of one traditional economic model in mathematical terms. In this example, individuals are assumed to take actions that increase their current well-being, their future well-being, or

> **BOX 3-1**
> **One Traditional Mathematical Economic**
> **Model of Decision Making**
>
> Rational decision making can be understood mathematically as behavior that maximizes what is known as the present value of expected utility: that is, it is a process of weighing the value and likelihood of obtaining possible benefits. In this model it is assumed that individuals make decisions that maximize a utility, or well-being, function as follows (Rabin, 2002; DellaVigna, 2009):
>
> $$\max_{x_i^t \in X} \sum_{t=0}^{\infty} \delta^t \sum_{s_t \in S} p(s_t) U(x_i^t \mid s_t)$$
>
> In this equation, $x(i,t)$ are the actions individual i takes at time t, given each possible future state of the world, s_t, that might occur. U represents utility in each future period (i.e., individual well-being) from each choice of x. The model assumes that an individual calculates the probability that each state of the world $p(s_t)$ will occur and then calculates a weighted average of utility in each of those possible future states. The model assumes that the individual will pick the x that maximizes utility in each such state of the world—that the individual will make the calculation of the "best" x to choose at each future period of life, so they maximize not just utility at each single future point, or well-being in one period, but in all future periods. Because individuals are assumed to care more about today's utility than future ones, the individual "discounts" well-being for each period in the future at a constant rate (delta, which is a parameter between 0 and 1).
>
> Thus, the model implies that rational people who are considering whether to save or spend a sum of money will decide to save in the present if their calculation of the value of consumption the savings will make possible in the future outweighs their calculation of the disadvantages of having less money in the present.

both. The future is uncertain, but the assumption is that people have an accurate perception of the probabilities associated with possible future events. In economists' terms, people "discount" the future—that is, they prefer well-being in the present to well-being in the future, everything else being equal—and they take current actions that maximize the discounted sum of well-being over the future. Their actions are consistent over time. This is a form of the well-known "expected utility" model, which Kahneman and Tversky argued is not the way humans behave (see Chapter 2).

There are many other types of models that extend this version of the traditional model in various ways. For example, some models incorporate the idea that individuals do not know the probabilities of future events with certainty but learn by observing events and constantly update their estimates of those probabilities over time. These are called learning models, and they are based on the assumption that individuals update their beliefs in a mathematically accurate fashion (Wald, 1950). Other models factor in the idea that beliefs are subjective and that individuals hold expectations about future events—expectations that can be measured (De Finetti, 1970; Manski, 2004).

In addition to these models of individual behavior, there are many models that incorporate the assumption that individual behaviors are influenced by those of others. Early work by Samuelson (1947) on consumption assumed that one person in a family represents all the other members in making consumer choices. This framework was later used by Becker (1981) and many others in the design of models of decision making within families (and in models that incorporate the idea of altruism). Other models that incorporate social interactions portray individuals as members of networks who share information and resources with each other (Schelling, 1978; Manski, 1993; Brock & Durlauf, 2001; Jackson, 2014).

Although these and other models developed by traditional economists address many important aspects of behavior, they do not capture the full spectrum of behavior that behavioral economists emphasize. Because they address other behavioral phenomena, behavioral economic models lead to policy recommendations that differ from those supported by traditional models. Decades of research have explored the possibilities for conducting economic analyses that incorporate behavioral concepts. In that work, formal modeling is used in order to improve predictions about the effects of policy interventions, explore new tools for analysis, and develop more accurate assessments of outcomes than traditional economic modeling could provide (Chetty, 2015).

FIVE CORE PRINCIPLES

There is no single definition of behavioral economics because the field arose from observations of a set of behaviors that appear to deviate from what is predicted by traditional models—not from the conceptualization of a new, all-encompassing theory of behavior. The committee identified five core principles, as behavioral economists have framed them, that have been the basis for large bodies of research designed to test behavioral hypotheses and develop strategies to influence behavior: limited attention and cognition, inaccurate beliefs, present bias, reference dependence and framing, and social preferences and norms.

This is necessarily a selective review of key behavioral principles for the development of policy. The five principles we highlight here do not capture all the behaviors and findings from the research on cognitive and social psychology, and this is not the only possible way to organize these ideas. A more comprehensive review can be found in the *Handbook of Behavioral Economics* (Bernheim, DellaVigna, & Laibson, 2019). However, these five have direct application to the kinds of decision making that behavioral economists study and the choices that policy makers hope to influence. We used them in analyzing the research on the six domains discussed in Part II and to assess what behavioral economics research has accomplished to date.

Limited Attention and Cognition	The extent to which people understand, pay attention to, and process information is crucial in any decision. Yet, individuals are able to pay only limited attention to important aspects of their environment, often have a difficult time processing information, and make cognitive errors even in simple situations.
Inaccurate Beliefs	Individuals often have incorrect perceptions of or information about the situations they are in, the incentives they face, their own abilities, and the beliefs of others, often as a result of limited attention or cognition.
Present Bias	People tend to disproportionately focus on issues that are before them in the present moment, paying less attention to future payoffs and consequences. This bias has important implications for decisions about consumption, payments, and utility.
Reference Dependence and Framing	Individuals tend to evaluate risk decisions by considering how the options relate to a particular reference point. That is, they assess whether an outcome would be a gain or a loss by comparing possible outcomes to a single reference point, such as the current status quo, rather than considering all alternative possibilities. Consequently, people are sensitive to the way decision problems are framed, which affects what possible outcomes come to their attention.
Social Preferences and Social Norms	An important aspect of the context for decision making is perceptions of how one's actions relate to those of others, including the well-being of others: people make comparisons between themselves and others, and they care about their social standing, how they signal their values and preferences to others, and how they conform with social norms.

Behavioral economics research illustrates how each of these core principles functions in the context of decision making.

Limited Attention and Cognition

One cannot overstate how important limited attention and cognitive difficulties are for public policy. To fully understand their role it is useful to step back and consider how economists have traditionally thought about designing public programs. Although no economist believes that people can pay perfect attention to everything and have infallible cognitive abilities, it is assumed that they are paying close enough attention and are sufficiently cognitively aware that policy recommendations can be based on the expectation that they will consistently respond in a "reasonable" way. Consequently, the key idea has been to put in place monetary incentives, such as taxes and subsidies, in order to induce individuals to change their behavior. Since it is in anyone's interest to take this economically relevant information into account, economists simply assumed that people do so.

Such incentive-based designs are intended to work in a variety of contexts. In designing tax rates, for example, economists assume that the tax elasticity—that is, the degree to which people respond to the imposition of a tax by changing their behavior—is nonzero. This assumption is critical for estimating who really pays a tax (e.g., if the behavioral response is to shift the cost to someone else) and whether there are unanticipated costs from imposing the tax (such as decreases in tax revenue). The tax subsidies in place for individual retirement accounts, for example, are intended to encourage lower-income filers to contribute to their retirement savings. The cost-sharing provisions that are part of many health care plans, such as deductibles or copayments, are designed to help align the incentives of consumers and insurers, with the goal of reducing health care spending by encouraging more cost-efficient utilization. In the field of energy, utilities often use nonlinear pricing, in which the marginal cost of energy or water increases with additional usage, to encourage customers to conserve. In all of these cases, the implicit assumption is that people are well informed of those features—they know the tax rate, the savings subsidy, the costs and benefits of health decisions, the price of energy consumption—and they take these incentives into account in making decisions.

Counterintuitive Responses to Incentives

Behavioral economists have carried out empirical research to determine whether and how these assumptions operate and to what extent limited attention and cognitive limitations may affect people's decisions. A first key lesson from this work is that people have a very limited understanding of tax, subsidy, and price incentives; moreover, they respond to the incentives they *perceive*, not necessarily to the incentives as they were designed to function. Multiple studies have shown that people often respond to the existence of incentive programs but not to their precise structure and that they miss features that are complex or not in plain sight.

For example, a study of the extent to which grocery store shoppers take into account state taxes when they make purchasing decisions showed that when the tax was explicitly identified as part of the price, consumers purchased less (Chetty, Looney, & Kroft, 2009). This finding violates the traditional economic model, which assumes that the total price should be the deciding factor, regardless of how much of the price is the tax. Instead, it was shown that making the tax *salient* affected people's behavior.

Another example concerns retirement savings (see Chapter 6). Research has shown that only a tiny fraction of low-income earners (1–2%) participated in individual retirement account savings plans despite tax incentives providing a substantial match for each dollar contributed. But when a similar subsidy was made salient—because it was newly offered through H&R Block at the time of tax filing—the response was about 10 times larger (Duflo et al., 2006). The key difference was the salience, the behavioral awareness, of the subsidy.

Other examples of the importance of salience come from research on health care and energy. For example, a health insurance company that imposed a high deductible for most care but no deductible for preventive care actually resulted in employees using less preventive care (Brot-Goldberg et al., 2017). That is, the employees responded to the change in incentive but disregarded the precise structure of the incentives, ignoring the special treatment of preventive care. Other work has shown that older individuals make many mistakes in their choice of Medicaid Plan D drug plans, though some do correct some of their mistakes over time (McFadden, 2006; Ketcham et al., 2012). Similarly, a study of energy utility consumers' responses to nonlinear pricing (which rewarded those who used less energy) showed that they did not respond to the marginal price of electricity, but rather to the average price, which undermined the conservation goal for the pricing structure (Ito, 2014). These examples show that people often respond to the existence of incentive programs but not to their precise structure.

Behavioral economists have developed models that accommodate the kinds of behaviors documented in these studies, and there is a vast and growing literature on such instances of limited attention and cognition. This work is also identifying which information is likely to be neglected and exploring settings in which information neglect can be mitigated (e.g., Gabaix, 2019). One key to the neglect of information is that it can stem from poor financial literacy (Lusardi & Mitchell, 2011). That is, people overlook, neglect, or misunderstand information that is in principle available to them, such as on instructions for taking advantage of tax incentives or maximizing mutual fund returns. Broadly, these behaviors deviate from those assumed in the most common traditional models (described in Box 3-1) because the individuals are not taking into account all the relevant incentives that matter for the utility maximization.

In this ongoing research, an open question is the extent to which limited attention can be understood as rational inattention (Sims, 2003; Maćkowiak, Matějka, & Wiederholt, 2023). That is, does the limited attention reflect a person's decision not to devote more attention to an economic opportunity because of the high cost of acquiring and processing information, or does it reflect a person's naïve inattention? In exploring the idea of rational inattention, researchers use models that allow for the possibility that people know that they have limited attention and that their time and effort is limited, and they choose which things to pay attention to for their own reasons. Providing more evidence on this margin—of the degree to which attention is allocated in accord with the perceived value of acquiring information—could be important in the future if it leads to policies that encourage people to pay more attention to opportunities or risks that are important to their well-being. For policy developers, however, both the behavioral economic models of limited attention and of rational inattention imply that processing of complex information is costly and that complex incentives, such as taxes, or the details of health insurance plans, will often be missed.

Varied Effects of Limited Attention

A second key lesson from the research on limited attention is that people's responses vary by their level of education and income. For example, in a study of a case in which a company accidentally offered health insurance plans that were demonstrably inferior compared with others they offered, the workers who stuck with the inferior plans—and incurred hundreds of dollars in losses—were likely to be low-wage employees (Bhargava, Loewenstein, & Sydnor, 2017). Similar results were found in a study of employer matches for retirement plans: lower-wage employees were much less likely to take advantage of the benefit than their higher-wage peers (Madrian & Shea, 2001). Below-median earners (of an already low-income sample) were more than twice as responsive to simplified notices (designed to overcome lapses in attention) as those with above-median incomes (Bharghava & Manoli, 2015). Another study showed that lower-income people systematically make poorer financial choices than do higher-income people: they have lower rates of participation in asset markets and consequent larger losses of the high historical investment returns in those markets (Campbell, 2016).

These results are surprising because lower-income individuals have the most to gain from such programs and incentives and can least afford to lose sources of income. One might expect that they would scrutinize financial options particularly closely. But lower-income people do not have the benefit of the same education or networks as do higher-income people, and they more often face pressing emergencies and challenges as they try to make ends meet (e.g., Mullainathan & Shafir, 2013). Thus, they spend less time on what could be important financial information for them. This research shows that, in general, misunderstanding of taxes, subsidies, and other complex programs is more common among people with relatively lower education and lower socioeconomic status and thus tends to increase inequality.

This research strongly suggests that simplifying communication about financial choices, such as those related to health insurance policies, taxes, subsidies, and the like—making the features that will have the most impact for consumers more salient—is an important strategy for limiting the inequitable effects of biases of limited attention and comprehension. If a policy is expressed in clear and plain language and if people are reminded at the moment they make a decision about the relevant features, they are significantly more likely to respond as the designers of the policy intended. This finding implies that the communication of public policy programs, including the work done in nudge units (see Chapter 2) that is focused on such communication, is of first-order importance. These small changes are inexpensive to implement but can yield sizable effects.

A study of communication about the Earned Income Tax Credit (EITC), which provides a large tax credit to low-income families with earnings if they file taxes, illustrates the importance of clarity in communication (see Chapter 7). Despite the large size of the benefits, about one-quarter of eligible people do not claim them. A study of possible solutions showed that when the Internal Revenue Service (IRS) sent letters to eligible households who had previously filed tax returns but had recently failed to take advantage of the EITC, the take-up of the benefit increased by more than 10 percent (Bhargava & Manoli, 2015). The letters were written in simple and clear language, illustrating the value of clarity in communication.

Similar results were found for communication about Medicare Part D plans, which cover drug costs for seniors. There is a large variety of plans designed to suit individuals with different health care needs, and the standard model assumes that individuals study the plans and choose the best option for them. Yet a clear communication to individuals about potential savings had a large impact on their plan choices: 11 percent of participants switched plans after receiving such information about the features of the plans, yielding an average savings of about $100 a year (Kling et al., 2012).

Inaccurate Beliefs

Holding inaccurate beliefs related to economic decisions—beliefs or understandings that do not objectively reflect the actual facts or situation—is a factor closely related to but distinct from cognitive and attentional issues. Inaccurate beliefs in this context does not mean occasional or unsystematic errors: as noted, above, traditional economic models assume that people do not have perfect information. Behavioral economists have focused on instances in which inaccurate beliefs are systematic and could be corrected with access to available information. (In the language of the traditional model in Box 3-1, this amounts to incorrect probabilities $p(s_t)$.)

One example is *overoptimism*: people tend to overestimate the positive aspects of their own lives, such as their likely success in a future job search effort or commitment to investing in retirement savings. For example, people who are unemployed overestimate the likelihood of finding a job compared with the actual empirical probability (e.g., Spinnewijn, 2015). Similarly, people who consider enrolling in a gym overestimate their future attendance (DellaVigna & Malmendier, 2006).

This kind of overestimation has consequences. For example, people who overestimate the likelihood that they will start saving later may save less in the present and fail to save enough to meet their retirement needs (Ganong & Noel, 2019; Gerard & Naritomi, 2021). Similarly, sales agents who overpredict future sales in their forecasts end up selling less than predicted (Huffman, Raymond, & Shvets, 2022). People who join a health club often pick the wrong membership contract because they overestimate how often they will go in the future (DellaVigna & Malmendier, 2006).

Why do people hold such overly positive beliefs in these instances? Two key factors seem at play: people like to have a positive opinion of themselves (positive ego utility), and they (consciously or not) tend to remember past events or behaviors as more positive than they were, which is an example of memory bias (see Chapter 2). For example, in one study, individuals were given (truthful) positive or negative feedback about how they did on an IQ-type test. One month later they accurately recalled the positive feedback but had largely forgotten the negative feedback (Zimmermann, 2020).

Indeed, in several of the empirical studies that have documented systematic overestimation, the overestimation was tied to biased memories. Sales agents who overestimated their future sales are also more likely to have an excessively rosy memory of their past sales (Huffman, Raymond, & Shvets, 2022). Gym club members who overestimated future attendance similarly were likely to recall more past gym visits than they actually made (Sial, Sydnor, & Taubinsky, 2023).

Similar findings of overestimation of future earnings have been found for gig workers, who typically experience more uncertainty than employees about future earnings because of variability in both hours worked and earnings per hour (Pires, 2022). The costs of vehicle use and depreciation are also an important part of net earnings. When asked to forecast a paycheck expected in the near future, gig workers overestimate it by an average of 30 percent (and even more if car depreciation is accounted for). This overestimation is related to selective memory, because gig workers also recall their past earnings as higher than they were. This study points out that this overestimation may be the reason gig workers continue in their work, for they claim they would be working in different jobs if their wages were as low as they actually are.

It is important to point out that the research does not suggest that individuals are overoptimistic all the time. The research on the elicitation of beliefs (e.g., Dominitz & Manski, 2004) suggests nuanced patterns, and it will be important to accumulate more evidence on settings in which overoptimism is at play versus others where individuals have on average accurate beliefs, or beliefs that diverge in unsystematic ways.

A second example of inaccurate beliefs, *recency bias*, or availability bias, occurs when people pay more attention to recent events than older ones, especially ones that they have directly experienced or witnessed. This phenomenon is illustrated in a study of people who own property in flood-prone areas: many who had available to them the entire history of floods in their areas nevertheless responded more directly to recent experiences (Gallagher, 2014). Homeowners who were not directly affected by a flood but witnessed other nearby properties affected by a flood were significantly more likely to purchase flood insurance the next year. This pattern is especially pronounced if the county of residence of the homeowner shares a media market with the county affected by the flood, which suggests that salience of the news in the media is largely responsible for the finding. In another example, investors who, by the traditional model, should incorporate all past investment returns of companies instead overweight their own experiences (Kaustia & Knüpfer, 2008). The study showed that Finnish investors who had previous investment experience with an initial public offering were more likely to invest again if they had earned a positive return from the earlier investment, despite the fact that it would be prudent to look at the average over all past returns.

That such personal, direct salient experiences can affect people for a long time is illustrated in a study showing that early exposure to traumatic financial episodes affected later risk taking (Malmendier & Nagel, 2011). The authors found, for example, that people who lived through the Great Depression in the 1930s were less likely to invest in stocks later in life than those who did not (holding wealth constant); they found similar results in other contexts. Such findings suggest that individuals are more responsive to recent or salient events, such as events in the media and personal experiences, than to accurate long-term information.

Another example of incorrect beliefs occurs in the context of predicting the future utility associated with a particular choice: individuals tend to assume that the future utility will be too close to the one they are currently experiencing. This phenomenon is called *projection bias* (Loewenstein, O'Donoghue, & Rabin, 2003). Examples of this include findings that people are more likely to purchase a convertible on an unusually hot day and to cancel solar energy contracts when the weather is cloudy

(Busse et al., 2015; Liao, 2020). Another example, from China, is that on days with (temporarily) high pollution, people are more likely to purchase health insurance, even though the health insurance does not take effect until later in the future, when the temporary pollution has faded (Chang, Huang, & Wang, 2018).

An important question is how researchers measure beliefs, and thus how they conclude that in some cases they are systematically incorrect. In some instances, the beliefs are inferred from the observed behavior (e.g., Chang, Huang, & Wang, 2018), but researchers also measure beliefs directly in order to compare them with the real situation, if possible. An example is a study in which people were asked what they remember about their past health club attendance, and the results were compared with administrative records of attendance for that person (Sial, Sydnor, & Taubinsky, 2023). Such studies follow an extensive literature on belief elicitation in economics, which predates behavioral economics research and provides evidence on methods for capturing beliefs (e.g., Manski, 2004; Hurd, 2009; Delavande, 2014). Some of the lessons from this important literature are captured in the recent *Handbook of Economic Expectations* (Bachmann, Topa, & van der Klaauw, 2022). One of the findings in this literature is the considerable heterogeneity in beliefs even within a group of seemingly similar individuals.

In the cases in which individuals have biased beliefs, a relevant question is how the biases in beliefs appear to be sustained over time, despite the opportunity for feedback. In some instances, the imperfect information that individuals have is consistent with optimal inattention: people disregard available information rationally, as the cost of information processing may exceed the value of the information (Sims, 2003; Caplin & Dean, 2015). However, in other cases it appears that behavioral forces are also at play (Schwartzstein, 2014; Gagnon-Bartsch, Rabin, & Schwartzstein, 2018). For example, people focus their attention on what they perceive as relevant and important, but if they misconceive what really matters, they may miss essential information (Hanna, Mullainathan, & Schwartzstein, 2014; Esponda, Oprea, & Yuksel, 2022). Studies have also shown that at times people make errors in evaluating information in order to maintain strongly held beliefs, such as a positive self-image or an ideologically motivated belief (Fryer, Harms, & Jackson, 2019; Santos-Pinto & de la Rosa, 2020; Thaler, 2021). Confirmation bias, which occurs when people discount information that contradicts their past choices and judgments, is a prominent example (Nickerson, 1998; Rabin & Schrag, 1999). People may also place more weight on favorable news than on unfavorable news (Eil & Rao, 2011; Möbius et al., 2014; Coutts, 2019). Furthermore, there is evidence that people have asymmetric memory recall, more easily recalling positive feedback than negative feedback (Enke, 2020; Zimmermann, 2020; Huffman, Raymond, & Shvets, 2022).

Present Bias

Limited attention, cognitive barriers, and incorrect beliefs are factors in the way people perceive and comprehend economic information and the probabilities of future events. Other cognitive traits affect the way individuals respond to the information and incentives that they perceive. Present bias is one of the most widely documented behavioral factors, and it is particularly important for the development of public policy. Box 3-2 shows how it is modeled by economists.

There are two key features of the way people perceive time-related issues that behavioral economists attempt to take account of in their work. First, most people are tempted to put off activities that are beneficial but require an immediate cost, such as going to the gym, writing a report, or filling out a tax return. At the same time, people are tempted by pleasant activities that may have a future cost, such as lighting one more cigarette or eating an extra scoop of ice cream. In planning for the future, people display tension: they would very much like their future selves to exercise, write reports, get their taxes done, stop smoking, and eat salads rather than

---

BOX 3-2
Modeling Present Bias

Economists typically model t, present bias (using the assumption that utility at time t is discounted), this way:

$$U_t = u_t + \beta\delta u_{t+1} + \beta\delta^2 u_{t+2} + \beta\delta^3 u_{t+3} + \ldots$$

(see, e.g., Laibson, 1997; O'Donoghue & Rabin, 1999), in which U is utility, β is the present bias factor, and δ is the long-term discount factor, which captures the traditional discounting in economic models. Each period further into the future is discounted by an extra term, delta < 1. The present bias factor, beta, drives a wedge between the present and future periods since it discounts all future utilities but not the present.

Intuitively, individuals experience immediate costs, or immediate benefits, more strongly than any future cost or benefit. There are dozens of estimates produced using this model, and the typical finding is that individuals have a present bias parameter around 0.8–0.9 (see, e.g., Augenblick, Niederle, & Sprenger, 2015). These models can account for the fact that individuals are at the same time patient in the longer term and highly impatient in the present.

ice cream, but they do not necessarily want to do those things right now. The tension is between the lure of immediate gratification in the present and longer-term hopes and goals for the future.

Behavioral economists have added a second, more subtle, component to understanding of present bias by making a distinction between the *naïveté* or *sophistication* that individuals bring to their assessments—or how aware they are of their present bias. A sophisticated individual is aware not only that they do not feel like filling out tax forms today but also that they will still dislike doing so in the future. A naïve person, in contrast, might expect their future self to not have the same present bias in the future and thus to be more willing to face those IRS forms at a later time.

Sophisticated and naïve individuals often behave quite differently. More sophisticated individuals, aware of their future selves' intended behavior, look for ways, such as commitment devices, to tie the hands of their future selves. They tend not to delay tasks on the to-do list because they are aware that things that do not get done today may not get done tomorrow either. Naïve individuals, in contrast, tend to have unrealistic expectations that their future selves will take on the hard tasks and thus are more likely to procrastinate. The evidence suggests that sophistication and naïveté are not crisp categories but are reflected in varying degrees in everyone—although naïveté may predominate (Augenblick & Rabin, 2019).

Present bias has important implications for understanding how people respond to public policy. Two key findings mirror each other: people are especially aversive to, and tend to delay, undertaking bureaucratic tasks, such as signing up for a benefit for which they are eligible; and people are not very sensitive to future benefits, even substantial ones, but are quite responsive to benefits perceived as immediate.

Aversiveness to bureaucratic tasks is a phenomenon almost anyone would likely recognize: in the face of tasks such as calculating one's taxes, signing up for the Supplemental Nutrition Assistance Program, or changing health insurance plans, the cost of the effort of figuring out complex forms and the administrative burden looms large. Especially when there is no clear deadline—and when naïveté is dominant—people will push the effort to the future under the (usually incorrect) assumption that it might be less unpleasant later and they will get to it at some future time.

Procrastination is a natural explanation for the very large default effects (tendency to accept whatever is the default option) that are found repeatedly in behavioral economics. For example (noted in Chapter 2 and further discussed in Chapter 6), employees are far more likely to enroll in 401(k) matching plans when opting in is set as the default choice. Similar work shows that individuals do not optimally adjust their retirement and health insurance choices over time, so that they get stuck in suboptimal plans (Handel, 2013; Bhargava, Loewenstein, & Sydnor, 2017). The health insurance example noted above as an example of limited attention also demonstrates present bias because even attentive workers might put off enrolling in better plans because they naïvely believe they will do it in the future. Similarly, people generally itemize deductions on their tax returns only when the amount of deductions they claim is hundreds of dollars higher than the standard deduction (Benzarti, 2020), even though they would benefit from itemization of smaller totals. This high avoidance of a seemingly clear benefit could be partly the result of limited attention, but present bias and naïve procrastination also play a role.

The evidence that individuals are not very sensitive to future benefits is also supported by research from Denmark that suggests that people do not respond at all in their savings decisions to variation in the rate at which their employers contribute to retirement savings, even though the traditional economic approach would predict substitution (Chetty et al., 2014). Interestingly, information about the benefit alone is not generally enough to stimulate action. Even people whose attention is directed to the possibility of receiving the employer's matching funds are slow to respond unless they have an opportunity to act right away as well as a deadline (Choi, Laibson, & Mandrian, 2011). In another case, the offer of a gift card did yield increased savings, but it is striking that employees responded far more substantially to an immediate incentive of $10 than to information on benefits worth thousands of dollars at retirement (Bhargava & Conell-Price, 2022).

Reference Dependence and Framing

One of the most influential models in behavioral economics is reference dependence, which is based on prospect theory (see Chapter 2). Prospect theory itself was based on observations of how people respond when faced with uncertain and risky choices. The traditional economic model assumes that people will rationally calculate the potential gains and losses under different scenarios, and will pick a riskier choice only if their average well-being could be significantly improved.[1] But, as discussed in Chapter 2, Kahneman and Tversky (1979) found that decisions involving risk often deviated from the traditional model. In facing risky choices that have only small magnitudes of gains and losses, people are more averse to risk than is predicted by the traditional model. For example, people often purchase insurance to protect themselves against losses (a risk-averse behavior) but simultaneously engage in risky lotteries that could bring gains or losses. Furthermore, if behaving according to expected utility, people

---

[1] The idea of rationally assessing the scenario that is most likely to yield overall benefit, given uncertainties, is captured in what is called *expected utility theory*, "a weighted average" of the potential utilities of various possible outcomes (Briggs, 2019).

would consider all aspects of a decision, integrating all relevant elements of the context. For example, in deciding to participate in a lottery, an individual should take into account their underlying wealth, including expected returns to any investments.

Kahneman and Tversky proposed that anomalies—deviations from expected utility–based behavior—could be explained by a simple theoretical model incorporating three key psychologically based insights. First, people exhibit *loss aversion*, which means that people respond more strongly to losses than the positive effect of equal-sized gains—this effect is much stronger than is predicted by the standard model. Second, people's choices are framed relative to a reference point, not in absolute terms, and are thus highly contextual (the reference point will depend on the context). A reference point could be a previous choice, a comparison group, or a default choice that is presented. (Reference dependence is an example of the influence of context discussed in Chapter 2.)

A third aspect of the model is an implicit assumption (made more explicit by recent research) of *narrow framing*: people tend to consider a particular decision in isolation, taking it as framed, instead of integrating it with all the other economically relevant factors. For example, consider an individual participating in a lottery that offers a 50 percent chance to gain $10 and a 50 percent chance to lose $8 (or the choice to opt out). The concept of narrow framing suggests that a person will consider this decision in isolation and not assess it in light of other aspects of their financial situation, such as wages or salary and returns from a portfolio investment. If those considerations were integrated with the lottery choice, the risk from the gamble would appear much smaller (or larger, if the amounts at stake were higher). Thus, the framing of a particular choice, and the reference point in particular, will affect how an option is perceived and thus the ensuing decision. An example of this was documented in a study of investors in 401(k) retirement accounts, which showed that they were more likely to take into account the asset allocations in their other investment accounts in making decisions about the 401(k) plan when they were prompted to do so (Choi, Laibson, & Madrian, 2009).

A classic example of reference dependence and loss aversion is the discrepancy between willingness to pay for an object and willingness to accept something in exchange for the object: this is the *endowment effect* described by Kahneman, Knetsch, & Thaler (1990). In studies of this phenomenon, subjects are randomly assigned either to receive an object (e.g., a mug) or not. The subjects who are given the mug are asked their willingness to accept something for parting from the mug, while the subjects without a mug are asked their willingness to pay to get a mug. These experiments have demonstrated that people's willingness to accept an exchange is generally larger than their willingness to pay. Models of reference dependence are natural explanations for this phenomenon, given that loss aversion increases willingness to accept (as the people would lose the object by selling) but not willingness to pay (see Marzilli Ericson & Fuster, 2014). If losses loom larger than gains, one would predict this disparity.[2]

An example of this behavior and the endowment effect arises in environmental evaluations. For example, after an oil spill, the compensation amount is decided on the basis of elicitations of willingness to accept an exchange and willingness to pay for clean water and clean beaches (e.g., Bishop et al., 2017). The research on endowment effects provides one reason that such evaluations will tend to be context dependent, as the elicitation is likely to depend on whether it is framed in terms of willingness to accept an exchange ("what would you need to be compensated to lose the clean water?") or as willingness to pay ("what would you be willing to pay to have clean water?").[3]

Another example of the impact of reference dependence through framing is *nominal wage rigidity*. Nominal (actual) wage cuts are rare, in comparison with real wage cuts (e.g., Card & Hyslop, 1997). That is, wage increases are common, but if inflation rates are high the result might still be a reduction in the value of earnings, a real wage cut. That is, if one's wages are increased by three percent when inflation is six percent, the value of one's wages is three percent lower than it had been. In part because of reference dependence and loss aversion, workers evaluate wages in nominal terms, comparing this year's pay to last year's, so a nominal wage cut is seen as a loss, while a real wage cut is not. A study conducted in India illustrates how nominal wage rigidity distorts the adjustment of markets to shocks (Kaur, 2019). An interview-based study suggesting that employers are unlikely to put in place nominal wage cuts because they damage worker morale supports this notion (Bewley, 1999). This is an example of reference-dependent statements of fairness documented by Kahneman, Knetsch, & Thaler (1986).

Other evidence comes from the housing market. Homeowners are typically averse to selling their houses at a (nominal) loss relative to the price at which they purchased their houses (Genesove & Mayer, 2001; Andersen et al., 2022). Other work showed that homeowners who purchase home insurance and pick low-deductible, high-premium plans even though the probability of a major loss is very small do so because they dislike the possibility of having to pay a high deductible in case of an accident: this finding also demonstrates loss aversion and that low-probability outcomes loom excessively large in people's perception (Sydnor, 2010).

---

[2] See also the work of Ellen Langer on the endowment effect (e.g., Maymin & Langer, 2021).

[3] A separate issue is that elicitations involve problems with validity and appropriateness of contingent valuation, but those problems do not affect the point being made here. We also note that willingness to pay is bounded by ability to pay.

In another example, unemployed workers looking for a job reduced their hours spent in job search efforts after their unemployment insurance benefits ran out (even taking into account unemployment insurance job search requirements) instead of increasing them, as the traditional economic model presumes (DellaVigna et al., 2017, 2022). The authors suggest that this occurred because the unemployed workers adjusted the reference point after their benefits ran out. A study of taxi drivers also demonstrated this phenomenon: those who experienced an above-average number of fares late in the day tended to stop work early, rather than taking advantage of the opportunity to earn even more, because they had already achieved or slightly exceeded the normal daily earnings, which they used as a reference point (Thakral & Tô, 2021, building on the work of Camerer et al., 1997).

Social Preferences and Social Norms

The textbook traditional economic model assumes that people act to enhance their own well-being and tend to ignore, in making decisions, both the consequences for others and social norms that are not directly reflected in economic payoffs. However, social psychologists have shown that an important aspect of the context for decision making is perceptions of how one's actions relate to those of others. People often care about the well-being of others. They make comparisons between themselves and others, and they care about their social standing, how they signal their values and preferences to others, and how they conform with social norms. People think about themselves (more or less consciously) in terms of social groups, compare themselves with others, are influenced by how others behave, and put considerable weight on how others perceive them. Behavioral economists have devoted considerable attention to exploring social interactions, peer effects, and conforming behavior, using variants of the traditional model. These models capture some elements of social preferences that come from social psychology and are consistent with some simple behavioral economics models. However, behavioral economists have explored how such socially based preferences affect choices and interactions with others in a deeper and more extensive way and have brought new conceptual models to the field.

Some of the earliest behavioral work in this area explored *social preferences,* the ways people care about other people's income and consumption, perhaps in relation to or in comparison with their own, in new ways. This work demonstrated the ways people's accrual choices diverge from those that would be driven by pure self-interest. For example, many people sacrifice their income and consumption to help others because they are altruistic or have a preference for fairness (Becker, 1974; Rabin, 1993). Nuanced studies of relative income (the impression of an income in comparison with a reference income) have pointed to the concept of *inequality aversion*: the idea that most people dislike inequality in outcomes relative to others' but are more disturbed by inequality when they earn less than others than when they earn more than others (e.g., Fehr & Schmidt, 1999; Chen & Li, 2009). Furthermore, people tend to display *reciprocity*—responding to being treated generously by behaving more generously themselves and vice versa if they are treated unkindly (Falk & Fischbacher, 2006). Behavioral economics has used such tools as the ultimatum game, the dictator game, and public goods games in studying people's behaviors in response to various challenges to their concepts of fairness (see, e.g., Houser & McCabe, 2014).[4] Researchers have also specifically studied social interactions within organizations (Ashraf & Bandiera, 2018).

Recent work in behavioral economics also goes beyond traditional models by suggesting that social preferences and other preferences that drive behavior derive from people's understanding of themselves within a social context and their identities and attachments to particular social groups. People care about following *social norms* more than can be accounted for by simple peer effects would suggest because those norms often indicate appropriate and inappropriate behavior for different settings. People also care about whether others view them as following the norms and as having values that align with the social group. These behaviors do not appear in traditional economic models.[5]

We emphasize two points from the research on social preferences and norms. The first is that people make choices to conform to social norms consistent with their identities, and thus conformity is especially pronounced in public spheres. A theoretical model of economic behavior that includes identity and social norms illustrates this point (Akerlof & Kranton, 2000). The model assigns each person an identity (or possibly multiple identities) that is associated with norms that prescribe behaviors in different settings. If a person with a particular identity does not follow the prescribed behavior, they pay a "disutility cost." Some traditional models might portray behavior related to social preferences in simple descriptive

---

[4]In an ultimatum game, one player is endowed with a sum of money and tasked with splitting it with another player. The first person decides how much to give the second person, who can accept or reject the offer. If the second person accepts the offer, the money is split as proposed; if the person rejects the offer, both players receive nothing. Both players know in advance the consequences of the second person accepting or rejecting the offer. The dictator game is a variation of the ultimatum game. In a public goods game, subjects secretly choose how many of their private tokens to put into a public pot. The tokens in this pot are multiplied by a set factor and this "public good" payoff is evenly divided among players. Players also keeps the tokens they do not contribute.

[5]There has been extensive work on these issues in the larger behavioral science literature mentioned earlier in this chapter. See, for example, the important work of Bicchieri (2005).

terms, but, in contrast, the Akerlof and Kranton models portray prescriptive behavior—they portray individuals' views of what they *should* do. Many studies of the role of social identity in academic performance demonstrate the importance of this factor. For example, there is evidence that students' decisions about their academic performance are different when they are visible to their peer groups (e.g., Hoff & Pandey, 2006; Bursztyn & Jensen, 2015). In a study of the influence of stereotypes on academic performance, the students performed better when stereotypes about their racial identity associated with strong academic performance were subtly highlighted in the testing context, but performed worse when other stereotypes they might identify with that are associated with weaker performance were invoked (Shih, Pittinsky, & Ambady, 1999). We note that the stereotypes do not have to be true, but if people have internalized them, they can have strong effects through identity and social norms.

People also care about whether they are *perceived* as altruistic as in social signaling models (Bénabou & Tirole, 2006). For example, people may behave more altruistically when they are being observed by others because they want to signal to others that they have this virtue. Other work shows that preferences for fairness and inequality aversion are group-based—that inequality aversion is much weaker toward participants who are outside one's own group and that people are more likely to make decisions that could harm others after seeing others in their group do so (Chen & Li, 2009; Shayo & Zussman, 2011; Bauer et al., 2018; Kranton et al., 2020).

A second key point from this body of work is that comparisons to others often trigger responses that are consistent with the importance of social norms and social comparisons of the type emphasized in behavioral economics. That is, people's behavior is often governed by their desire to have the good opinion of others and to maintain positive relationships (e.g., Cialdini & Trost, 1998). Efforts to harness this desire to promote socially desirable choices in numerous contexts illustrate this idea (see Chapter 8). For example, people respond to social pressure by reducing their energy use when informed about the average energy use by others (e.g., Allcott, 2011). Presenting taxpayers with the message that the vast majority of their peers pay on time has been effective at increasing on-time filing (Luttmer & Singhal, 2014).[6]

---

[6]The existing literature on social interactions and social networks emphasizes what is called the "general equilibrium" nature of the problem, referring to the fact that when individuals respond to other individuals' actions and beliefs, those other individuals respond in kind, multiplying the effect. All the behavioral forces identified in this section would also have those effects.

CONCLUSION

Insights about human behavior from work in cognitive psychology, social psychology, and behavioral economics (and other fields) have been integrated in the development of a sophisticated portrait of how people make decisions. Drawing on this work, behavioral economists have identified similar and overlapping concepts and have developed distinct ways of framing questions and findings. The integration of work from behavioral domains with economic analysis has demonstrated that decision processes are dynamic, malleable, and context dependent, often shaped by what would ordinarily be considered irrelevant factors and by people's mental representations of the world.

Conclusion 3-1: Foundational work in behavioral economics, drawing on the fields of economics, psychology, social psychology, and others, suggests the importance of five principles to consider in designing policy interventions to modify human behavior: limited attention and cognition, inaccurate beliefs, present bias, reference dependence and framing, and social preferences and social norms.

REFERENCES

Akerlof, G. A., & Kranton, R. E. (2000). Economics and identity. *The Quarterly Journal of Economics*, 115(3), 715–753. https://doi.org/10.1257/aer.20150742

Allcott, H. (2011). Social norms and energy conservation. *Journal of Public Economics*, 95(9–10), 1082–1095. https://doi.org/10.1016/j.jpubeco.2011.03.003

Andersen, S., Badarinza, C., Liu, L., Marx, J., & Ramadorai, T. (2022). *Reference dependence in the housing market*. SSRN. https://dx.doi.org/10.2139/ssrn.3396506

Ashraf, N., & Bandiera, O. (2018). Social incentives in organizations. *Annual Review of Economics*, 10, 439–463. https://doi.org/10.1146/annurev-economics-063016-104324

Augenblick, N., Niederle, M., & Sprenger, C. (2015). Working over time: Dynamic inconsistency in real effort tasks. *The Quarterly Journal of Economics*, 130(3), 1067–1115. https://doi.org/10.1093/qje/qjv020

Augenblick, N., & Rabin, M. (2019). An experiment on time preference and misprediction in unpleasant tasks. *Review of Economic Studies*, 86(3), 941–975. https://doi.org/10.1093/restud/rdy019

Bachmann, R., Topa, G., & van der Klaauw, W. (Eds.). (2022). *Handbook of economic expectations*. Elsevier.

Bauer, M., Cahlíková, J., Chytilová, J., & Želinský, T. (2018). Social contagion of ethnic hostility. *Proceedings of the National Academy of Sciences*, 115(19), 4881–4886. https://doi.org/10.1073/pnas.1720317115

Becker, G. S. (1974). A theory of social interactions. *Journal of Political Economy*, 82, 1063–1093. https://econweb.ucsd.edu/~jandreon/PhilanthropyAndFundraising/Volume%201/3%20Becker%201974.pdf

———. (1981). Altruism in the family and selfishness in the market place. *Economica*, 48(189), 1–15. https://doi.org/10.2307/2552939

Bénabou, R., & Tirole, J. (2006). Incentives and prosocial behavior. *American Economic Review*, 96 (5), 1652–1678. https://doi.org/10.1257/aer.96.5.1652

Benzarti, Y. (2020). How taxing is tax filing? Using revealed preferences to estimate compliance costs. *American Economic Journal: Economic Policy, 12*(4), 38–57. https://doi.org/10.1257/pol.20180664

Bernheim, B. D., DellaVigna, S., & Laibson, D. (2019). *Handbook of behavioral economics—Foundations and applications, 2*. Elsevier.

Bewley, T. F. (1999). *Work motivation*. Cowles Foundation Discussion Paper 1457. https://elischolar.library.yale.edu/cowles-discussion-paper-series/1457

Bhargava, S., & Conell-Price, L. (2022). Serenity now, save later? Evidence on retirement savings puzzles from a 401(k) field experiment. SSRN. https://dx.doi.org/10.2139/ssrn.4056407

Bhargava, S., & Manoli, D. (2015). Psychological frictions and the incomplete take-up of social benefits: Evidence from an IRS field experiment. *American Economic Review, 105*(11), 3489–3529. https://doi.org/10.1257/aer.20121493

Bhargava, S., Loewenstein, G., & Sydnor, J. (2017). Choose to lose: Health plan choices from a menu with dominated option. *The Quarterly Journal of Economics, 132*(3), 1319–1372. https://doi.org/10.1093/qje/qjx011

Bicchieri, C. (2005). *The grammar of society: The nature and dynamics of social norms*. Cambridge University Press.

Bishop, R. C., Boyle, K. J., Carson, R. T., Chapman, D., Hanemann, W. M., Kanninen, B., Kopp, R. J., Krosnick, J., List, J., Meade, N., Paterson, R., Presser, S., Smith, V. K., Tourangeau, R., Welsh, M., Wooldridge, J. M., De Bell, M., Donovan, C., Konopka, M., & Scherer, N. (2017). Contingent valuation: Flawed logic?-Response. *Science, 357*(6349), 363–364. https://doi.org/10.1126/science.aao0197

Briggs, R. A., (2019). Normative theories of rational choice: Expected utility. *Stanford encyclopedia of philosophy*. Stanford University. https://plato.stanford.edu/archives/fall2019/entries/rationality-normative-utility

Brock, W. A., & Durlauf, S. N. (2001). Interactions-based models. *Handbook of econometrics, 5*, 3297–3380. Elsevier.

Brot-Goldberg, Z. C., Chandra, A., Handel, B. R., & Kolstad, J. T. (2017). What does a deductible do? The impact of cost-sharing on health care prices, quantities, and spending dynamics. *The Quarterly Journal of Economics, 132*(3), 1261–1318. https://doi.org/10.1093/qje/qjx013

Bursztyn, L., & Jensen, R. (2015). How does peer pressure affect educational investments? *The Quarterly Journal of Economics, 130*(3), 1329–1367. https://doi.org/10.1093/qje/qjv021

Busse, M. R., Pope, D. G., Pope, J. C., & Silva-Risso, J. (2015). The psychological effect of weather on car purchases. *The Quarterly Journal of Economics, 130*(1), 371–414. https://www.jstor.org/stable/26372602

Camerer, C., Babcock, L., Loewenstein, G., & Thaler, R. (1997). Labor supply of New York City cabdrivers: One day at a time. *The Quarterly Journal of Economics, 112*(2), 407–441. https://doi.org/10.1162/003355397555244

Campbell, J. Y. (2016). Restoring rational choice: The challenge of consumer financial regulation. *American Economic Review, 106*(5), 1–30. https://doi.org/10.1257/aer.p20161127

Caplin, A., & Dean, M. (2015). Revealed preference, rational inattention, and costly information acquisition. *American Economic Review, 105*(7), 2183–2203. https://doi.org/10.1257/aer.20140117

Card, D., & Hyslop, D. (1997). Does inflation "grease the wheels of the labor market"? *Reducing inflation: Motivation and strategy*, 71–122. University of Chicago Press. http://www.nber.org/chapters/c8882

Chang, T. Y., Huang, W., & Wang, Y. (2018). Something in the air: Pollution and the demand for health insurance. *The Review of Economic Studies, 85*(3),1609–1634. https://doi.org/10.1093/restud/rdy016

Chen, Y., & Li, S. X. (2009). Group identity and social preferences. *American Economic Review*, 99(1), 431–457. https://doi.org/10.1257/aer.99.1.431

Chetty, R. (2015). Behavioral economics and public policy: A pragmatic perspective. *American Economic Review*, 105(5), 1–33. https://doi.org/10.1257/aer.p20151108

Chetty, R., Looney, A., & Kroft, K. (2009). Salience and taxation: Theory and evidence. *American Economic Review*, 99(4), 1145–1177. https://doi.org/10.1257/aer.99.4.1145

Chetty, R., Friedman, J. N., Leth-Petersen, S., Nielsen, T. H., & Olsen, T. (2014). Active vs. passive decisions and crowd-out in retirement savings accounts: Evidence from Denmark. *The Quarterly Journal of Economics*, 129(3), 1141–1219. https://doi.org/10.1093/qje/qju013

Choi, J. J., Laibson, D., & Madrian, B. C. (2009). Mental accounting in portfolio choice: Evidence from a flypaper effect. *American Economic Review*, 99(5), 2085–2095. https://doi.org/10.1257/aer.99.5.2085

———. (2011). $100 bills on the sidewalk: Suboptimal investment in 401(k) plans. *Review of Economics and Statistics*, 93(3), 748–763. https://doi.org/10.1162/REST_a_00100

Cialdini, R. B., & Trost, M. R. (1998). Social influence: Social norms, conformity and compliance. *The handbook of social psychology*, 151–192. McGraw-Hill.

Coutts, A. (2019). Good news and bad news are still news: Experimental evidence on belief updating. *Experimental Economics*, 22(2), 369–395. https://doi.org/10.1007/s10683-018-9572-5

De Finetti, B. (1970). Logical foundations and measurement of subjective probability. *Acta Psychologica*, 34, 129–145. https://doi.org/10.1016/0001-6918(70)90012-0

Delavande, A. (2014). Probabilistic expectations in developing countries. *Annual Review of Economics*, 6(1), 1–20. https://doi.org/10.1146/annurev-economics-072413-105148

DellaVigna, S. (2009). Psychology and economics: Evidence from the field. *Journal of Economic Literature*, 47(2), 315–372. https://doi.org/10.1257/jel.47.2.315

DellaVigna, S., & Malmendier, U. (2006). Paying not to go to the gym. *American Economic Review*, 96(3), 694–719. https://doi.org/10.1257/aer.96.3.694

DellaVigna, S., Lindner, A., Reizer, B., & Schmieder, J. F. (2017). Reference-dependent job search: Evidence from Hungary. *The Quarterly Journal of Economics*, 132(4), 1969–2018. https://doi.org/10.1093/qje/qjx015

DellaVigna, S., Heining, J., Schmieder, J. F., & Trenkle, S. (2022). Evidence on job search models from a survey of unemployed workers in Germany. *The Quarterly Journal of Economics*, 137(2), 1181–1232. https://doi.org/10.1093/qje/qjab039

Dominitz, J., & Manski, C. F. (2004). How should we measure consumer confidence? *Journal of Economic Perspectives*, 18(2), 51–66. https://doi.org/10.1257/0895330041371303

Duflo, E., Gale, W., Liebman, J., Orszag, P., & Saez, E. (2006). Saving incentives for low-and middle-income families: Evidence from a field experiment with H&R Block. *The Quarterly Journal of Economics*, 121(4), 1311–1346. https://doi.org/10.1093/qje/121.4.1311

Eil, D., & Rao, J. M. (2011). The good news-bad news effect: Asymmetric processing of objective information about yourself. *American Economic Journal: Microeconomics*, 3(2), 114–138. https://doi.org/10.1257/mic.3.2.114

Enke, B. (2020). What you see is all there is. *The Quarterly Journal of Economics*, 135(3), 1363–1398. https://doi.org/10.1093/qje/qjaa012

Esponda, I., Oprea, R., & Yuksel, S. (2022). *Discrimination without reason: Biases in statistical discrimination*. Mimeo. https://faculty.econ.ucsb.edu/~sevgi/EspondaOpreaYuksel.pdf

Falk, A., & Fischbacher, U. (2006). A theory of reciprocity. *Games and Economic Behavior*, 54(2), 293–315. https://doi.org/10.1016/j.geb.2005.03.001

Fehr, E., & Schmidt, K. S. (1999). A theory of fairness, competition, and cooperation. *The Quarterly Journal of Economics*, 114(3), 817–868. https://doi.org/10.1162/003355399556151

Fryer Jr., R. G., Harms, P., & Jackson, M. O. (2019). Updating beliefs when evidence is open to interpretation: Implications for bias and polarization. *Journal of the European Economic Association, 17*(5), 1470–1501. https://doi.org/10.1093/jeea/jvy025

Gabaix, X. (2019). Behavioral inattention. *Handbook of behavioral economics: Applications and foundations, 2,* 261–343. North-Holland. https://doi.org/10.1016bs.hesbe.2018.11.001

Gagnon-Bartsch, T., Rabin, M., & Schwartzstein, J. (2018). *Channeled attention and stable errors.* Harvard Business School.

Gallagher, J. (2014). Learning about an infrequent event: Evidence from flood insurance take-up in the United States. *American Economic Journal: Applied Economics, 6*(3), 206–233. https://www.jstor.org/stable/43189495

Ganong, P., & Noel, P. (2019). Consumer spending during unemployment: Positive and normative implications. *American Economic Review, 109*(7), 2383–2424. https://doi.org/10.1257/aer.20170537

Genesove, D., & Mayer, C. (2001). Loss aversion and seller behavior: Evidence from the housing market. *The Quarterly Journal of Economics, 116*(4), 1233–1260. https://doi.org/10.1162/003355301753265561

Gerard, F., & Naritomi, J. (2021). Job displacement insurance and (the lack of) consumption-smoothing. *American Economic Review, 111*(3), 899–942. https://doi.org/10.1257/aer.20190388

Handel, B. R. (2013). Adverse selection and inertia in health insurance markets: When nudging hurts. *American Economic Review, 103*(7), 2643–2682. https://doi.org/10.1257/aer.103.7.2643

Hanna, R., Mullainathan, S., & Schwartzstein, J. (2014). Learning through noticing: Theory and evidence from a field experiment. *The Quarterly Journal of Economics, 129*(3), 1311–1353. https://doi.org/10.1093/qje/qju015

Hoff, K., & Pandey, P. (2006). Discrimination, social identity, and durable inequalities. *American Economic Review, 96*(2), 206–211. https://pubs.aeaweb.org/doi/pdf/10.1257/000282806777212611

Houser, D., & McCabe, K. (2014). Experimental economics and experimental game theory. *Neuroeconomics.* (2nd ed.). Elsevier Academic Press. https://www.sciencedirect.com/topics/neuroscience/ultimatum-game

Huffman, D., Raymond, C., & Shvets, J. (2022). Persistent overconfidence and biased memory: Evidence from managers. *American Economic Review, 112*(10), 3141–3175. https://doi.org/10.1257/aer.20190668

Hurd, M. (2009). Subjective probabilities in household surveys. *Annual Review of Economics, 1*(1), 543–562. https://doi.org/10.1146/annurev.economics.050708.142955

Ito, K. (2014). Do consumers respond to marginal or average price? Evidence from nonlinear electricity pricing. *American Economic Review, 104*(2), 537–563. https://doi.org/10.1257/aer.104.2.537

Jackson, M. O. (2014). Networks in the understanding of economic behaviors. *Journal of Economic Perspectives, 28*(4), 3–22. https://doi.org/10.1257/jep.28.4.3

Kahneman, D., & Tversky, A. (1979). Prospect theory: An analysis of decision under risk. *Econometrica, 47*(2), 263–291. https://doi.org/10.2307/1914185

Kahneman, D., Knetsch, J. L., & Thaler, R. (1986). Fairness as a constraint on profit seeking: Entitlements in the market. *The American Economic Review, 76*(4), 728–741. https://www.jstor.org/stable/1806070

———. (1990). Experimental tests of the endowment effect and the Coase theorem. *Journal of Political Economy, 98*(6), 1325–1348. https://doi.org/10.1086/261737

Kaur, S. (2019). Nominal wage rigidity in village labor markets. *American Economic Review, 109*(10), 3585–3616. https://doi.org/10.1257/aer.20141625

Kaustia, M., & Knüpfer, S. (2008). Do investors overweight personal experience? Evidence from IPO subscriptions. *The Journal of Finance, 63*(6), 2679–2702. https://doi.org/10.1111/j.1540-6261.2008.01411.x

Ketcham, J. D., Lucarelli, C., Miravete, E. J., & Roebuck, M. C. (2012). Sinking, swimming, or learning to swim in Medicare Part D. *American Economic Review, 102*(6), 2639–2673. https://doi.org/10.1257/aer.102.6.2639

Kling, J. R., Mullainathan, S., Shafir, E., Vermeulen, L. C., & Wrobel, M. V. (2012). Comparison friction: Experimental evidence from Medicare drug plans. *The Quarterly Journal of Economics, 127*(1), 199–235. https://doi.org/10.1093/qje/qjr055

Kranton, R., Pease, M., Sanders, S., & Huettel, S. (2020). Deconstructing bias in social preferences reveals groupy and not-groupy behavior. *Proceedings of the National Academy of Sciences, 117*(35), 21185–21193. https://doi.org/10.1073/pnas.1918952117

Laibson, D. (1997). Golden eggs and hyperbolic discounting. *The Quarterly Journal of Economics, 112*(2), 443–478. https://doi.org/10.1162/003355397555253

Liao, Y. (2020). Weather and the decision to go solar: Evidence on costly cancellations. *Journal of the Association of Environmental and Resource Economists, 7*(1), 1–33. https://doi.org/10.1086/705592

Loewenstein, G., O'Donoghue, T., & Rabin, M. (2003). Projection bias in predicting future utility. *The Quarterly Journal of Economics, 118*(4), 1209–1248. https://doi.org/10.1162/003355303322552784

Lusardi, A., & Mitchell, O. (2011). Financial literacy around the world: An overview. *Journal of Pension Economics & Finance, 10*(4), 497–508. https://doi.org/10.1017/S1474747211000448

Luttmer, E., & Singhal, M. (2014). Tax morale. *Journal of Economic Perspectives, 28*(4), 149–168. https://doi.org/10.1257/jep.28.4.149

Maćkowiak, B., Matějka, F., & Wiederholt, M. (2023). Rational inattention: A review. *Journal of Economic Literature, 61*(1), 226–273. https://doi.org/10.1257/jel.20211524

Madrian, B. C. (2014). Applying insights from behavioral economics to policy design. *Annual Review of Economics, 6*(1), 663–688. https://doi.org/10.1146/annurev-economics-080213-041033

Madrian, B. C., & Shea, D. F. (2001). The power of suggestion: Inertia in 401(k) participation and savings behavior. *The Quarterly Journal of Economics, 116*(4), 1149–1187. https://doi.org/10.1162/003355301753265543

Malmendier, U., & Nagel, S. (2011). Depression babies: Do macroeconomic experiences affect risk taking? *The Quarterly Journal of Economics, 126*(1), 373–416. https://doi.org/10.1093/qje/qjq004

Manski, C. F. (1993). Identification of endogenous social effects: The reflection problem. *The Review of Economic Studies, 60*(3), 531–542. https://doi.org/10.2307/2298123

———. (2004). Measuring expectations. *Econometrica, 72*(5), 1329–1376. https://doi.org/10.1111/j.1468-0262.2004.00537.x

Marzilli Ericson, K. M., & Fuster, A. (2014). The endowment effect. *Annual Review of Economics, 6*(1), 555–579. https://www.annualreviews.org/doi/abs/10.1146/annurev-economics-080213-041320

Maymin, P. Z., & Langer, E. J. (2021). Cognitive biases and mindfulness. *Humanities and Social Sciences Communication, 8*(40). https://doi.org/10.1057/s41599-021-00712-1

McFadden, D. (2006). Free markets and fettered consumers. *American Economic Review, 96*(1), 5–29. https://doi.org/10.1257/000282806776157542

Möbius, M. M., Niederle, M., Niehaus, P., & Rosenblat, T. S. (2014). *Managing self-confidence*. NBER Working Paper 17014. National Bureau of Economic Research. http://web.stanford.edu/~niederle/Mobius.Niederle.Niehaus.Rosenblat.paper.pdf

Mullainathan, S., & Shafir, E. (2013). *Scarcity: Why having too little means so much.* Macmillan.
Nickerson, R. S. (1998). Confirmation bias: A ubiquitous phenomenon in many guises. *Review of General Psychology, 2*(2), 175–220. https://doi.org/10.1037/1089-2680.2.2.175
O'Donoghue, T., & Rabin, M. (1999). Doing it now or later. *American Economic Review, 89*(1), 103–124. https://doi.org/10.1257/aer.89.1.103
Pires, P. (2022). How much can you make? Misprediction and biased memory in gig jobs [Draft]. https://pedropires.io/s/Pires_JMP_HowMuchCanYouMake.pdf
Rabin, M. (1993). Incorporating fairness into game theory and economics. *The American Review, 83*(5), 1281–1302. http://www.jstor.org/stable/2117561
———. (2002). Inference by believers in the law of small numbers. *The Quarterly Journal of Economics, 117*(3), 775–816. https://doi.org/10.1162/003355302760193896
———. (2002). A perspective on psychology and economics. *European Economic Review, 46*(4–5), 657–685. https://doi.org/10.1016/S0014-2921(01)00207-0
Samuelson, P. A. (1947). *Foundations of economic analysis.* Harvard University Press.
Santos-Pinto, L., & de la Rosa, L. E. (2020). Overconfidence in labor markets. *Handbook of labor, human resources and population economics,* 1–42. Springer. https://doi.org/10.1007/978-3-319-57365-6_117-1
Schelling, T. C. (1978). *Micromotives and macrobehavior.* WW Norton & Company.
Schwartzstein, J. (2014). Selective attention and learning. *Journal of the European Economic Association, 12*(6), 1423–1452. https://doi.org/10.1111/jeea.12104
Shayo, M., & Zussman, A. (2011). Judicial ingroup bias in the shadow of terrorism. *The Quarterly Journal of Economics, 126*(3), 1447–1484. https://doi.org/10.1093/qje/qjr022
Shih, M., Pittinsky, T. L., & Ambady, N. (1999). Stereotype susceptibility: Identity salience and shifts in quantitative performance. *Psychological Science, 10*(1), 80–83. https://doi.org/10.1111/1467-9280.00111
Sial, A. Y., Sydnor, J. R., & Taubinsky, D. (2023). *Biased memory and perceptions of self-control.* NBER Working Paper 30825. National Bureau of Economic Research. https://doi.org/10.3386/w30825
Sims, C. A. (2003). Implications of rational inattention. *Journal of Monetary Economics, 50*(3), 665–690. https://doi.org/10.1016/S0304-3932(03)00029-1
Spinnewijn, J. (2015). Unemployed but optimistic: Optimal insurance design with biased beliefs. *Journal of the European Economic Association, 13*(1), 130–167. https://doi.org/10.1111/jeea.12099
Sydnor, J. (2010). (Over) insuring modest risks. *American Economic Journal: Applied Economics, 2*(4), 177–199. https://doi.org/10.1257/app.2.4.177
Thakral, N., & Tô, L. T. (2021). Daily labor supply and adaptive reference points. *American Economic Review, 111*(8), 2417–2443. https://doi.org/10.1257/aer.20170768
Thaler, M. (2021). The supply of motivated beliefs. *arXiv.* https://doi.org/10.48550/arXiv.2111.06062
Wald, A. (1950). *Statistical decision functions.* Wiley.
Zimmermann, F. (2020). The dynamics of motivated beliefs. *American Economic Review, 110*(2), 337–363. https://doi.org/10.1257/aer.20180728

4

The Behavioral Economics Toolkit: Policy Levers and Intervention Strategies

The theoretical foundations of behavioral economics discussed in Chapter 3 have been used to design policies aimed at changing behavior. An outstanding question, however, is *how* these principles are translated into interventions and behavior change strategies, including so-called nudges, in real-world settings.

A nudge is defined in the context of behavioral economics as a low-cost, light-touch change in choice architecture—the structures and contexts within which and through which a choice is presented—that shifts people's behavior without explicitly regulating it and without imposing significant (financial) rewards or punishments (Thaler & Sunstein, 2009). Multiple elements of choice architecture can be altered: the number of options, the framing of options, the information provided about the options, the placement of options in a physical or digital space, and the way people's attention is drawn to some options (or features of options) more than others (Münscher, Vetter, & Scheuerle, 2016; Johnson, 2021). Many different aspects of choice architecture have been targeted using nudge strategies: they include changing default options; providing information about the behavior of peers or neighbors; simplifying forms or instructions for decision making; and a variety of ways to increase the salience of the desired option, such as changing the order or convenience of options in a decision menu. This approach to behavioral change is sometimes called "libertarian paternalism," in that the designer of the nudge has determined that one choice would be better than another—would benefit individuals or society—but is not imposing that choice through regulation or other requirements (see Chapter 2).

Researchers, policy makers, and practitioners in many domains have designed and tested interventions that leverage these principles, efforts that have been documented in decades of research. Interventions are planned and coordinated sets of activities designed to change specific behaviors or behavior patterns (Michie, Van Stralen, & West, 2011). Behaviorally informed interventions are those that have been selected or designed specifically to address a behavioral barrier, biased tendency, or decision error that can be explained by the foundational principles of behavioral economics discussed in Chapter 3.[1]

Interventions can be designed and implemented by different actors (corporate, governmental, institutional) in different policy domains (e.g., health, education, finance) and take diverse forms (e.g., the design of a promotional brochure or reminder letter, a policy about enrollment or late fees, or a physical change to a choice environment). Interventions can be targeted at the general population or at specific subgroups of interest, may comprise one-time or repeated exposures, and may range from very obvious to quite invisible.

In this chapter we review a necessarily selected group of these intervention strategies or approaches. We focus on the strategies that are most commonly used and for which there is some evidence of effectiveness. We note here that some of these strategies work by leveraging the common cognitive biases and heuristics that affect people's decision making, such as present bias, availability heuristic, and loss aversion (see Chapters 2 and 3); others work by countering, mitigating, or decreasing the effects of those same biases and heuristics. This latter type can be referred to as a way of de-biasing individuals or counteracting specific sources of bias. We note that the research on the effectiveness of de-biasing is just beginning, and its findings to date are inconclusive (Borchardt, Kamzabek, & Lovallo, 2022).

In addition to drawing heavily on psychology, many of the intervention strategies discussed below also rely on theories and practices from communication, education, and human-centered design[2] to most effectively either leverage or counter the impact of behavioral factors, such as reference dependence and present bias, on behavior. The emerging interdisciplinary field of behavioral design brings together the findings and methods from all of these fields to optimize intervention designs as effective solutions

---

[1]The committee uses the phrase "behaviorally informed" to distinguish between interventions that are specifically designed to address a behavioral attribute and other, possibly very similar, interventions that were not. For example, incentives are recognized as key factors in economic decisions, but, while in some cases they are straightforward (e.g., offering financial rewards for taking an action), in others they are designed to address behavioral factors such as those discussed in Chapter 3.

[2]Human-centered design is an approach to problem-solving that focuses on users' perspectives, emotions, and needs in the design of products and services.

to behavior change challenges (Datta & Mullainathan, 2014; Niedderer, Clune, & Ludden, 2017; Bucher, 2020). Indeed, behavioral design of markets and institutions is also emerging as an important area of research on the optimal design of institutions—such as matching markets for medical interns (Roth & Sotomayor, 1992; Roth, 2015) and school choice mechanisms (Pathak, 2017)—that incorporate behavioral elements (also see McFadden, 2009; Duflo, 2017). Similarly, behavioral public policy and behavioral governance focus attention on the ways in which policy makers themselves may be subject to biases and heuristic thinking in the policy formulation process and on how to productively incorporate behavioral insights into that process (see Chapter 13; Grimmelikhuijsen et al., 2017; Gofen et al., 2021).

As we discuss in Part III, more research is needed on many aspects of these kinds of interventions, including studies of their efficacy and effectiveness; implementation; replication; subgroup analyses and explorations of differential responses; and ways to ensure the best fit between intervention strategy and target, context, and behavior type. For all of the strategies we discuss, the evidence is mixed: it is possible to find studies with null effects, failures to replicate, or nuanced results suggesting subgroup effects and contextually specific results, as well as evidence of positive effects. For example, it is likely that some behaviorally informed interventions are more effective for changing a one-off behavior than for creating and sustaining a habit (Neal et al., 2016; Wood & Neal, 2016; Carden & Wood, 2018; Venema et al., 2020). Similarly, while there are settings and situations in which individual behavior decisions are made in isolation, many other settings are characterized by feedback loops, "gaming," or other interpersonal and networked behaviors that may influence the effectiveness or effects of an individually targeted intervention. More research and discussion are also needed on the limitations of behaviorally informed interventions (especially for the narrow nudge form) and on how focusing on individual behavior change could preclude or crowd out focus on structural or system change (Loewenstein & Chater, 2017; Chater & Loewenstein, 2022).

Although there is much more to learn, the work to date has produced an impressive toolkit for influencing behavior in a policy context. While different fields use different terms for the contents of a toolkit (tools, strategies, approaches), we refer to them as "intervention strategies." For simplicity, we have chosen to align the intervention strategies covered in this chapter with the foundational principles discussed in Chapter 3. However, most successful intervention strategies take into account more than one of these principles. Our mapping of strategies to the foundational principles is shown in Table 4-1. The rest of the chapter discusses some of the leading intervention strategies that have been developed applying these principles.

TABLE 4-1 Intervention Strategies Mapped to the Five Foundational Principles

Strategies	Foundational Principle and Everyday Meaning				
	Limited Attention and Cognition	Inaccurate Beliefs	Present Bias	Reference Dependence and Framing	Social Preferences and Social Norms
	"I don't know what I want"	"I think I know what I want"	"I want it now"	"I want this more than I want that"	"I want to do what others are doing"
Altruism Primes			X		X
Behaviorally Informed Incentives, Including Microincentives	X		X	X	
Choice Sets and Active Choice	X	X		X	
Commitment Devices			X		
Defaults	X		X	X	
Feedback	X			X	X
Foot-in-the-Door			X	X	
Framing	X	X		X	
Fresh Start Effects			X	X	
Hassle Factors		X	X		X
Implementation Intentions			X		
Mental Models		X	X	X	
Planning Prompts			X		
Reciprocity Primes					X
Reminders	X		X		
Salience Primes	X				
Scarcity	X		X	X	
Simplification	X		X	X	
Slack	X				
Social Influence	X	X		X	X
Social Proof	X	X	X	X	X
Switching Costs			X	X	
Temptation Bundling			X		

ADDRESSING LIMITED ATTENTION AND COGNITION

To address limited attention and cognition, the behavioral challenge for policy makers is that individuals pay only limited attention to important aspects of policy situations, often have a hard time processing information, and make cognitive errors even in simple situations. To meet this challenge, interventions have used defaults, active choice, salience primes, simplification, choice sets, and creating slack.

Defaults

Setting a default (e.g., a default level of salary deduction for a retirement plan, or a healthy default side dish on a restaurant menu) is among the most powerful strategies for behavioral change. Defaults have been shown in several systematic reviews and meta-analyses to have larger effect sizes than other intervention approaches. Defaults work through multiple mechanisms but are particularly effective in conditions of limited attentional or cognitive bandwidth, when individuals cannot or will not take the time to evaluate options and make a fully informed choice (Johnson & Goldstein, 2003). Examples of effective defaults include opt-out or opt-in 401(k) retirement plan enrollments for employees (Madrian & Shea, 2001; see Chapter 10), defaults for prescribing generic medications (Patel et al., 2016b), and default menu options to encourage healthy food choices (Vecchio & Cavallo, 2019).

Active Choice

When it is not possible (or perceived as not ethical) to implement a true default, an *active choice* intervention can also focus limited attention. Active choice interventions create a stopping point in a process that requires an individual to make a choice before proceeding. A common one is the requirement to elect or decline travel insurance when purchasing a plane or train ticket. A study of HIV testing decisions found that an active choice intervention resulted in testing rates between those of opt-out (default) and opt-in interventions (Montoy, Dow, & Kaplan, 2016).

Salience Primes

When inattention and cognitive load create barriers to behavior change, it can be an effective strategy to make crucial information or features of a choice set more salient (see Chapter 3). Salience prime interventions have been shown to be effective in many domains, as shown in two examples discussed in Chapter 3: the study showing that grocery store price tags that made state taxes more salient significantly decreased purchases for taxable products (compared with price tags that did include taxes; Chetty, Looney, & Kroft, 2009), and the study showing the importance of providing clear descriptions of the options included in Medicare Part D plans (Kling et al., 2012).

Simplification

As discussed in Chapter 3, interventions that simplify the presentation of information allow people's limited attentional resources to be directed at a smaller amount of information. In a field experiment conducted in cooperation with the Internal Revenue Service (IRS), different versions of letters were sent to 35,000 taxpayers who filed returns and were eligible for the Earned Income Tax Credit but had not yet claimed it (Bhargava & Manoli, 2015). Remarkably, just a simplification of the two-page notice sent from the IRS with clearer wording increased the take-up in this group by over 10 percent, suggesting the importance of clear communication about government programs.

One popular form of simplification that also reduces cognitive burden and can nudge individuals toward a focused set of tasks in a set order is a checklist. A systematic review of checklists used to improve health care delivery quality found significant reductions in surgical complications and medication errors associated with checklists (Boyd, Wu, & Stelfox, 2017).

Choice Sets

Limited attention for choices can also be focused through the creation, arrangement, and framing through *choice sets* (Johnson, 2021). Reducing the number of choices available has been shown to improve the selection process and increase people's satisfaction with their choices (Gourville & Soman, 2005; Reutskaja et al., 2020, 2022). Studies of health insurance plan choice have highlighted how plan choice can be strongly influenced by how different plan options are described and displayed, often leading to suboptimal choices (Bhargava, Loewenstein, & Sydnor, 2017). Choice sets can be designed to reduce comparison friction—the cognitive burden caused by having to compare choices across multiple attributes without sufficient information—or other psychological frictions that impede accessing information or taking up benefits (Kling et al., 2012; Bhargava & Manoli, 2015).

Creating Slack

A final category of intervention strategies to counteract limited attention and cognition is the creation of slack: that is, providing more space or flexibility for people's responses. Creating slack is particularly effective for those experiencing scarcity of any kind (time, material resources, even social interaction), because scarcity can make decisions about immediate tasks more costly and challenging, while also amplifying the negative consequences of poor or short-sighted decisions (Mullainathan & Shafir, 2013). Techniques to create slack include introducing buffers of extra time or extra financial resources and reducing the cost of errors or poor decisions by establishing safeguards and backstops or otherwise "replacing cliffs with slopes" (Daminger et al., 2015, pp. 34–35).

ADDRESSING INACCURATE BELIEFS

To address inaccurate beliefs, the behavioral challenge for policy makers is that people often have inaccurate perceptions of the situation, of incentives, of their own abilities, and about the beliefs of others. Intervention strategies that address inaccurate beliefs or perceptions can replace or update inaccurate beliefs with new beliefs or reduce the effect of the inaccurate beliefs on optimal decision making. Several of the strategies mentioned above are relevant here, including framing, defaults, reference groups, simplification (e.g., of complex incentive schemes), choice sets, peer feedback, and social proof.

In addition to those interventions, two others are important for meeting the challenge of inaccurate beliefs: de-biasing and mental models, which are people's representations of the world.

De-biasing

The primary type of intervention for correcting beliefs is de-biasing. For example, an overoptimism bias—the tendency for a person to believe they will perform better than the average or that good things will be more likely to come their way and bad things less likely—can be addressed through salient presentation of statistics related to past performance of either an individual or a relevant reference group. In a systematic review of interventions to de-bias health-related decisions, two-thirds of the studies designed to counter overoptimism bias were successful (Ludolph & Schulz, 2018). De-biasing approaches have been categorized into motivational, cognitive, affective, and technological strategies, with emerging research showing nuanced evidence about which approaches are the most successful in different contexts (Larrick, 2004; Larrick & Soll, 2008; Croskerry, Singhal, & Mamede, 2013; Soll, Milkman, & Payne, 2015; Delavande, 2023; Fuster & Zafar, 2023; Haaland, Roth, & Wohlfart, 2023).

Mental Models

A large literature on mental models suggests that people's mental representations of how the world works can strongly influence decisions and behaviors in diverse domains, including health, climate change, and management (Johnson-Laird, 2004; Pfeffer, 2005; Kealey & Berkman, 2010; Wong-Parodi & Bruine de Bruin, 2017). For example, multiple studies have shown that people have powerful mental models of the epidemiology of COVID-19 and of the effectiveness and acceptability of mitigation strategies, including masking, social distancing, and vaccination (Southwell et al., 2020; Greenhalgh, 2021; Berg et al., 2022; de Ridder et al., 2022). While mental models can be useful decision-making heuristics, they can also induce inertia and are susceptible to bias (Guiette & Vandenbempt, 2013; Hovmand et al., 2021). Biased or inaccurate mental models can be a target for interventions, including de-biasing interventions, although research suggests that replacing or updating mental models can be challenging. Techniques to revise or update mental models include visualizations, experiencing surprise, analogies, simulation, and critical reflection (Bostrom, 2008; Gary & Wood, 2011; Thacker & Sinatra, 2019; Vink et al., 2019).

ADDRESSING PRESENT BIAS

To address present bias, the behavioral challenge for policy makers is that people tend to disproportionately focus on present consumption, payments, and general utility, and pay less attention to future payoffs and consequences. Present bias creates a tendency to procrastinate and to choose immediate rewards over longer-term benefits.

Whether this tendency is perceived as laziness or hyperbolic discounting, there are several evidence-based strategies to counter present bias. Disregard of future benefits is likely related to inattention, as described above: that is, individuals simply are not paying attention to future benefits. For this reason, many of the strategies discussed above as remedies to limited attention and cognition are also applicable here, particularly defaults and simplification. Defaults and simplification make it harder for an individual to procrastinate by reducing options and limiting overwhelming and distracting information. Interestingly, however, even when attention is focused on future benefits (e.g., employer matches for retirement savings), there may be minimal take-up of the future-oriented benefit in the moment without an opportunity to act right away and a deadline (Choi, Laibson, & Madrian, 2011).

In addition to these strategies, five others are particularly appropriate to meet the challenge of present bias: reducing friction and hassle factors, behaviorally informed financial or nonfinancial incentives, lottery-based incentives, commitment devices, and reminders.

Friction and Hassle Factors

Removing friction reduces people's tendency to procrastinate by reducing the immediate costs (in the form of time or inconvenience) of a behavior. Researchers across diverse domains have studied the response to strategies or interventions that remove sources of friction (also called "hassle factors"), reduce administrative burdens, or reduce switching costs. Because present bias leads individuals to delay action when they experience friction, hassle factors, or administrative burden, reducing those factors can substantially increase compliance. Examples of such interventions include providing individualized information about a benefit so that participants do not have to seek that information themselves (Kling et al., 2012), transitioning cumbersome paper-based benefits administration to electronic formats (Vasan et al., 2021), and allowing users to complete an action online instead of by mail or in person (Bhanot, 2021).

The highly successful Moving to Opportunity (MTO) program, which provides an opportunity for low-income families to move to better neighborhoods using a voucher, demonstrates the importance of hassle factors. Despite robust evidence on the effectiveness of the program, take-up is low. In a subsample of MTO recipients who were randomized to receive services that reduce the hassle costs of moving, the proportion of movers increased from 15 percent without the services to 53 percent with the services that reduced hassle factors (Bergman, Chan, & Kapor, 2020). In contrast, even sizable increases in the value of the voucher did not have large effects, suggesting that the key factor is the disutility from navigating bureaucracy and other transaction costs.

Behaviorally Informed Financial or Nonfinancial Incentives

Many people who read about behavioral economics in the lay press assume the term refers to financial incentives or paying individuals to change their behavior. It is certainly the case that many well-known behavioral economics studies leverage incentives to counter present bias. Because present bias leads people to focus on immediate costs and benefits of an action at the expense of future costs and benefits, a financial incentive that is delivered in the present can make benefits feel more immediate and can counter immediate costs (time, hassle, etc.). Financial incentives are also well-suited to incorporating other behavioral principles, including loss aversion, regret aversion, and reference dependence, into the design of interventions.

A common query, particularly from economists, is whether financial incentives should be considered as part of the behavioral economics toolkit. After all, what's "behavioral" about changing the cost of taking some action and expecting a response to that change? For example, a frequently cited study showed that a $750 incentive prompted 15 percent of employees of a large private firm to quit smoking: in comparison, only five percent quit smoking in a control group that received only information about cessation and available cessation programs (Volpp et al., 2009). While this result may seem obvious—of course it makes sense that people who were paid to quit did so more frequently than those who were not—it is important to note that for most habitual smokers, the financial savings that accrue from quitting exceed $750 very soon after quitting. It violates assumptions of traditional economics that an offer of $750 would be much more effective at prompting quitting (than no financial incentive). Similarly, participants offered a $10 incentive to take up 401(k) retirement savings enrollment increased their savings more than participants who received information about the future benefits of retirement savings that were worth far more (Bhargava & Conell-Price, 2022).

The distinction that behavioral economists point to is between incentives that are specifically designed to capitalize on knowledge of behavioral characteristics and those that simply increase the benefits or change the price of a particular option. An illustration of this distinction is a study that showed that consumers react more strongly to a tax if it is made more salient to them: in this case, if the consumer saw a price tag on an alcoholic beverage that specified the tax rather than having the opportunity to notice a tax of the same amount being applied at the cash register (Chetty, Looney, & Kroft, 2009). The accumulated evidence suggests that behaviorally informed microincentives are a promising way to motivate actions in settings in which the future benefits of an action (or the current costs of inaction) may otherwise be ignored.

Lottery-Based Incentives

Many variations of financial incentives have also been tested, with features that further leverage behavioral research findings to boost effectiveness. Lottery-based incentive programs leverage the fact that participants may be more motivated by the small probability of winning a large prize than by a guaranteed incentive of a much smaller prize. This phenomenon results from base rate neglect (see below), a manifestation of reference dependence. A regret lottery further leverages regret aversion, the tendency to strongly dislike the possibility of regret, which motivates behaviors that avoid future regret. In regret lotteries, participants are eligible to "win" the lottery (i.e., have their winning number drawn) but are only eligible for the prize if they have already taken some specified action by the time their lucky number is drawn (Zeelenberg & Pieters, 2004; Haff et al., 2015; Patel et al., 2016a). Deposit contracts leverage the notion of loss aversion or the endowment effect (see section on reference dependence, below; see also Chapter 3) by asking participants to put up their own money in a bet against a future behavioral outcome. If the behavior is achieved, the participant keeps the deposit (and possibly earns additional incentives). If the participant fails to achieve the behavioral target, the deposit is forfeited (Volpp et al., 2008; Barankay et al., 2020).

These examples of variations on financial incentives highlight the importance of behavioral design, given the many design elements required in an incentives program, including the size, conditionality, currency, probabilistic or guaranteed nature, and framing of the incentive. While financial incentives have been shown to be effective for many behaviors, particularly one-off behaviors where procrastination is a key barrier, there is less evidence that they can lead to sustained behavior change after the incentive is removed or can boost motivation for behaviors with which a person has considerable experience or strong preferences (Mantzari et al., 2015; Thirumurthy, Asch, & Volpp, 2019; Luong et al., 2021). There is also mixed evidence about the effectiveness of lotteries in the handful of studies that directly compare lottery-based incentives to a fixed or guaranteed payment (Halpern et al., 2011; Meiselman et al., 2022).

Commitment Devices

A different way to counter present bias is to commit a future self to an action that is difficult to evade or delay when the moment comes. This can be accomplished through commitment devices (such as when Odysseus tied himself to the mast) that can be harder or softer depending on the degree of enforceability of the device (Ashraf, Karlan, & Yin, 2006; Bryan, Karlan, & Nelson, 2010; Schwartz et al., 2014). Commitment devices (also called commitment contracts) can take the form of a savings vehicle that restricts when and how you can access your savings or a deposit you put down that is forfeited if you fail to exert self-control over an undesired or unhealthy behavior (e.g., smoking). An important policy question related to the effectiveness of commitment devices is whether they are only useful for "sophisticated" people (those with accurate beliefs about their degree of self-control or present bias) and much less effective for "naïve" people who hold inaccurate beliefs (see Chapter 3). Naïve people may pay for a commitment device that they are unlikely to benefit from (Bai et al., 2021).

Prompting individuals to make a plan with planning prompts or guiding them to state their implementation intentions to complete a behavior has also been shown to boost completion of a task and overcome present bias (Milkman et al., 2013; Rogers et al., 2015; Yeomans & Reich, 2017; Mazar, Mochon, & Ariely, 2018; Silva et al., 2018; Ahn, Hu, & Vega, 2021; Robitaille, House, & Mazar, 2021). A well-known example of the effect of planning and implementation prompts can be found in the literature on motivating voting behavior (Nickerson & Rogers, 2010). In another domain, a study demonstrated that a simple planning prompt on a postcard significantly increased use of an employee vaccination clinic in comparison with a postcard that only reminded participants of the clinic dates (Milkman et al., 2011). Pairing a more desired and a less desired action together, known as temptation bundling, can also counter present bias that leads to putting off the less desired action (Milkman, Minson, & Volpp, 2014).

Reminders

Finally, simple reminders can also counter the tendency to delay costly behaviors, especially when they mention a future goal or desired state (Karlan et al., 2016). Reminders also cut through inattention, remedy prospective memory failures (i.e., forgetting), and increase salience of the desired behavior. A systematic review of reminders for health behaviors found moderate effectiveness, with the strongest evidence of effectiveness from reminders that are frequent and those that are accompanied by personal contact with a health care provider or counselor (Neff & Fry, 2009). In a powerful example of the effectiveness of reminders, researchers have been able to reduce failures to appear in court following an arrest summons with behaviorally informed reminders about court dates sent in text messages (Fishbane, Ouss, & Shah, 2020).

ADDRESSING REFERENCE DEPENDENCE AND FRAMING

To address reference dependence and framing, the behavioral challenge for policy makers is to recognize that individuals evaluate risk decisions in terms of a specific reference point and may not treat risk according to traditional economic utility theory. Thus, they are sensitive to the framing of decision problems.

Behavioral research has shown that people do not evaluate decisions in a vacuum or using absolute standards. They are highly influenced by reference points, particularly when considering tradeoff decisions (now or later, sell or buy, etc.) or evaluating risk. Reference dependence implies that policy designers can guide choices by creating or highlighting a specific reference group, drawing attention to a temporal reference point, or using framing to prompt a comparison to a reference point. In addition to the strategy of choice sets discussed above, three other strategies are especially relevant to reference dependence: framing, foot in the door, and fresh start effects.

Framing

A common framing strategy for behavioral interventions is a loss frame, which leverages loss aversion and the endowment effect by drawing attention to the negative consequences of inaction (i.e., the bad things that will happen if you do not do something), which may be more motivating than a gain frame (i.e., the good things that will happen if you do something). Loss-frame messages promoting health behaviors are often more effective for some groups than others—for example, for those more at risk of the consequences of a behavior and those in a positive affective state (Keller, Lipkus, & Rimer, 2003; Cho & Boster, 2008). There is also robust evidence that loss-frame messages are more effective for screening or disease detection behaviors, while gain-frame messages are more effective for prevention behaviors (Rothman et al., 2006) or prosocial behaviors (Castelo et al., 2015).

Foot in the Door

Self-perception theory and the literature on people's preference for consistent actions are the basis for the use of foot-in-the-door techniques, which invite individuals to agree to a smaller request before presenting a larger one, thus resetting the reference point for the larger decision. While much of the foot-in-the-door literature concerns fundraising or civic behavior, foot-in-the-door interventions have also increased engagement with health promotion activities (Dolin & Booth-Butterfield, 1995; Ybarra et al., 2014).

Fresh Start Effects

The fresh start effect is the tendency to be more motivated to set or achieve goals related to key personal or cultural milestones, such as birthdays; holidays; or the start of a new year, month, or week (Dai, Milkman, & Riis, 2014). Simply sending a reminder or inviting goal setting at a fresh start moment can increase engagement. There is some evidence that framing a message around a fresh start—which encourages individuals to reflect on these temporal landmarks—can increase the intention to pursue a goal (Dai, Milkman, & Riis, 2015).

ADDRESSING SOCIAL PREFERENCES AND SOCIAL NORMS

To address social preferences and social norms, the behavioral opportunity for policy makers is that people often care deeply about the well-being of others and how their own behavior and social standing compares with those of others, and the social environment has a significant influence on people's decision making. This finding from behavioral research does not align with the most common traditional economic model, which assumes that individuals care most about their own well-being and ignore the actions of others in society when making their decisions (but some traditional models do; see Chapter 3).

Many intervention strategies specifically leverage the importance and salience of social norms (detailed below) and people's perceptions of their social standing. Four intervention strategies are particularly relevant for taking advantage of social preferences and social norms: social proof, social comparison, social influence, and reciprocity and altruism. As with all behavioral strategies, interventions related to social norms can be nuanced and may backfire; careful attention to this possibility during both the design and evaluation of these interventions is crucial (Bicchieri, 2016; Bicchieri & Dimant, 2022; Constantino et al., 2022).

Social Proof

Social proof interventions provide descriptive data about other people's choices and behaviors, such as the number of drinks most students consume at a party (Perkins, 2002) or how many other voters plan to vote or have already voted (Gerber & Rogers, 2009). These interventions have been used to reduce risky or harmful behaviors, such as binge drinking among students, and to increase positive behaviors, such as voter engagement. The mechanisms underlying these interventions include motivating conformity and serving as a simplifying decision-making heuristic.

Social Comparison

Social comparison interventions explicitly compare an individual's performance with a relevant comparison or reference group. The evidence on social comparison is mixed, with several instances of successful interventions, as well null results and even backfire effects (Beshears et al., 2015). A particularly strong response may be triggered by social comparisons with others if the comparison is not anonymous and individuals are publicly compared with others.

A controversial version of a social comparison intervention provides the information for an individual and a comparison between the individual and a relevant peer group, as in a voting intervention that reminded voters about their own voting record and the voting rate of their neighbors (Gerber, Green, & Larimer, 2008). In this study, the social comparison mailer further informed voters that they are likely to receive an updated mailer later with the updated voter turnout record. This mailer led to a dramatic 8 percentage point increase in voter turnout, probably the largest such finding in the literature. Voters anticipated that their turnout choice would be shared with neighbors and wanted to be sure to vote so they would be seen by neighbors as public good providers. Social comparison can also be implemented as feedback about peer performance, a common strategy for changing clinicians' behaviors related to adherence to evidence-based guidelines (Hallsworth et al., 2016; Meeker et al., 2016).

Social Influence

Social influence, which is also known as social modeling, involves having celebrities or respected opinion leaders endorse or model a desired behavior, which also leverages the importance of injunctive or prescriptive social norms. This strategy has been studied extensively for recycling behaviors: in that context, social comparison is more effective than information provision alone, but it does not work better than financial incentives (Osbaldiston & Schott, 2012; Varotto & Spagnolli, 2017).

Reciprocity and Altruism

The importance of social relationships can also be invoked by interventions that leverage reciprocity and altruism. Traditional economic models assume self-interest, but studies of human behavior suggest that people feel motivated and rewarded when they reciprocate and act altruistically. While many laboratory experiments have successfully used altruism appeals to increase prosocial behavioral intentions (e.g., to get vaccinated), there is less evidence from real-world or field studies (Hershey et al., 1994; Rieger, 2020; Cucciniello et al., 2022; for evidence related to organ donation, see also Sallis, Harper, & Sanders, 2018; Robitaille et al., 2021).

CONCLUSION

The range of behaviorally based economic interventions is large and expanding. It includes strategies for which there is excellent empirical evidence of effectiveness (defaults, framing) and others for which the evidence is mixed or less robust (incentives, planning prompts). However, the interventions are not well defined: that is, many of the strategies are defined differently by researchers and practitioners in different policy domains and from different academic disciplines and fields.[3] The field of behavioral eco-

---

[3]For a detailed discussion of this problem, see National Academies of Sciences, Engineering, and Medicine (2022).

nomics has also not yet developed or embraced rigorous design methods for characterizing behavioral barriers in specific contexts and then selecting or matching interventions or strategies for addressing those barriers. It is impossible to know now whether this laudable goal can ever be achieved, given the importance of context and the unique characteristics of many behavior change targets. Published studies describing behavioral interventions often fail to describe the source of the behavioral intervention tested or the design process that produced it, if any. True collaboration among behavioral economists, other behavioral scientists, and behavioral designers (i.e., practitioners and researchers focused on developing behavioral solutions to meet specific needs) has been rare.

Conclusion 4-1: Research is needed to advance methods used to characterize barriers to a specific behavior and then to design behaviorally informed interventions that address those barriers. Such research can address the pressing policy demand for guidance about when to use different behavioral strategies and how to match a policy challenge to an intervention strategy and evidence about the optimal level at which to target behavioral interventions: individuals, practitioners and providers, firms and organizations, or government entities.

REFERENCES

Ahn, J. N., Hu, D., & Vega, M. (2021). Changing pace: Using implementation intentions to enhance social distancing behavior during the COVID-19 pandemic. *Journal of Experimental Psychology: Applied, 27*(4), 762–772. https://psycnet.apa.org/doi/10.1037/xap0000385

Ashraf, N., Karlan, D., & Yin, W. (2006). Tying Odysseus to the mast: Evidence from a commitment savings product in the Philippines. *The Quarterly Journal of Economics, 121*(2), 635–672. https://doi.org/10.1162/qjec.2006.121.2.635

Bai, L., Handel, B., Miguel, E., & Rao, G. (2021). Self-control and demand for preventive health: Evidence from hypertension in India. *Review of Economics and Statistics, 103*(5), 835–856. https://doi.org/10.1162/rest_a_00938

Barankay, I., Reese, P. P., Putt, M. E., Russell, L. B., Loewenstein, G., Pagnotti, D., Yan, J., Zhu, J., McGilloway, R., Brennan, T., & Finnerty, D. (2020). Effect of patient financial incentives on statin adherence and lipid control: A randomized clinical trial. *Journal of the American Medical Association Network Open, 3*(10), e2019429. https://doi.org/10.1001/jamanetworkopen.2020.19429

Berg, S. H., Shortt, M. T., Thune, H., Røislien, J., O'Hara, J. K., Lungu, D. A., & Wiig, S. (2022). Differences in comprehending and acting on pandemic health risk information: A qualitative study using mental models. *BioMed Central Public Health, 22*(1), 1–15. https://doi.org/10.1186/s12889-022-13853-y

Bergman, P., Chan, E. W., & Kapor, A. (2020). *Housing search frictions: Evidence from detailed search data and a field experiment.* NBER Working Paper 27209. National Bureau of Economic Research. https://doi.org/10.3386/w27209

Beshears, J., Choi, J. J., Laibson, D., Madrian, B. C., & Milkman, K. L. (2015). The effect of providing peer information on retirement savings decisions. *The Journal of Finance, 70*(3), 1161–1201. https://doi.org/10.1111/jofi.12258

Bhanot, S. P. (2021). Good for you or good for us? A field experiment on motivating citizen behavior change. *Journal of Behavioral Public Administration*, 4(1). https://doi.org/10.30636/jbpa.41.207

Bhargava, S., & Conell-Price, L. (2022). *Serenity now, save later? Evidence on retirement savings puzzles from a 401(k) field experiment*. SSRN. https://dx.doi.org/10.2139/ssrn.4056407

Bhargava, S., & Manoli, D. (2015). Psychological frictions and the incomplete take-up of social benefits: Evidence from an IRS field experiment. *American Economic Review*, 105(11), 3489–3529. https://doi.org/10.1257/aer.20121493

Bhargava, S., Loewenstein, G., & Sydnor, J. (2017). Choose to lose: Health plan choices from a menu with dominated option. *The Quarterly Journal of Economics*, 132(3), 1319–1372. https://doi.org/10.1093/qje/qjx011

Bicchieri, C. (2016). *Norms in the wild: How to diagnose, measure, and change social norms*. Oxford University Press.

Bicchieri, C., & Dimant, E. (2022). Nudging with care: The risks and benefits of social information. *Public Choice*, 191(3–4), 443–464. https://doi.org/10.1007/s11127-019-00684-6

Borchardt, W., Kamzabek, T., & Lovallo, D. (2022). Behavioral strategy in the wild. *Management Research Review*, 45(9). https://doi.org/10.1108/MRR-12-2021-0876

Bostrom, A. (2008). Lead is like mercury: Risk comparisons, analogies and mental models. *Journal of Risk Research*, 11(1–2), 99–117. https://doi.org/10.1080/13669870701602956

Boyd, J. M., Wu, G., & Stelfox, H. T. (2017). The impact of checklists on inpatient safety outcomes: A systematic review of randomized controlled trials. *Journal of Hospital Medicine*, 12(8), 675–682. https://doi.org/10.12788/jhm.2788

Bryan, G., Karlan, D., & Nelson, S. (2010). Commitment devices. *Annual Review of Economics*, 2(1), 671–698. https://doi.org/10.1146/annurev.economics.102308.124324

Bucher, A. (2020). *Engaged: Designing for behavior change*. Rosenfeld Media.

Carden, L., & Wood, W. (2018). Habit formation and change. *Current Opinion in Behavioral Sciences*, 20, 117–122. https://doi.org/10.1016/j.cobeha.2017.12.009

Castelo, N., Hardy, E., House, J., Mazar, N., Tsai, C., & Zhao, M. (2015). Moving citizens online: Using salience & message framing to motivate behavior change. *Behavioral Science & Policy*, 1(2), 57–68. https://doi.org/10.1353/bsp.2015.0018

Chater, N., & Loewenstein, G. (2022). The i-frame and the s-frame: How focusing on individual-level solutions has led behavioral public policy astray. *Behavioral and Brain Sciences*, 1–60. https://doi.org/10.1017/S0140525X22002023

Chetty, R., Looney, A., & Kroft, K. (2009). Salience and taxation: Theory and evidence. *American Economic Review*, 99(4), 1145–1177. https://doi.org/10.1257/aer.99.4.1145

Cho, H., & Boster, F. J. (2008). Effects of gain versus loss frame antidrug ads on adolescents. *Journal of Communication*, 58(3), 428–446. https://doi.org/10.1111/j.1460-2466.2008.00393.x

Choi, J. J., Laibson, D., & Madrian, B. C. (2011). $100 bills on the sidewalk: Suboptimal investment in 401(k) plans. *The Review of Economics and Statistics*, 93(3), 748–763. https://doi.org/10.1162/REST_a_00100

Constantino, S. M., Sparkman, G., Kraft-Todd, G. T., Bicchieri, C., Centola, D., Shell-Duncan, B., Vogt, S., & Weber, E. U. (2022). Scaling up change: A critical review and practical guide to harnessing social norms for climate action. *Psychological Science in the Public Interest*, 23(2), 50–97. https://doi.org/10.1177/15291006221105279

Croskerry, P., Singhal, G., & Mamede, S. (2013). Cognitive debiasing 2: Impediments to and strategies for change. *British Medical Journal Quality & Safety*, 22(Suppl 2), ii65–ii72. http://dx.doi.org/10.1136/bmjqs-2012-001713

Cucciniello, M., Pin, P., Imre, B., Porumbescu, G. A., & Melegaro, A. (2022). Altruism and vaccination intentions: Evidence from behavioral experiments. *Social Science & Medicine*, 292, 114195. https://doi.org/10.1016/j.socscimed.2021.114195

Dai, H., Milkman, K. L., & Riis, J. (2014). The fresh start effect: Temporal landmarks motivate aspirational behavior. *Management Science, 60*(10), 2563–2582. https://doi.org/10.1287/mnsc.2014.1901

———. (2015). Put your imperfections behind you: Temporal landmarks spur goal initiation when they signal new beginnings. *Psychological Science, 26*(12), 1927–1936. https://doi.org/10.1177/0956797615605818

Daminger, A., Hayes, J., Barrows, A., & Wright, J. (2015). Poverty interrupted: Applying behavioral science to the context of chronic scarcity. *Ideas, 42*, 1–49. http://www.ideas42.org/wp-content/uploads/2015/05/I42_PovertyWhitePaper_Digital_FINAL-1.pdf

Datta, S., & Mullainathan, S. (2014). Behavioral design: A new approach to development policy. *Review of Income and Wealth, 60*(1), 7–35. https://doi.org/10.1111/roiw.12093

de Ridder, D. T., van den Boom, L. A., Kroese, F. M., Moors, E. H., & van den Broek, K. L. (2022). How do people understand the spread of COVID-19 infections? Mapping mental models of factors contributing to the pandemic. *Psychology & Health*. https://doi.org/10.1080/08870446.2022.2129054

Delavande, A. (2023). Expectations in development economics. *Handbook of economic expectations*, 261–291. Academic Press. https://doi.org/10.1016/B978-0-12-822927-9.00016-1

Dolin, D. J., & Booth-Butterfield, S. (1995). Foot-in-the-door and cancer prevention. *Health Communication, 7*(1), 55–66. https://doi.org/10.1207/s15327027hc0701_4

Duflo, E. (2017). The economist as plumber. *American Economic Review, 107*(5), 1–26.

Fishbane, A., Ouss, A., & Shah, A. K. (2020). Behavioral nudges reduce failure to appear for court. *Science, 370*(6517), eabb6591. https://doi.org/10.1126/science.abb6591

Fuster, A., & Zafar, B. (2023). Survey experiments on economic expectations. *Handbook of economic expectations*, 107–130. Academic Press. https://doi.org/10.1016/B978-0-12-822927-9.00010-0

Gary, M. S., & Wood, R. E. (2011). Mental models, decision rules, and performance heterogeneity. *Strategic Management Journal, 32*(6), 569–594. https://doi.org/10.1002/smj.899

Gerber, A. S., Green, D. P., & Larimer, C. W. (2008). Social pressure and voter turnout: Evidence from a large-scale field experiment. *American Political Science Review, 102*(1), 33–48. https://doi.org/10.1017/S000305540808009X

Gerber, A. S., & Rogers, T. (2009). Descriptive social norms and motivation to vote: Everybody's voting and so should you. *The Journal of Politics, 71*(1), 178–191. https://doi.org/10.1016/j.jdeveco.2022.102995

Gofen, A., Moseley, A., Thomann, E., & Kent Weaver, R. (2021). Behavioural governance in the policy process: Introduction to the special issue. *Journal of European Public Policy, 28*(5), 633–657. https://doi.org/10.1080/13501763.2021.1912153

Gourville, J. T., & Soman, D. (2005). Overchoice and assortment type: When and why variety backfires. *Marketing Science, 24*(3), 382–395. https://doi.org/10.1287/mksc.1040.0109

Greenhalgh, T. (2021). Miasmas, mental models and preventive public health: Some philosophical reflections on science in the COVID-19 pandemic. *Interface Focus, 11*(6), 20210017. https://doi.org/10.1098/rsfs.2021.0017

Grimmelikhuijsen, S., Jilke, S., Olsen, A. L., & Tummers, L. (2017). Behavioral public administration: Combining insights from public administration and psychology. *Public Administration Review, 77*(1), 45–56. https://doi.org/10.1111/puar.12609

Guiette, A., & Vandenbempt, K. (2013). Exploring team mental model dynamics during strategic change implementation in professional service organizations. A sensemaking perspective. *European Management Journal, 31*(6), 728–744. https://doi.org/10.1016/j.emj.2013.07.002

Haaland, I., Roth, C., & Wohlfart, J. (2023). Designing information provision experiments. *Journal of Economic Literature, 61*(1), 3–40. https://doi.org/10.1257/jel.20211658

Haff, N., Patel, M. S., Lim, R., Zhu, J., Troxel, A. B., Asch, D. A., & Volpp, K. G. (2015). The role of behavioral economic incentive design and demographic characteristics in financial incentive-based approaches to changing health behaviors: A meta-analysis. *American Journal of Health Promotion, 29*(5), 314–323. https://doi.org/10.4278/ajhp.140714-LIT-333

Hallsworth, M., Chadborn, T., Sallis, A., Sanders, M., Berry, D., Greaves, F., Clements, L., & Davies, S. C. (2016). Provision of social norm feedback to high prescribers of antibiotics in general practice: A pragmatic national randomised controlled trial. *The Lancet, 387*(10029), 1743–1752. https://doi.org/10.1016/S0140-6736(16)00215-4

Halpern, S. D., Kohn, R., Dornbrand-Lo, A., Metkus, T., Asch, D. A., & Volpp, K. G. (2011). Lottery-based versus fixed incentives to increase clinicians' response to surveys. *Health Services Research, 46*(5), 1663–1674. https://doi.org/10.1111/j.1475-6773.2011.01264.x

Hershey, J. C., Asch, D. A., Thumasathit, T., Meszaros, J., & Waters, V. V. (1994). The roles of altruism, free riding, and bandwagoning in vaccination decisions. *Organizational Behavior and Human Decision Processes, 59*(2), 177–187. https://doi.org/10.1006/obhd.1994.1055

Hovmand, P. S., Pronk, N. P., Kyle, T. K., Nadglowski, J., Nece, P. M., & Lynx, C. T. (2021). Obesity, biased mental models, and stigma in the context of the obesity COVID-19 syndemic. *NAM Perspectives.* https://doi.org/10.31478%2F202104a

Johnson, E. J. (2021). *The elements of choice: Why the way we decide matters.* Penguin.

Johnson, E. J., & Goldstein, D. (2003). Do defaults save lives? *Science, 302*(5649), 1338–1339. https://doi.org/10.1126/science.1091721

Johnson-Laird, P. N. (2004). The history of mental models. *Psychology of reasoning*, 189–222. Psychology Press.

Karlan, D., McConnell, M., Mullainathan, S., & Zinman, J. (2016). Getting to the top of mind: How reminders increase saving. *Management Science, 62*(12), 3393–3411. https://doi.org/10.1287/mnsc.2015.2296

Kealey, E., & Berkman, C. S. (2010). The relationship between health information sources and mental models of cancer: Findings from the 2005 Health Information National Trends Survey. *Journal of Health Communication, 15*(Suppl 3), 236–251. https://doi.org/10.1080/10810730.2010.522693

Keller, P. A., Lipkus, I. M., & Rimer, B. K. (2003). Affect, framing, and persuasion. *Journal of Marketing Research, 40*(1), 54–64. https://doi.org/10.1509/jmkr.40.1.54.19133

Kling, J. R., Mullainathan, S., Shafir, E., Vermeulen, L. C., & Wrobel, M. V. (2012). Comparison friction: Experimental evidence from Medicare drug plans. *The Quarterly Journal of Economics, 127*(1), 199–235. https://doi.org/10.1093/qje/qjr055

Larrick, R. P. (2004). Debiasing. *Blackwell handbook of judgment and decision making*, 316–337. Blackwell Publishing.

Larrick, R. P., & Soll, J. B. (2008). The MPG illusion. *Science, 320*(5883), 1593–1594. https://doi.org/10.1126/science.1154983

Loewenstein, G., & Chater, N. (2017). Putting nudges in perspective. *Behavioural Public Policy, 1*(1), 26–53. https://doi.org/10.1017/bpp.2016.7

Ludolph, R., & Schulz, P. J. (2018). Debiasing health-related judgments and decision making: A systematic review. *Medical Decision Making, 38*(1), 3–13. https://doi.org/10.1177/0272989X17716672

Luong, M. L. N., Hall, M., Bennell, K. L., Kasza, J., Harris, A., & Hinman, R. S. (2021). The impact of financial incentives on physical activity: A systematic review and meta-analysis. *American Journal of Health Promotion, 35*(2), 236–249. https://doi.org/10.1177/0890117120940133

Madrian, B. C., & Shea, D. F. (2001). The power of suggestion: Inertia in 401(k) participation and savings behavior. *The Quarterly Journal of Economics, 116*(4), 1149–1187. https://doi.org/10.1162/003355301753265543

Mantzari, E., Vogt, F., Shemilt, I., Wei, Y., Higgins, J. P., & Marteau, T. M. (2015). Personal financial incentives for changing habitual health-related behaviors: A systematic review and meta-analysis. *Preventive Medicine, 75*, 75–85. https://doi.org/10.1016/j.ypmed.2015.03.001

Mazar, N., Mochon, D., & Ariely, D. (2018). If you are going to pay within the next 24 hours, press 1: Automatic planning prompt reduces credit card delinquency. *Journal of Consumer Psychology, 28*(3), 466–476. https://doi.org/10.1002/jcpy.1031

McFadden, D. (2009). The human side of mechanism design: A tribute to Leo Hurwicz and Jean-Jacque Laffont. *Review of Economic Design, 13*(1), 77–100.

Meeker, D., Linder, J. A., Fox, C. R., Friedberg, M. W., Persell, S. D., Goldstein, N. J., Knight, T. K., Hay, J. W., & Doctor, J. N. (2016). Effect of behavioral interventions on inappropriate antibiotic prescribing among primary care practices: A randomized clinical trial. *Journal of the American Medical Association, 315*(6), 562–570. https://doi.org/10.1001/jama.2016.0275

Meiselman, B. S., Weigel, C., Ferraro, P. J., Masters, M., Messer, K. D., Savchenko, O. M., & Suter, J. F. (2022). Lottery incentives and resource management: Evidence from the Agricultural Data Reporting Incentive Program (AgDRIP). *Environmental and Resource Economics, 82*(4), 847–867. https://doi.org/10.1007/s10640-022-00690-1

Michie, S., Van Stralen, M. M., & West, R. (2011). The behaviour change wheel: A new method for characterising and designing behaviour change interventions. *Implementation Science, 6*(1), 1–12. https://doi.org/10.1186/1748-5908-6-42

Milkman, K. L., Beshears, J., Choi, J. J., Laibson, D., & Madrian, B. C. (2011). Using implementation intentions prompts to enhance influenza vaccination rates. *Proceedings of the National Academy of Sciences, 108*(26), 10415–10420. https://doi.org/10.1073/pnas.1103170108

———. (2013). Planning prompts as a means of increasing preventive screening rates. *Preventive Medicine, 56*(1), 92. https://doi.org/10.1016/j.ypmed.2012.10.021

Milkman, K. L., Minson, J. A., & Volpp, K. G. (2014). Holding the hunger games hostage at the gym: An evaluation of temptation bundling. *Management Science, 60*(2), 283–299. https://doi.org/10.1287/mnsc.2013.1784

Montoy, J. C. C., Dow, W. H., & Kaplan, B. C. (2016). Patient choice in opt-in, active choice, and opt-out HIV screening: Randomized clinical trial. *British Medical Journal, 352*. https://doi.org/10.1136/bmj.h6895

Mullainathan, S., & Shafir, E. (2013). *Scarcity: Why having too little means so much*. Picador.

Münscher, R., Vetter, M., & Scheuerle, T. (2016). A review and taxonomy of choice architecture techniques. *Journal of Behavioral Decision Making, 29*(5), 511–524. https://doi.org/10.1002/bdm.1897

National Academies of Sciences, Engineering, and Medicine. (2022). *Ontologies in the behavioral sciences: Accelerating research and the spread of knowledge*. The National Academies Press.

Neal, D., Vujcic, J., Burns, R., Wood, W., & Devine, J. (2016). *Nudging and habit change for open defecation: New tactics from behavioral science*. World Bank Group. https://documents.worldbank.org/curated/en/905011467990970572/pdf/104328-WP-PUBLIC-OD-Habit-and-Nudging-Catalyst-Behavioral-Sciences-022916.pdf

Neff, R., & Fry, J. (2009). Periodic prompts and reminders in health promotion and health behavior interventions: Systematic review. *Journal of Medical Internet Research, 11*(2), e1138. https://doi.org/10.2196/jmir.1138

Nickerson, D. W., & Rogers, T. (2010). Do you have a voting plan? Implementation intentions, voter turnout, and organic plan making. *Psychological Science, 21*(2), 194–199. https://doi.org/10.1177/0956797609359326

Niedderer, K., Clune, S., & Ludden, G. (Eds.). (2017). *Design for behaviour change: Theories and practices of designing for change*. Routledge.

Osbaldiston, R., & Schott, J. P. (2012). Environmental sustainability and behavioral science: Meta-analysis of proenvironmental behavior experiments. *Environment and Behavior*, 44(2), 257–299. https://doi.org/10.1177/0013916511402673

Patel, M. S., Asch, D. A., Troxel, A. B., Fletcher, M., Osman-Koss, R., Brady, J., Wesby, L., Hilbert, V., Zhu, J., Wang, W., & Volpp, K. G. (2016a). Premium-based financial incentives did not promote workplace weight loss in a 2013–15 Study. *Health Affairs*, 35(1), 71–79. https://doi.org/10.1377/hlthaff.2015.0945

Patel, M. S., Day, S. C., Halpern, S. D., Hanson, C. W., Martinez, J. R., Honeywell, S., & Volpp, K. G. (2016b). Generic medication prescription rates after health system–wide redesign of default options within the electronic health record. *Journal of the American Medical Association Internal Medicine*, 176(6), 847–848. https://doi.org/10.1001/jamainternmed.2016.1688

Pathak, P. A. (2017). What really matters in designing school choice mechanisms. *Advances in Economics and Econometrics*, 1, 176–214.

Perkins, H. W. (2002). Social norms and the prevention of alcohol misuse in collegiate contexts. *Journal of Studies on Alcohol*, (Suppl 14), 164–172. https://doi.org/10.15288/jsas.2002.s14.164

Pfeffer, J. (2005). Changing mental models: HR's most important task. *Human Resource Management*, 44(2), 123–128. https://doi.org/10.1002/hrm.20053

Reutskaja, E., Iyengar, S., Fasolo, B., & Misuraca, R. (2020). *Cognitive and affective consequences of information and choice overload*. Routledge.

Reutskaja, E., Cheek, N. N., Iyengar, S., & Schwartz, B. (2022). Choice deprivation, choice overload, and satisfaction with choices across six nations. *Journal of International Marketing*, 30(3), 18–34. https://doi.org/10.1177/1069031X211073821

Rieger, M. O. (2020). Triggering altruism increases the willingness to get vaccinated against COVID-19. *Social Health and Behavior*, 3(3), 78. https://doi.org/10.4103/SHB.SHB_39_20

Robitaille, N., House, J., & Mazar, N. (2021). Effectiveness of planning prompts on organizations' likelihood to file their overdue taxes: A multi-wave field experiment. *Management Science*, 67(7), 4327–4340. https://doi.org/10.1287/mnsc.2020.3744

Robitaille, N., Mazar, N., Tsai, C. I., Aviv, A. M., & Hardy, E. (2021). Increasing organ donor registrations with behavioral interventions: A field experiment. *Journal of Marketing*, 85(3). https://doi.org/10.1177/0022242921990070

Rogers, T., Milkman, K. L., John, L. K., & Norton, M. I. (2015). Beyond good intentions: Prompting people to make plans improves follow-through on important tasks. *Behavioral Science & Policy*, 1(2), 33–41. https://doi.org/10.1353/bsp.2015.0011

Roth, A. E. (2015). *Who gets what—And why: The new economics of matchmaking and market design*. Houghton Mifflin Harcourt.

Roth, A. E., & Sotomayor, M. (1992). Two-sided matching. *Handbook of game theory with economic applications*, 1, 485–541. North-Holland.

Rothman, A. J., Bartels, R. D., Wlaschin, J., & Salovey, P. (2006). The strategic use of gain-and loss-framed messages to promote healthy behavior: How theory can inform practice. *Journal of Communication*, 56(Suppl 1), S202–S220. https://doi.org/10.1111/j.1460-2466.2006.00290.x

Sallis, A., Harper, H., & Sanders, M. (2018). Effect of persuasive messages on National Health Service Organ Donor Registrations: A pragmatic quasi-randomised controlled trial with one million UK road taxpayers. *Trials*, 19, 1–10. https://doi.org/10.1186/s13063-018-2855-5

Schwartz, J., Mochon, D., Wyper, L., Maroba, J., Patel, D., & Ariely, D. (2014). Healthier by precommitment. *Psychological Science*, 25(2), 538–546. https://doi.org/10.1177/0956797613510950

Silva, M. A. V. D., Sao-Joao, T. M., Brizon, V. C., Franco, D. H., & Mialhe, F. L. (2018). Impact of implementation intentions on physical activity practice in adults: A systematic review and meta-analysis of randomized clinical trials. *PLoS One, 13*(11), e0206294. https://doi.org/10.1371/journal.pone.0206294

Soll, J. B., Milkman, K. L., & Payne, J. W. (2015). A user's guide to debiasing. *The Wiley Blackwell handbook of judgment and decision making, 2*, 924–951. Blackwell. https://doi.org/10.1002/9781118468333.ch33

Southwell, B. G., Kelly, B. J., Bann, C. M., Squiers, L. B., Ray, S. E., & McCormack, L. A. (2020). Mental models of infectious diseases and public understanding of COVID-19 prevention. *Health Communication, 35*(14), 1707–1710. https://doi.org/10.1080/10410236.2020.1837462

Thacker, I., & Sinatra, G. M. (2019). Visualizing the greenhouse effect: Restructuring mental models of climate change through a guided online simulation. *Education Sciences, 9*(1), 14. https://doi.org/10.3390/educsci9010014

Thaler, R. H., & Sunstein, C. R. (2009). *Nudge: Improving decisions about health, wealth, and happiness.* Penguin.

Thirumurthy, H., Asch, D. A., & Volpp, K. G. (2019). The uncertain effect of financial incentives to improve health behaviors. *Journal of the American Medical Association, 321*(15), 1451–1452. https://doi.org/10.1001/jama.2019.2560

Varotto, A., & Spagnolli, A. (2017). Psychological strategies to promote household recycling. A systematic review with meta-analysis of validated field interventions. *Journal of Environmental Psychology, 51*, 168–188. https://doi.org/10.1016/j.jenvp.2017.03.011

Vasan, A., Kenyon, C. C., Feudtner, C., Fiks, A. G., & Venkataramani, A. S. (2021). Association of WIC participation and electronic benefits transfer implementation. *Journal of the American Medical Association Pediatrics, 175*(6), 609–616. https://doi.org/10.1001/jamapediatrics.2020.6973

Vecchio, R., & Cavallo, C. (2019). Increasing healthy food choices through nudges: A systematic review. *Food Quality and Preference, 78*, 103714. https://doi.org/10.1016/j.foodqual.2019.05.014

Venema, T. A., Kroese, F. M., Verplanken, B., & de Ridder, D. T. (2020). The (bitter) sweet taste of nudge effectiveness: The role of habits in a portion size nudge, a proof of concept study. *Appetite, 151*, 104699. https://doi.org/10.1016/j.appet.2020.104699

Vink, J., Edvardsson, B., Wetter-Edman, K., & Tronvoll, B. (2019). Reshaping mental models—Enabling innovation through service design. *Journal of Service Management, 30*(1), 75–104. https://doi.org/10.1108/JOSM-08-2017-0186

Volpp, K. G., John, L. K., Troxel, A. B., Norton, L., Fassbender, J., & Loewenstein, G. (2008). Financial incentive–based approaches for weight loss: A randomized trial. *Journal of the American Medical Association, 300*(22), 2631–2637. https://doi.org/10.1001/jama.2008.804

Volpp, K. G., Troxel, A. B., Pauly, M. V., Glick, H. A., Puig, A., Asch, D. A., Galvin, R., Zhu, J., Wan, F., DeGuzman, J., & Corbett, E. (2009). A randomized, controlled trial of financial incentives for smoking cessation. *New England Journal of Medicine, 360*, 699–709. https://doi.org/10.1056/NEJMsa0806819

Wong-Parodi, G., & Bruine de Bruin, W. (2017). Informing public perceptions about climate change: A "mental models" approach. *Science and Engineering Ethics, 23*(5), 1369–1386. https://doi.org/10.1007/s11948-016-9816-8

Wood, W., & Neal, D. T. (2016). Healthy through habit: Interventions for initiating & maintaining health behavior change. *Behavioral Science and Policy, 2*(1), 71–83. https://doi.org/10.1353/bsp.2016.0008

Ybarra, M. L., Holtrop, J. S., Prescott, T. L., & Strong, D. (2014). Process evaluation of a mHealth program: Lessons learned from Stop My Smoking USA, a text messaging-based smoking cessation program for young adults. *Patient Education and Counseling*, 97(2), 239–243. https://doi.org/10.1016/j.pec.2014.07.009

Yeomans, M., & Reich, J. (2017). Planning prompts increase and forecast course completion in massive open online courses. *Proceedings of the Seventh International Learning Analytics & Knowledge Conference*, 464–473. Association for Computing Machinery. https://doi.org/10.1145/3027385.3027416

Zeelenberg, M., & Pieters, R. (2004). Consequences of regret aversion in real life: The case of the Dutch postcode lottery. *Organizational Behavior and Human Decision Processes*, 93(2), 155–168. https://doi.org/10.1016/j.obhdp.2003.10.001

Part II

Evidence from Selected Policy Domains

5

Health

For decades, policy makers have sought to influence health-related behaviors that contribute substantially to both morbidity and early mortality. Significant successes in influencing health behaviors—such as the multifaceted public health campaign that yielded a 58 percent decline in smoking in the United States between 1964 and the early 2000s—have fueled research attention to influences on health behaviors (Institute of Medicine [IOM], 2007). It is not only the choices that individuals make about their own health that are important to public health goals: understanding of the behavior and decision making of health care providers can help in the design of interventions to reduce medical errors, promote the implementation of evidence-based medicine, and influence outcomes for patients in other ways.

Health researchers have been designing and testing interventions grounded in core behavioral economics principles to encourage positive outcomes for individuals and patients and support provider decision making for more than 20 years. A wide range of behavioral ideas have been tested in varied settings. The committee explored the research in three domains that highlight both landmark work and knowledge gaps that point to research priorities for the future: behaviors that can have substantial effects on cardiovascular health, healthy individuals' engagement with preventive care, and clinicians' behaviors.

CARDIOVASCULAR DISEASE RISK

Cardiovascular disease is the leading cause of morbidity and mortality in much of the world, and a great number of intervention studies have explored ways to lower risk for this disease. Three behaviors—smoking, physical activity, and adherence to medication regimes—have a demonstrated impact on cardiovascular disease and are potentially amenable to interventions grounded in behavioral economics, such as behaviorally informed incentives and use of structured defaults.

Smoking Cessation

It is well known that smoking significantly increases the risk of cardiovascular conditions, including atherosclerosis, coronary heart disease, stroke, peripheral arterial disease, and abdominal aneurysm (Centers for Disease Control and Prevention, n.d.). Smoking is extremely habit forming, and there are numerous strategies people can use to try to break the habit. Policy approaches have included increasing the price of cigarettes by imposing taxes (a traditional economic intervention) or not allowing smoking in public buildings. Strategies that rely on individual behavior have primarily focused on the design, timing, and form of incentives to stop smoking.

Financial incentives to change behavior may be thought of as addressing present bias (see Chapter 3), as well as related internalities. (Economists define internalities as the costs people impose on their future selves, while externalities are the costs imposed on others, such as the effects on others of second-hand smoke.) A 2019 meta-analysis reviewed the long-term effectiveness of financial incentives on smoking cessation, identifying 33 mixed-population, randomized controlled trials (Notley et al., 2019). The studies that met the criteria for inclusion used incentives that ranged significantly in value, from programs in which people deposited their own money in accounts and would lose the funds if they did not meet their self-imposed goals, to rewards worth more than $1,000. Looking across the studies, the authors found strong evidence that even modest incentives could improve rates of smoking cessation and that those rates were sustained after the withdrawal of the incentive.

Notable studies covered in the meta-analysis included a large clinical trial showing that programs in which participants were required to put down a financial deposit in order to ultimately receive a reward were less appealing to participants than ones where they could receive an incentive without having to make an up-front deposit. Overall, the authors of the meta-analysis found that incentives for smoking cessation are effective, with several large-scale studies showing roughly a tripling in long-term smoking cessation rates. However, there are still important questions about optimal design and about whether carrots (reward-based incentives) or sticks (loss-framed incentives) are more effective. When individuals were given the option of participating in an incentive program in which they could put their own money at risk, which would be matched roughly four to one but could be lost, it was highly efficacious for those who choose to participate. However, participation rates were only about 14 percent; thus, a standard gain-based incentive may be on balance more effective (Halpern et al., 2015). Loss framing of incentives tied to smoking cessation in the form of higher premiums for smokers may be more palatable and thereby more widely used in employer and other settings (Volpp & Galvin, 2014). This work overall is a good illustration of how behaviorally informed incentives are distinct from traditional economic incentives.

Medication Adherence

Numerous studies have shown that adherence to medications prescribed by a physician is well below 100 percent. For example, in the year following a heart attack, adherence to the recommended cardiovascular medications has been estimated at 39–45 percent (Choudhry et al., 2011). A wide variety of explanations have been suggested: forgetfulness, inattention, emotions, misinformation about the benefits and risks of the medication, side effects or fear of side effects, and present-biased preferences that result in decisions that are not consistent with what might be in a patient's longer-term self-interest (Volpp & Pauly, 2022).

One approach to improving medication adherence is to change some of the underlying defaults to make it easier for patients to follow their physician's instructions. For example, reducing the frequency with which refills are needed through 90-day prescriptions rather than 30-day prescriptions appears to significantly improve adherence (Rymer et al., 2021). Refilling prescriptions is a complex organizational task for patients taking multiple medications, so synchronized refills in which all medications are on the same refill schedule can also be helpful (Doshi et al., 2016).

Automatic refill programs also increase the ease of obtaining refills. Although entry into such programs can be set up as a default choice, credit card charges are involved, so this approach requires approval from participants before joining, unlike some other default arrangements (see Chapter 10). In one study, however, using an active choice approach in which patients were given the option of signing up every time they refilled a prescription, but in which the convenience of automatic refills was highlighted, roughly doubled the rate of sign-ups (Keller et al., 2011). Increasing social accountability may also be effective in improving adherence. For example, one study showed an increase of 33 percentage points in adherence for posttransplant patients who were told that their adherence would be reported to their transplant physician, although blood samples measuring immunosuppressant levels suggested that some of the measured difference was spurious (Reese et al., 2017).

A significant body of research has shown that requirements in health plans for out-of-pocket payments can discourage utilization of health care services (e.g., Manning et al., 1987). Unfortunately, patients are not always able to differentiate between lower-value and higher-value care, and patient cost-sharing may have detrimental effects in the context of medications and services that are of high value and low cost, such as those used to manage blood pressure or elevated cholesterol. Value-based insurance design, in which patient cost-sharing for high-value services varies on the basis of the particular health care service, was inspired by research that showed the use of higher copayments significantly reduced the use of medications: this approach resulted in saving money on pharmaceuticals without reducing overall health care costs while raising mortality because lower rates of medication adherence led to higher rates of emergency department visits and adverse outcomes (Hsu et al., 2006).

However, lowering copayments has had only modest effects on medication adherence, typically increasing it by 3 to 6 percentage points (Tang, Ghali, & Manns, 2014; Volpp & Pauly, 2022). Even among patients who had recent heart attacks and were given their cardiovascular medications for free, average adherence was only 45 percent, only about six percentage points higher than that seen with regular copayments (Choudhry et al., 2011). A recent clinical trial showed that providing patients who had experienced acute myocardial infarction with financial vouchers that reduced their out-of-pocket costs to zero increased adherence by 2.3 percent but had no effect on the rate of adverse cardiovascular event outcomes one year later (Wang et al., 2019). One reason for these disappointing results is the "dog that didn't bark" problem (Loewenstein, Asch, & Volpp, 2013). People who are nonadherent do not notice that their copays have been reduced because they are not using (and thus are not paying for) the service. In addition, the small effects of reducing copayments reflect that framing matters and that losses (in the form of higher copayments) generally have greater effects than gains (lowered copayments) do (Volpp & Pauly, 2022).

Other sorts of financial incentives regarding medication adherence have been studied. A review of 15 randomized and six nonrandomized studies showed that behaviorally informed financial incentive interventions (in this case, ones that have been framed to address behavioral reasons people fail to adhere) significantly improved medication adherence. This review also found that larger effects were seen in interventions that offered larger incentives, provided at least weekly reinforcement, and were longer in duration (Petry et al., 2012). Researchers hoping to build on these findings by providing more frequent feedback have tested a daily lottery-based reward for adherence. This work is based on the notion that lotteries might have outsize effectiveness in two ways: by leveraging insights from prospect theory that people overestimate very low probabilities, and by incorporating anticipated regret in the design of the systems (participants are both told whether they won or whether they would have won had they been adherent; e.g., Kimmel et al., 2012; Barankay et al., 2020; Volpp & Pauly, 2022). While some results have been promising, there have been a number of published studies with negative results (and likely many more unpublished ones; see Chapter 12). Researchers have noted the importance of confirming positive results with testing of expected physiological effects of medication adherence (such as reductions in low-density lipoprotein cholesterol), of focusing these efforts on patients who are demonstrably nonadherent at baseline, and of tying these approaches into other evidence-based approaches.

While various intervention strategies have shown promise, there is no single strategy that has been shown to "solve" medication nonadherence at scale (Zullig et al., 2018).[1] The fact that earlier work showing the effectiveness of incentives in improving outcomes has not been confirmed in more recent studies—even when the incentives offered were worth up to $1,024 per year—highlights several points. First, rigorous randomized testing is critical, and it is necessary to measure both adherence and related medical outcomes. Second, interventions involving patients who are discharged from hospitals highlight the importance of enrolling patients in interventions right at the time of discharge, when they are likely to be most vulnerable. Structural approaches that address barriers to adherence (such as forgetfulness, inattention, inaccurate or incomplete information, and logistical challenges with obtaining refills) appear to be the most valuable. These approaches include synchronizing refills and providing 90-day prescriptions and automatic refills. Removing financial barriers is useful but not a panacea and might best be coupled with low-cost approaches to using technology to increase social accountability. All of these are promising areas for future research.

Physical Activity

The many health benefits of physical activity include reductions in risk for cardiovascular disease and related mortality rates—a relationship that has been well established in the literature (Nystoriak & Bhatnagar, 2018). Researchers have explored the effectiveness of behavioral economic strategies at increasing physical activity in a number of contexts. Studies have suggested that sustained behavior change is achievable through a variety of behavioral mechanisms, including classic habit formation, learning by doing, information acquisition, addressing status quo bias, discovery of new

---

[1] That is, no approach has achieved effects in large populations, in contrast with laboratory settings or other controlled experimental circumstances.

tastes, changes in norms or network effects, and changes in choice environments (Volpp & Loewenstein, 2020). However, the most studied approach has been the use of behaviorally informed financial incentives.

A frequently cited study examined the use of behaviorally informed incentives provided to college students to go to the gym frequently for 1 month and then compared the effect on the longer-term behavior of students who received the incentives and those who did not. Those who received the incentives for multiple visits attended roughly 25 percent more often than those who did not receive the incentives, both during the intervention and after it was over. As in other contexts, there is evidence that incentives provided relatively immediately following a desired action are more effective than incentives provided after a time delay. In addition, incentives delivered using loss framing are more effective than those using gain framing (Finkelstein et al., 2016; Patel et al., 2016; Adams et al., 2017; Chokshi et al., 2018).

Studies focused on lottery incentives suggest that an approach that combines significant odds of winning a small award with low odds of winning a large award are more effective than either alone and that incentives based on a combination of group and individual performance are more effective than incentives offered on the basis of only individual or group performance (Patel et al., 2016, 2018).[2] This body of work highlights that while the magnitude of incentives is important, behaviorally informed design often plays a big role in determining effectiveness.

Another approach that has been studied is gamification, which has been used to encourage physical activity through the application of such behavioral principles as variable reinforcement, loss aversion, the endowment effect, social accountability, and anticipated regret, using contests, progress charts, scoring, and other game-like activities. Examples include an intervention with families to encourage them to meet daily step goals using a system of points and levels, in which individuals start with a moderate level of status that they can lose if they do not meet sufficient daily goals (team members are chosen to represent their team daily at random) and in which there is a built-in social accountability mechanism through the ongoing notification of other team members (Patel et al., 2019). Another promising approach encourages people to commit to a target activity, applying the concept of temptation bundling (or combining *wants* with *shoulds*), such as by encouraging people to listen to tempting audio novels while exercising, using iPods available only at the gym (Milkman, Minson, & Volpp, 2014).

---

[2]Evidence for the effectiveness of lotteries is mixed. For example, recent efforts to use them to increase rates of COVID-19 vaccination did not show effectiveness or were mixed (Acharya & Dhakal, 2021; Law et al., 2022).

Taken together, these studies suggest that many approaches hold promise, but they have not yet shown the optimal incentive design for time-limited interventions that will result in sustained behavior change. Three important questions to be considered are what later effects can be expected after the intervention is terminated; whether it is cost-effective for the intervention to be continued indefinitely; and, if so, whether its effectiveness wanes over time.

PROMOTING PREVENTIVE CARE

Behavioral economics findings have been applied in interventions to encourage people to engage in a wide variety of other preventive activities to promote health. We identified three examples with a substantial evidence base: colorectal cancer screening, HIV prevention and treatment, and vaccination. The findings from this work can yield helpful insights about the effects of behavioral economics approaches on health behavior change.

Colorectal Cancer Screening

Cancer is a high-burden condition worldwide. A key approach to secondary prevention is screening, particularly for cancers for which a cost-effective and acceptable screening method exists and for which early detection makes a difference for treatment options and prognosis. Evidence-based screening programs for colorectal and other cancers are in place in many countries and have reduced mortality from these conditions (Smith et al., 2019; Aoki et al., 2020). The general population benefits of screening can only be achieved if individuals comply and complete recommended screening, yet many behavioral barriers prevent patients from seeking screening services or from following up on a clinician's recommendations, referrals, or prescriptions for screening.

Present bias, inaccurate information, and social norms appear to be especially relevant behavioral factors in this context. For example, people may underestimate their risk from cancer because of optimism bias. The screening process itself may be unpleasant, embarrassing, or simply a hassle, and these factors may be perceived as outweighing the possible long-term benefits. Present bias may lead people to overweight those immediate costs and underweight the benefits of screening, which are intangible, probabilistic, and in the future. Finally, people may not be aware of how accepted screening is in their own social network and may be unlikely to get feedback about this from their network.

Interventions have been designed to address such barriers and increase colorectal cancer screening rates. Behaviorally informed approaches to referral and scheduling procedures, incentives, and reminders have been tested in diverse settings and with diverse populations. A recent systematic review of studies testing such interventions found that default or opt-out interventions were the most successful, with incentives studies showing mixed results and salience interventions being the least successful (Taylor et al., 2022). In one low-cost intervention that led to higher rates of response, providers mailed fecal immunochemical test kits to patients if they did not explicitly say "no" (opt out) rather than sending the kits only to those who explicitly requested them. A separate systematic review and meta-analysis of studies found that financial incentives added onto a mail outreach program may also have modest benefit (Facciorusso et al., 2021). Individual studies point to potential benefits from many low-cost interventions, such as including an endorsement from a primary care physician on invitations for screening and addressing women's frequent preference for a same-sex screener by including a picture of a female provider on an appointment scheduling website, thus decreasing the perceived cognitive effort of scheduling.

The research to date points to the promise of low-touch,[3] low-cost behavioral interventions, as well as the challenge of realizing that potential. Replication studies, systematic reviews and meta-analyses, and the preregistration and publication of all relevant studies are needed to confirm effects and inform implementation and scale efforts.

HIV Prevention and Treatment

The global HIV epidemic has been transformed in the last decade by the availability of highly effective antiretroviral treatment and by the widespread dissemination and adoption of primary and secondary prevention approaches, including self-testing, medical male circumcision, and preexposure prophylaxis. Theories and principles from behavioral economics can help explain why those at highest risk for HIV might be reluctant to test, or why adherence to antiretroviral therapy may be challenging (Linnemayr, 2017; Linnemayr, Stecher, & Mukasa, 2017; George, Maughan-Brown, & Thirumurthy, 2021). In a setting with substantial HIV prevalence, HIV prevention requires sustained attention and motivation; if the salience of HIV risk is low, limited attentional resources may be allocated elsewhere. Present bias, relevant for all prevention behaviors, may lead to procrastination or avoidance of short-term hassles or time costs if people underweight the future benefits of prevention. Researchers have also investigated the role that other behavioral constructs may play in HIV prevention and treatment decisions, including risk assessment heuristics, social norms, status quo bias, salience, scarcity, information avoidance, optimism bias, and mental models

---

[3]Low-touch interventions are those that involve comparatively little interaction or interference with the recipient, requiring minimal effort to implement.

(Hutchinson, Mahlalela, & Yukich, 2007; Carey et al., 2011; Dalal et al., 2011; Thirumurthy et al., 2015; Montoy, Dow, & Kaplan, 2018; Pettifor et al., 2020; Buttenheim et al., 2022a). A growing body of evidence has demonstrated the success of interventions that address these decision-making factors using a behavioral lens, including behaviorally informed financial incentives (Thirumurthy et al., 2014; Linnemayr, Stecher, & Mukasa, 2017), promotion of testing and treatment services (Chamie et al., 2018), behaviorally framed HIV risk and treatment effectiveness information (Dupas, 2011; Smith et al., 2021), and interventions that leverage social norms to counter HIV-related stigma (Hutchinson, Mahlalela, & Yukich, 2007; Thornton, 2008).

A meta-analysis of 22 studies of financial incentives to support HIV care goals showed that incentives significantly improved HIV testing take-up, antiretroviral therapy adherence, and continuity of care (Krishnamoorthy, Rehman, & Sakthivel, 2021). A second review, focused on demand-side incentives, showed moderate effects for treatment adherence and substantial effects for voluntary male medical circumcision (Choko et al., 2018). A review of behaviorally informed financial incentives to promote HIV testing found that incentives were effective, whether the incentives included a guaranteed monetary reward; a lottery; or nonmonetary rewards, such as a food voucher (Lee et al., 2014). It is important to note that these systematic reviews did not exclude studies that offered purely financial or transactional incentives: that is, only some of the interventions included in these reviews incorporated behavioral factors into the design and delivery of the incentives. However, several studies of incentives for HIV-related behaviors demonstrated that larger incentives do not always produce larger effect sizes than smaller incentives, supporting an underlying behavioral mechanism (Thornton, 2008; Thirumurthy et al., 2014).

Vaccination

Resistance to vaccines has been a reality since long before federal or other government agencies began routinely requiring programs of regular vaccination for a variety of diseases; that resistance reflects complex social factors (Conis, 2015). In more than 20 years of study, researchers have identified aspects of decisions about vaccination (made either for oneself or on behalf of a child) that can be explained by behavioral concepts (Buttenheim & Asch, 2016; Brewer et al., 2017a).

Vaccination decisions involve time-inconsistent preferences: the benefits are in the future and are both probabilistic and intangible. Yet the costs are immediate, certain, and salient. Vaccination decisions are strongly influenced by social norms and are susceptible to predictable errors or biases in risk assessment. Specifically, for example, researchers have examined omission bias, status quo bias, and availability heuristic as drivers of negative vaccination decisions (Meszaros et al., 1996; Connolly & Reb, 2003; Opel & Omer, 2015; Chen & Stevens, 2017).[4]

Numerous interventions have been studied to encourage people who do not intend to be vaccinated to do so (i.e., to increase motivation or intentions), to address the gap between intention and follow-through, or both. A recent systematic review (Reñosa et al., 2021) found that the most promising behavioral evidence for increasing rates of vaccination (where it is not required) points to three strategies: making information about vaccines more salient (e.g., Milkman et al., 2011; Chen et al., 2020; Szilagyi et al., 2020), offering incentives (e.g., Banerjee et al., 2010; Chetty-Makkan et al., 2022: Schneider et al., 2023), and changing defaults (e.g., Brewer et al., 2017b). Individual studies have also found support for social proof interventions—ways of communicating expert or social group endorsement of vaccination (e.g., Bartoš et al., 2022).

A detailed review of the determinants of vaccine take-up and proposed interventions to address concluded that interventions to establish the intention to get vaccinated—including providing information about benefits, boosting trust in the vaccine itself and in sources of information about it, and combating misinformation—are both necessary and effective (Brody, Saccardo, & Dai, 2022). This finding adds valuable insights to the current state of thinking about behavioral approaches to this persistent health care challenge. For people who already intend to get vaccinated, reminders, prompts that assist with planning, and addressing specific barriers (e.g., simplifying access to vaccination) are most effective.

A second key takeaway from the research to date on vaccine acceptance, which is relevant for many other health topics and diverse policy domains, is that the effectiveness of specific behavioral interventions will vary depending on underlying participant characteristics (including a person's motivation to get vaccinated and beliefs and attitudes about vaccination) and contextual factors (e.g., the geographic location of the intervention or the epidemiologic characteristics of the vaccine-preventable disease). For example, an experiment conducted in eight countries tested a message about the harm that could come to others who might be infected if the population is not thoroughly vaccinated against the flu—in order to tap prosocial motivations (Li et al., 2016). This intervention was more effective among people who had not received a vaccine the previous year than among those

---

[4]Omission bias is the tendency to consider negative outcomes caused by actions as worse than those caused by a failure to act. Status quo bias is the tendency to prefer things as they are over making a change. The availability heuristic is a term for the tendency to rely on information that is readily available in making a decision rather than seeking information that might be more relevant or helpful.

who had, suggesting that this approach was more likely to show results with people who had a lower motivation to be vaccinated in the first place.

One study provides particularly concrete evidence of this phenomenon. In a head-to-head comparison of multiple nudge-type text messaging interventions designed to increase take-up of the flu vaccine (Milkman et al., 2021), the strategy with the largest estimated effect size was a "reserved for you" or ownership message. These results were supported by an even larger-scale study at a retail pharmacy chain, in which the message was changed slightly to refer to the vaccine "waiting for you" (Milkman et al., 2022). Although this ownership strategy notably did not significantly outperform many of the other tested nudges, many local public health agencies applied the "reserved for you" message in COVID-19 vaccine promotion campaigns based on this promising signal, desperate for strategies that could motivate vaccination and bolster demand. Further analyses of the original study (Buttenheim et al., 2022b; Patel et al., 2022), as well as multiple attempts to apply ownership messages in the COVID-19 vaccine context (Dai et al., 2021; Rabb et al., 2022), have demonstrated that the results are more nuanced, succeeding in some settings, for some populations, and at some moments in a vaccination campaign more than in others. This points to the importance of selecting and designing interventions that are carefully tailored to the barriers to take-up identified in a target population, testing the same intervention in diverse settings and contexts, and evaluating mechanisms of action and subgroup responses wherever possible.

PROVIDER BEHAVIOR

It has been well documented in many countries that patients often either receive too little or too much health care relative to what is clinically indicated. For example, more than 20 percent of care provided may actually be unnecessary (IOM, 2013; Carrol, 2017; Lyu et al., 2017). In some cases, clinicians make errors, despite training and treatment protocols. More generally, clinicians clearly respond to traditional economic incentives: they provide more services when they are paid per service than when they are paid through such arrangements as salary or full-risk capitation, which raises concerns about potential conflicts with their patients' best interests (Larkin & Loewenstein, 2017). In addition, there is growing recognition that clinicians, like other people, are affected by behavioral factors when they make decisions. Clinicians often work in busy settings that place multiple demands on their attention and must make frequent, often high-stakes decisions under time pressure. Such conditions mean that factors including the structure of choices and defaults, cognitive biases, and decision fatigue are likely to play a significant role in clinicians' decision making.

A number of behavioral interventions to address these challenges have been explored. A 2020 review of 17 behavioral interventions in the United States found that the interventions most studied were changing default settings (such as encouraging prescribing of generic medications) and using information on relative performance to influence behavior using social norms (prescribing behavior was the most frequently targeted behavior; Wang & Groene, 2020). Both of these interventions were found to be consistently effective at modifying clinicians' behavior to be more consistent with existing guidelines; the effects were often quite large with minimal costs. However, the authors caution that more research is needed to clarify the mechanisms and determine the optimal approaches to support wider implementation.

Checklists can be seen as a way of both creating a social norm and changing defaults. In essence, a requirement to complete a checklist shifts the default from an opt-in (need to remember each order to write when admitting a patient) to an opt-out (the most relevant orders are listed and the clinician can opt out or modify): the opt-out approach makes it much more difficult to forget something. The many documented benefits of checklists in improving quality and safety in health care include nearly eliminating catheter infections that used to kill about 30,000 Americans per year (Pronovost et al., 2006; Gawande, 2010).

Other work has pointed to the potential for active-choice interventions. In such interventions, decisions about specific treatments for specific patients are made more salient. For example, one study examined the effects of identifying for providers the patients for whom statins may be appropriate and asking them to select whether to prescribe or not; it showed an increase in prescribing rates (Patel et al., 2018). This study also showed that providing feedback on prescribing rates relative to their clinical peers contributed to higher prescribing rates. Similar approaches have also been effective in increasing rates of cancer screenings (Patel et al., 2016).

Some social incentive interventions have had large effects, but the results have been highly variable. For example, rates of inappropriate prescribing of antibiotics were brought close to zero when clinicians were asked to provide a justification in a free-text response for treatment decisions or provided with peer comparisons (Meeker et al., 2016). These effects were much larger than those observed in some other efforts to use social norms and social comparisons to motivate behavior change. One possible reason for the large effect is that physicians are highly motivated not to appear below average or to be seen as practicing inappropriately by their peers. In contrast, an example of a smaller effect comes from the use of Opower, a software platform that uses artificial intelligence to apply behavioral principles that was developed to support utilities in helping consumers reduce energy usage by making more energy-efficient choices. In this case, the Opower social comparisons only showed consumers how their own household compares with others and therefore invokes significantly less social accountability than the physician's peer comparisons.

Other studies have shown more mixed results. For example, sending clinicians letters comparing their prescribing rates with those of other local practices had less effect than the study described above (Hallsworth et al., 2016). A recent study by Gauri and colleagues (2021) tested a performance-contingent social recognition intervention to increase performance in the tracking of income and expenditures at primary care clinics in Nigeria. Weekly performance was posted by use of the number of stars on a prominently displayed certificate of excellence, with the best-performing facility promised a public award ceremony with the secretary of health. In one state there were consistent and large effects on performance (roughly 18 percent), but in the other state there was no detectable effect. Differences in observable characteristics between the facilities did not explain the cross-state differences in impacts. In short, it is not clear why some of the interventions that use social incentives to motivate clinician behavior have larger effects than others. That variability may relate to such factors as the timing of interventions, the comparison groups used, the salience of the information provided, the source of information, the fidelity of implementation, or the degree to which comparative information provided new information.

Finally, a number of studies have examined the use of financial incentives, such as bonuses for improved quality, as an enhancement to the existing fee-for-service payment system. These types of incentives are structured as separate incentives or bonuses (rather than simply folded into salaries) to more specifically target behaviors, but the effects have typically been modest. Despite efforts to increase the use of such value-based payment arrangements, standard fee for-service arrangements still account for roughly 70 percent of compensation for both primary and specialist physicians (Reid et al., 2022). Open questions include how to optimally simplify incentive systems that adequately reflect the quality of care but avoid choice overload; how to distribute incentives among individual physicians in practice groups; the magnitude of incentives needed to change different types of behaviors; and how to optimally combine financial and nonfinancial strategies. All of these questions highlight the need for different approaches to be carefully tested and evaluated (Emanuel et al., 2016).

FINDINGS

The committee's review of behaviorally based interventions in the three selected areas of health care demonstrate strong effects for many of them. Looking across the work in the areas we examined, we saw considerable support for the effectiveness of interventions that address the five core principles discussed in Chapter 3. Although it is difficult to generalize across this large volume of work, we note that present bias, limited attention, and social norms were all repeatedly identified as intervention targets. Specific findings from this body of work include the following:

- Structural approaches to lowering barriers to medication adherence (such as forgetfulness, inattention, and inaccurate or incomplete information) appear to be the most promising interventions.
- Behaviorally informed incentives using loss framing show promise for increasing physical activity.
- Default or opt-out interventions were the most successful among interventions tried for increasing rates of colorectal cancer screening.
- Behaviorally informed financial incentives, promotion of testing and treatment services, and provision of information about HIV risk and treatment effectiveness were all promising interventions for increasing HIV prevention and adherence to treatment.
- The most promising behavioral evidence for increasing vaccination has been found for three strategies: making information about vaccines more salient, offering incentives, and changing defaults.
- To modify clinicians' behavior to be more in line with guidelines, the most frequently studied interventions have been changing default settings and providing comparative information on the performance of peers to influence behavior.

Although health is one of the policy domains with the largest evidence base for policy interventions, many important questions and challenges remain. Below we list priorities for follow-up work, but we stress that, while rigorous testing of conceptually based interventions remains critically important to map out the comparative effectiveness of different approaches in improving health or the value of health care delivery, assessment of how to tie together approaches that demonstrate efficacy into effective population health solutions might benefit from collaboration with experts in innovation and implementation science.

Four topics present important opportunities for further research: making behavior changes stick, preventing nudge fatigue, precision nudging, and designing for scaling and planned replication.

Making Behavior Changes Stick

There are hundreds of published studies demonstrating significant positive (and sometimes large) effects of time-limited behaviorally informed interventions. Evidence of sustained and sustainable behavior change is rarer, unfortunately, although there are good examples from the areas of smoking cessation and financial incentives, among others. Evidence-based strategies for changes that are sustained are badly needed and might benefit from drawing on some of the different mechanistic approaches for achieving sustained behavior change, such as classic habit formation, learning by doing, information acquisition, addressing status quo bias, discovery of new tastes, changes in norms or network effects, and changes in choice environments (Volpp & Loewenstein, 2020).

Preventing Nudge Fatigue

In some health care settings, many clinicians may be finding there are too many nudges, which runs the risk of diminishing the incremental effectiveness of each such approach (see, e.g., Ancker et al., 2017; Blecker et al., 2019; Kwan et al., 2020; Chen et al., 2022). There are only so many electronic health record pop-ups, best practice alerts, or peer-comparison dashboards that clinicians can take in during a busy day. Attention is needed to the problem of making such nudges less intrusive and for prioritization of the most effective strategies for use at an organizational level.

Precision Nudging

Interventions informed by behavioral economics rarely work equally well for all. Uncovering heterogeneous treatment effects—especially those that widen rather than close health disparities—is an important but sometimes neglected aspect of intervention trials in health and health care. Machine learning and related approaches to identifying variations in treatment effects can support better targeting and tailoring of interventions for maximum impact. While this identification typically requires large samples for adequately powered subgroup analyses, this approach could make possible the tailoring of interventions to different populations, increasing the amount of benefit for the resources expended.

Designing for Scaling and Planned Replication

Recent popular books, such as *The Voltage Effect: How to Make Good Ideas Great and Great Ideas Scale* by John List, have highlighted that promising ideas often do not scale because the initial demonstration of efficacy may represent a best-case scenario. Replication testing is typically not adequately rewarded in academia, but it is critically important in determining whether a given intervention actually is effective before any decisions are made about further scaling. Careful consideration should be given to the assessment of context and execution, with researchers working together with implementation scientists to design a path for advancing promising ideas that show efficacy to increasingly pragmatic tests of effectiveness in different populations to determine the effectiveness and cost-effectiveness of any given intervention before the decision is made to use it more widely.

REFERENCES

Acharya, B., & Dhakal, C. (2021). Implementation of state vaccine incentive lottery programs and uptake of COVID-19 vaccinations in the United States. *The Journal of the American Medical Association Network Open*, 4(12), e2138238. https://doi.org/10.1001/jamanetworkopen.2021.38238

Adams, M. A., Hurley, J. C., Todd, M., Bhuiyan, N., Jarrett, C. L., Tucker, W. J., Hollingshead, K. E., & Angadi, S. S. (2017). Adaptive goal setting and financial incentives: A 2 × 2 factorial randomized controlled trial to increase adults' physical activity. *BioMed Central Public Health*, 17(1), 1–16. https://doi.org/10.1186/s12889-017-4197-8

Ancker, J. S., Edwards, A., Nosal, S., Hauser, D., Mauer, E., & Kaushal, R. (2017). Effects of workload, work complexity, and repeated alerts on alert fatigue in a clinical decision support system. *BioMed Central Medical Informatics and Decision Making*, 17(1), 1–9. https://doi.org/10.1186/s12911-017-0430-8

Aoki, E. S., Yin, R., Li, K., Bhatla, N., Singhal, S., Ocviyanti, D., Saika, K., Suh, M., Kim, M., & Termrungruanglert, W. (2020). National screening programs for cervical cancer in Asian countries. *Journal of Gynecologic Oncology*, 31(3). https://doi.org/10.3802%2Fjgo.2020.31.e55

Banerjee, A. V., Duflo, E., Glennerster, R., & Kothari, D. (2010). Improving immunisation coverage in rural India: Clustered randomised controlled evaluation of immunisation campaigns with and without incentives. *British Medical Journal*, 340. https://doi.org/10.1136/bmj.c2220

Barankay, I., Reese, P. P., Putt, M. E., Russell, L. B., Loewenstein, G., Pagnotti, D., Yan, J., Zhu, J., McGilloway, R., Brennan, T., & Finnerty, D. (2020). Effect of patient financial incentives on statin adherence and lipid control: A randomized clinical trial. *The Journal of the American Medical Association Network Open*, 3(10), e2019429. https://doi.org/10.1001/jamanetworkopen.2020.19429

Bartoš, V., Bauer, M., Cahlíková, J., & Chytilová, J. (2022). Communicating doctors' consensus persistently increases COVID-19 vaccinations. *Nature*, 606(7914), 542–549. https://doi.org/10.1038/s41586-022-04805-y

Blecker, S., Austrian, J. S., Horwitz, L. I., Kuperman, G., Shelley, D., Ferrauiola, M., & Katz, S. D. (2019). Interrupting providers with clinical decision support to improve care for heart failure. *International Journal of Medical Informatics*, 131, 103956. https://doi.org/10.1016/j.ijmedinf.2019.103956

Brewer, N. T., Chapman, G. B., Rothman, A. J., Leask, J., & Kempe, A. (2017a). Increasing vaccination: Putting psychological science into action. *Psychological Science in the Public Interest*, 18(3), 149–207. https://doi.org/10.1177/1529100618760521

Brewer, N. T., Hall, M. E., Malo, T. L., Gilkey, M. B., Quinn, B., & Lathren, C. (2017b). Announcements versus conversations to improve HPV vaccination coverage: A randomized trial. *Pediatrics*, 139(1). https://doi.org/10.1542/peds.2016-1764

Brody, I., Saccardo, S., & Dai, H. (2022). *One size does not fit all: Behavioral intervention to promote vaccination.* SSRN. https://dx.doi.org/10.2139/ssrn.4139702

Buttenheim, A. M., & Asch, D. A. (2016). Leveraging behavioral insights to promote vaccine acceptance: One year after Disneyland. *The Journal of the American Medical Association Pediatrics*, 170(7), 635–636. https://doi.org/10.1001/jamapediatrics.2016.0192

Buttenheim, A. M., Schmucker, L., Marcus, N., Phatsoane, M., Msolomba, V., Rhagnath, N., Majam, M., Venter, F., & Thirumurthy, H. (2022a). Planning and commitment prompts to encourage reporting of HIV self-test results: A cluster randomized pragmatic trial in Tshwane District, South Africa. *PLOS Global Public Health*, 2(10), e0001196. https://doi.org/10.1371/journal.pgph.0001196

Buttenheim, A., Milkman, K. L., Duckworth, A. L., Gromet, D. M., Patel, M., & Chapman, G. (2022b). Effects of ownership text message wording and reminders on receipt of an influenza vaccination: A randomized clinical trial. *Journal of the American Medical Association Network Open, 5*(2), e2143388. https://doi.org/10.1001/jamanetworkopen.2021.43388

Carey, K. B., Scott-Sheldon, L. A., Carey, M. P., Cain, D., Mlobeli, R., Vermaak, R., Mthembu, J., Simbayi, L. C., & Kalichman, S. C. (2011). Community norms for HIV risk behaviors among men in a South African township. *Journal of Behavioral Medicine, 34*(1), 32–40. https://doi.org/10.1007/s10865-010-9284-6

Carrol, A. E. (2017). The high costs of unnecessary care. *Journal of the American Medical Association, 318*(18), 1748–1749. https://doi.org/10.1001/jama.2017.16193

Centers for Disease Control and Prevention. (n.d.). *Smoking and cardiovascular disease.* https://www.cdc.gov/tobacco/data_statistics/sgr/50th-anniversary/pdfs/fs_smoking_CVD_508.pdf

Chamie, G., Schaffer, E. M., Ndyabakira, A., Emperador, D. M., Kwarisiima, D., Camlin, C. S., Havlir, D. V., Kahn, J. G., Kamya, M. R., & Thirumurthy, H. (2018). Comparative effectiveness of novel non-monetary incentives to promote HIV testing: A randomized trial. *AIDS, 32*(11), 1443. https://doi.org/10.1097%2FQAD.0000000000001833

Chen, F., & Stevens, R. (2017). Applying lessons from behavioral economics to increase flu vaccination rates. *Health Promotion International, 32*(6), 1067–1073. https://doi.org/10.1093/heapro/daw031

Chen, N., Trump, K. S., Hall, S., & Le, Q. (2020). The effect of postcard reminders on vaccinations among the elderly: A block-randomized experiment. *Behavioural Public Policy*, 1–26. https://doi.org/10.1017/bpp.2020.34

Chen, Y., Harris, S., Rogers, Y., Ahmad, T., & Asselbergs, F. W. (2022). Nudging within learning health systems: Next generation decision support to improve cardiovascular care. *European Heart Journal, 43*(13), 1296–1306. https://doi.org/10.1093/eurheartj/ehac030

Chetty-Makkan, C. M., Thirumurthy, H., Bair, E. F., Bokolo, S., Day, C., Wapenaar, K., Werner, J., Long, L., Maughan-Brown, B., Miot, J., & Pascoe, S. J. (2022). Quasi-experimental evaluation of a financial incentive for first-dose COVID-19 vaccination among adults aged≥ 60 years in South Africa. *British Medical Journal Global Health, 7*(12), e009625. http://dx.doi.org/10.1136/bmjgh-2022-009625

Choko, A. T., Nanfuka, M., Birungi, J., Taasi, G., Kisembo, P., & Helleringer, S. (2018). A pilot trial of the peer-based distribution of HIV self-test kits among fishermen in Bulisa, Uganda. *PloS One, 13*(11), e0208191.

Chokshi, N. P., Adusumalli, S., Small, D. S., Morris, A., Feingold, J., Ha, Y. P., Lynch, M. D., Rareshide, C. A., Hilbert, V., & Patel, M. S. (2018). Loss-framed financial incentives and personalized goal-setting to increase physical activity among ischemic heart disease patients using wearable devices: The ACTIVE REWARD randomized trial. *Journal of the American Heart Association, 7*(12), e009173. https://doi.org/10.1161/JAHA.118.009173

Choudhry, N. K., Avorn, J., Glynn, R. J., Antman, E. M., Schneeweiss, S., Toscano, M., Reisman, L., Fernandes, J., Spettell, C., Lee, J. L., & Levin, R. (2011). Full coverage for preventive medications after myocardial infarction. *New England Journal of Medicine, 365*(22), 2088–2097. https://doi.org/10.1056/NEJMsa1107913

Conis, E. (2015). Vaccination resistance in historical perspective. *The American Historian.* https://www.oah.org/tah/issues/2015/august/vaccination-resistance/

Connolly, T., & Reb, J. (2003). Omission bias in vaccination decisions: Where's the "omission"? Where's the "bias"? *Organizational Behavior and Human Decision Processes, 91*(2), 186–202. https://doi.org/10.1016/S0749-5978(03)00057-8

Dai, H., Saccardo, S., Han, M. A., Roh, L., Raja, N., Vangala, S., Modi, H., Pandya, S., Sloyan, M., & Croymans, D. M. (2021). Behavioural nudges increase COVID-19 vaccinations. *Nature*, *597*(7876), 404–409. https://doi.org/10.1038/s41586-021-03843-2

Dalal, S., Lee, C. W., Farirai, T., Schilsky, A., Goldman, T., Moore, J., & Bock, N. N. (2011). Provider-initiated HIV testing and counseling: Increased uptake in two public community health centers in South Africa and implications for scale-up. *PloS One*, *6*(11), e27293. https://doi.org/10.1371/journal.pone.0027293

Doshi, J. A., Lim, R., Li, P., Young, P. P., Lawnicki, V.F., State, J. J., Troxel, A. B., & Volpp, K. G. (2016). A synchronized prescription refill program improved medication adherence. *Health Affairs*, *35*(8), 1504–1512. https://doi.org/10.1377/hlthaff.2015.1456

Dupas, P. (2011). Do teenagers respond to HIV risk information? Evidence from a field experiment in Kenya. *American Economic Journal: Applied Economics*, *3*(1), 1–34. https://doi.org/10.1257/app.3.1.1

Emanuel, E. J., Ubel, P. A., Kessler, J. B., Meyer, G., Muller, R. W., Navathe, A. S., Patel, P., Pearl, R., Rosenthal, M. B., Sacks, L., & Sen, A. P. (2016). Using behavioral economics to design physician incentives that deliver high-value care. *Annals of Internal Medicine*, *164*(2), 114–119. https://doi.org/10.7326/M15-1330

Facciorusso, A., Demb, J., Mohan, B. P., Gupta, S., & Singh, S. (2021). Addition of financial incentives to mailed outreach for promoting colorectal cancer screening: A systematic review and meta-analysis. *The Journal of the American Medical Association Network Open*, *4*(8), e2122581. https://doi.org/10.1001/jamanetworkopen.2021.22581

Finkelstein, E. A., Haaland, B. A., Bilger, M., Sahasranaman, A., Sloan, R. A., Nang, E. E. K., & Evenson, K. R. (2016). Effectiveness of activity trackers with and without incentives to increase physical activity (TRIPPA): A randomised controlled trial. *The Lancet Diabetes & Endocrinology*, *4*(12), 983–995. https://doi.org/10.1016/S2213-8587(16)30284-4

Gauri, V., Jamison, J. C., Mazar, N., & Ozier, O. (2021) Motivating bureaucrats through social recognition: External validity—A tale of two states. *Organizational Behavior and Human Decision Processes*, *163*, 117–131. https://doi.org/10.1016/j.obhdp.2019.05.005

Gawande, A. (2010). *The checklist manifesto*. Picadur.

George, G., Maughan-Brown, B., & Thirumurthy, H. (2021). Behavioural science to improve effectiveness of HIV programmes, South Africa. *Bulletin of the World Health Organization*, *99*(11), 840. https://doi.org/10.2471%2FBLT.21.285626

Hallsworth, M., Chadborn, T., Sallis, A., Sanders, M., Berry, D., Greaves, F., Clements, L., & Davies, S. C. (2016). Provision of social norm feedback to high prescribers of antibiotics in general practice: A pragmatic national randomised controlled trial. *The Lancet*, *387*(10029), 1743–1752. https://doi.org/10.1016/S0140-6736(16)00215-4

Halpern, S. D., French, B., Small, D. S., Saulsgiver, K., Harhay, M. O., Audrain-McGovern, J., Loewenstein, G., Brennan, T. A., Asch, D. A., & Volpp, K. G. (2015). Randomized trial of four financial-incentive programs for smoking cessation. *New England Journal of Medicine*, *372*, 2108–2117. https://doi.org/10.1056/NEJMoa1414293

Hsu, E. B., Thomas, T. L., Bass, E. B., Whyne, D., Kelen, G. D., & Green, G. B. (2006). Healthcare worker competencies for disaster training. *BioMed Central Medical Education*, *6*(1), 1–9. https://doi.org/10.1186/1472-6920-6-19

Hutchinson, P. L., Mahlalela, X., & Yukich, J. (2007). Mass media, stigma, and disclosure of HIV test results: Multilevel analysis in the Eastern Cape, South Africa. *AIDS Education and Prevention*, *19*(6), 489. https://doi.org/10.1521/aeap.2007.19.6.489

Institute of Medicine (IOM). (2007). *Ending the tobacco problem: A blueprint for the nation*. The National Academies Press. https://doi.org/10.17226/11795

———. (2013). *Best care at lower cost: The path to continuously learning health care in America*. The National Academies Press. https://doi.org/10.17226/13444

Keller, P. A., Harlam, B., Loewenstein, G., & Volpp, K. G. (2011). Enhanced active choice: A new method to motivate behavior change. *Journal of Consumer Psychology*, *21*(4), 376–383. https://doi.org/10.1016/j.jcps.2011.06.003

Kimmel, S. E., Troxel, A. B., Loewenstein, G., Brensinger, C. M., Jaskowiak, J., Doshi, J. A., Laskin, M., & Volpp, K. (2012). Randomized trial of lottery-based incentives to improve warfarin adherence. *American Heart Journal, 164*(2), 268–274. https://doi.org/10.1016/j.ahj.2012.05.005

Krishnamoorthy, Y., Rehman, T., & Sakthivel, M. (2021). Effectiveness of financial incentives in achieving UNAID fast-track 90-90-90 and 95-95-95 target of HIV care continuum: A systematic review and meta-analysis of randomized controlled trials. *AIDS and Behavior, 25*(3), 814–825. https://doi.org/10.1007/s10461-020-03038-2

Kwan, J. L., Lo, L., Ferguson, J., Goldberg, H., Diaz-Martinez, J. P., Tomlinson, G., Grimshaw, J. M., & Shojania, K. G. (2020). Computerised clinical decision support systems and absolute improvements in care: Meta-analysis of controlled clinical trials. *British Medical Journal, 370*. https://doi.org/10.1136/bmj.m3216

Larkin, I., & Loewenstein, G. (2017). Business model–related conflict of interests in medicine: Problems and potential solutions. *Journal of the American Medical Association, 317*(17), 1745–1746. https://doi.org/10.1001/jama.2017.2275

Law, A. C., Peterson, D., Walkey, A. J., & Bosch, N. A. (2022). Lottery-based incentives and COVID-19 vaccination rates in the US. *The Journal of the American Medical Association Internal Medicine, 182*(2), 235–237. https://doi.org/10.1001/jamainternmed.2021.7052

Lee, R., Cui, R. R., Muessig, K. E., Thirumurthy, H., & Tucker, J. D. (2014). Incentivizing HIV/STI testing: A systematic review of the literature. *AIDS and Behavior, 18*(5), 905–912. https://doi.org/10.1007/s10461-013-0588-8

Li, M., Taylor, E. G., Atkins, K. E., Chapman, G. B., & Galvani, A. P. (2016). Stimulating influenza vaccination via prosocial motives. *PloS One, 11*(7), e0159780. https://doi.org/10.1371/journal.pone.0159780

Linnemayr, S. (2017). Behavioral economics and HIV: A review of existing studies and potential future research area. *Behaviors: Key concepts and current research*. Routledge. https://doi.org/10.4324/9781315637938

Linnemayr, S., Stecher, C., & Mukasa, B. (2017). Behavioral economic incentives to improve adherence to antiretroviral medication. *AIDS, 31*(5), 719. https://doi.org/10.1097%2FQAD.0000000000001387

Loewenstein, G., Asch, D. A., & Volpp, K. G. (2013). Behavioral economics holds potential to deliver better results for patients, insurers, and employers. *Health Affairs, 32*(7), 1244–1250. https://doi.org/10.1377/hlthaff.2012.1163

Lyu, H., Xu, T., Brotman, D., Mayer-Blackwell, B., Cooper, M., Daniel, M., Wick, E. C., Saini, V., Brownlee, S., & Makary, M. A. (2017). Overtreatment in the United States. *PLoS One 12*(9), e0181970. https://doi.org/10.1371/journal.pone.0181970

Manning, W. G., Newhouse, J. P., Duan, N., Keeler, E. B., & Leibowitz, A. (1987). Health insurance and the demand for medical care: Evidence from a randomized experiment. *The American Economic Review, 77*(3), 251–277. https://www.jstor.org/stable/1804094

Meeker, D., Linder, J. A., Fox, C. R., Friedberg, M. W., Persell, S. D., Goldstein, N. J., Knight, T. K., Hay, J. W., & Doctor, J. N. (2016). Effect of behavioral interventions on inappropriate antibiotic prescribing among primary care practices: A randomized clinical trial. *Journal of the American Medical Association, 315*(6), 562–570. https://doi.org/10.1001/jama.2016.0275

Meszaros, J. R., Asch, D. A., Baron, J., Hershey, J. C., Kunreuther, H., & Schwartz-Buzaglo, J. (1996). Cognitive processes and the decisions of some parents to forego pertussis vaccination for their children. *Journal of Clinical Epidemiology, 49*(6), 697–703. https://doi.org/10.1016/0895-4356(96)00007-8

Milkman, K. L., Beshears, J., Choi, J. J., Laibson, D., & Madrian, B. C. (2011). Using implementation intentions prompts to enhance influenza vaccination rates. *Proceedings of the National Academy of Sciences, 108*(26), 10415–10420. https://doi.org/10.1073/pnas.1103170108

Milkman, K. L., Minson, J. A., & Volpp, K. G. (2014). Holding the hunger games hostage at the gym: An evaluation of temptation bundling. *Management Science*, 60(2), 283–299. https://doi.org/10.1287/mnsc.2013.1784

Milkman, K. L., Patel, M. S., Gandhi, L., Graci, H. N., Gromet, D. M., Ho, H., Kay, J. S., Lee, T. W., Akinola, M., Beshears, J., & Bogard, J. E. (2021). A megastudy of text-based nudges encouraging patients to get vaccinated at an upcoming doctor's appointment. *Proceedings of the National Academy of Sciences*, 118(20), e2101165118. https://doi.org/10.1073/pnas.2101165118

Milkman, K. L., Gandhi, L., Patel, M. S., Graci, H. N., Gromet, D. M., Ho, H., Kay, J. S., Lee, T. W., Rothschild, J., Bogard, J. E., & Brody, I. (2022). A 680,000-person megastudy of nudges to encourage vaccination in pharmacies. *Proceedings of the National Academy of Sciences*, 119(6), e2115126119.

Montoy, J. C. C., Dow, W. H., & Kaplan, B. C. (2018). Cash incentives versus defaults for HIV testing: A randomized clinical trial. *PloS One*, 13(7), e0199833. https://doi.org/10.1371/journal.pone.0199833

Notley, C., Gentry, S., Livingstone-Banks, J., Bauld, L., Perera, R., & Hartmann-Boyce, J. (2019). Incentives for smoking cessation. *Cochrane Database of Systematic Reviews*. https://doi.org/10.1002/14651858.CD004307.pub6

Nystoriak, M. A., & Bhatnagar, A. (2018). Cardiovascular effects and benefits of exercise. *Frontiers in Cardiovascular Medicine*, 5, 135. https://doi.org/10.3389/fcvm.2018.00135

Opel, D. J., & Omer, S. B. (2015). Measles, mandates, and making vaccination the default option. *The Journal of the American Medical Association Pediatrics*, 169(4), 303–304. https://doi.org/10.1001/jamapediatrics.2015.0291

Patel, M. S., Asch, D. A., Rosin, R., Small, D. S., Bellamy, S. L., Heuer, J., Sproat, S., Hyson, C., Haff, N., Lee, S. M., & Wesby, L. (2016). Framing financial incentives to increase physical activity among overweight and obese adults: A randomized, controlled trial. *Annals of Internal Medicine*, 164(6), 385–394.

Patel, M. S., Volpp, K. G., Rosin, R., Bellamy, S. L., Small, D. S., Heuer, J., Sproat, S., Hyson, C., Haff, N., Lee, S. M., & Wesby, L. (2018). A randomized, controlled trial of lottery-based financial incentives to increase physical activity among overweight and obese adults. *American Journal of Health Promotion*, 32(7), 1568–1575. https://doi.org/10.1177/0890117118758932

Patel, M. S., Small, D. S., Harrison, J. D., Fortunato, M. P., Oon, A. L., Rareshide, C. A., Reh, G., Szwartz, G., Guszcza, J., Steier, D., & Kalra, P. (2019). Effectiveness of behaviorally designed gamification interventions with social incentives for increasing physical activity among overweight and obese adults across the United States: The STEP UP randomized clinical trial. *The Journal of the American Medical Association Internal Medicine*, 179(12), 1624–1632. https://doi.org/10.1001/jamainternmed.2019.3505

Patel, M. S., Milkman, K. L., Gandhi, L., Graci, H. N., Gromet, D., Ho, H., Kay, J. S., Lee, T. W., Rothschild, J., Akinola, M., & Beshears, J. (2022). A randomized trial of behavioral nudges delivered through text messages to increase influenza vaccination among patients with an upcoming primary care visit. *American Journal of Health Promotion*. https://doi.org/10.1177/08901171221131021

Petry, N. M., Rash, C. J., Byrne, S., Ashraf, S., & White, W. B. (2012). Financial reinforcers for improving medication adherence: Findings from a meta-analysis. *The American Journal of Medicine*, 125(9), 888–896.

Pettifor, A., Lippman, S. A., Kimaru, L., Haber, N., Mayakayaka, Z., Selin, A., Twine, R., Gilmore, H., Westreich, D., Mdaka, B., & Wagner, R. (2020). HIV self-testing among young women in rural South Africa: A randomized controlled trial comparing clinic-based HIV testing to the choice of either clinic testing or HIV self-testing with secondary distribution to peers and partners. *eClinicalMedicine*, 21, 100327. https://doi.org/10.1016/j.eclinm.2020.100327

Pronovost, P., Needham, D., Berenholtz, S., Sinopoli, D., Chu, H., Cosgrove, S., Sexton, B., Hyzy, R., Welsh, R., Roth, G., & Bander, J. (2006). An intervention to decrease catheter-related bloodstream infections in the ICU. *New England Journal of Medicine, 355*(26), 2725–2732. https://doi.org/10.1056/NEJMoa061115

Rabb, N., Swindal, M., Glick, D., Bowers, J., Tomasulo, A., Oyelami, Z., Wilson, K. H., & Yokum, D. (2022). Evidence from a statewide vaccination RCT shows the limits of nudges. *Nature, 604*(7904), E1–E7. https://doi.org/10.1038/s41586-022-04526-2

Reese, P. P., Bloom, R. D., Trofe-Clark, J., Mussell, A., Leidy, D., Levsky, S., Zhu, J., Yang, L., Wang, W., Troxel, A., & Feldman, H. I. (2017). Automated reminders and physician notification to promote immunosuppression adherence among kidney transplant recipients: A randomized trial. *American Journal of Kidney Diseases, 69*(3), 400–409. https://doi.org/10.1053/j.ajkd.2016.10.017

Reid, R. O., Tom, A. K., Ross, R. M., Duffy, E. L., & Damberg, C. L. (2022). Physician compensation arrangements and financial performance incentives in US health systems. *Journal of the American Medical Association Health Forum, 3*(1), e214634. https://doi.org/10.1001/jamahealthforum.2021.4634

Reñosa, M. D. C., Landicho, J., Wachinger, J., Dalglish, S. L., Bärnighausen, K., Bärnighausen, T., & McMahon, S. A. (2021). Nudging toward vaccination: A systematic review. *British Medical Journal Global Health, 6*(9), e006237. http://dx.doi.org/10.1136/bmjgh-2021-006237

Rymer, J. A., Fonseca, E., Bhandary, D. D., Kumar, D., Khan, N. D., & Wang, T. Y. (2021). Difference in medication adherence between patients prescribed a 30-day versus 90-day supply after acute myocardial infarction. *Journal of the American Heart Association, 10*(1), e016215. https://doi.org/10.1161/JAHA.119.016215n

Schneider, F. H., Campos-Mercade, P., Meier, S., Pope, D., Wengström, E., & Meier, A. N. (2023). Financial incentives for vaccination do not have negative unintended consequences. *Nature, 613*, 526–533. https://doi.org/10.1038/s41586-022-05512-4

Smith, P., Buttenheim, A., Schmucker, L., Bekker, L. G., Thirumurthy, H., & Davey, D. L. J. (2021). Undetectable = untransmittable (U = U) messaging increases uptake of HIV testing among men: Results from a pilot cluster randomized trial. *AIDS and Behavior, 25*(10), 3128–3136. https://doi.org/10.1007/s10461-021-03284-y

Smith, R. A., Andrews, K. S., Brooks, D., Fedewa, S. A., Manassaram-Baptiste, D., Saslow, D., & Wender, R. C. (2019). Cancer screening in the United States, 2019: A review of current American Cancer Society guidelines and current issues in cancer screening. *CA: A Cancer Journal for Clinicians, 69*(3), 184–210.

Szilagyi, P. G., Albertin, C., Casillas, A., Valderrama, R., Duru, O. K., Ong, M. K., Vangala, S., Tseng, C. H., Rand, C. M., Humiston, S. G., & Evans, S. (2020). Effect of patient portal reminders sent by a health care system on influenza vaccination rates: A randomized clinical trial. *Journal of the American Medical Association Internal Medicine, 180*(7), 962–970. https://doi.org/10.1001/jamainternmed.2020.1602

Tang, K. L., Ghali, W A., & Manns, B. J. (2014). Addressing cost-related barriers to prescription drug use in Canada. *Canadian Medical Association Journal, 186*(4), 276–280. https://doi.org/10.1503/cmaj.121637

Taylor, L. C., Kerrison, R. S., Herrmann, B., & Stoffel, S. T. (2022). Effectiveness of behavioural economics-based interventions to improve colorectal cancer screening participation: A rapid systematic review of randomised controlled trials. *Preventive Medicine Reports, 26*. https://doi.org/10.1016%2Fj.pmedr.2022.101747

Thirumurthy, H., Masters, S. H., Rao, S., Bronson, M. A., Lanham, M., Omanga, E., Evens, E., & Agot, K. (2014). Effect of providing conditional economic compensation on uptake of voluntary medical male circumcision in Kenya: A randomized clinical trial. *The Journal of the American Medical Association, 312*(7), 703–711. https://doi.org/10.1001/jama.2014.9087

Thirumurthy, H., Hayashi, K., Linnemayr, S., Vreeman, R. C., Levin, I. P., Bangsberg, D. R., & Brewer, N. T. (2015). Time preferences predict mortality among HIV-infected adults receiving antiretroviral therapy in Kenya. *PloS One, 10*(12), e0145245. https://doi.org/10.1371/journal.pone.0145245

Thornton, R. L. (2008). The demand for, and impact of, learning HIV status. *American Economic Review, 98*(5), 1829–1863. https://doi.org/10.1257/aer.98.5.1829

Volpp, K. G., & Galvin, R. (2014). Reward-based incentives for smoking cessation: How a carrot became a stick. *The Journal of the American Medical Association, 311*(9), 909–910. https://doi.org/10.1001/jama.2014.418

Volpp, K. G., & Loewenstein, G. (2020). What is a habit? Diverse mechanisms that can produce sustained behavior change. *Organizational Behavior and Human Decision Processes, 161*, 36–38. https://doi.org/10.1016/j.obhdp.2020.10.002

Volpp, K., & Pauly, M. (2022). Evidence on ways to bring about effective consumer and patient engagement. *Seemed like a good idea: Alchemy versus evidence-based approaches to healthcare management innovation*, 274–300. Cambridge University Press.

Wang, S. Y., & Groene, O. (2020). The effectiveness of behavioral economics-informed interventions on physician behavioral change: A systematic literature review. *PLoS One, 15*(6), e0234149. https://doi.org/10.1371/journal.pone.0234149

Wang, T. Y., Kaltenbach, L. A., Cannon, C. P., Fonarow, G. C., Choudhry, N. K., Henry, T. D., Cohen, D. J., Bhandary, D., Khan, N. D., Anstrom, K. J., & Peterson, E. D. (2019). Effect of medication co-payment vouchers on $P2Y_{12}$ inhibitor use and major adverse cardiovascular events among patients with myocardial infarction: The ARTEMIS randomized clinical trial. *The Journal of the American Medical Association, 321*(1), 44–55. https://doi.org/10.1001/jama.2018.19791

Zullig, L. L., Blalock, D. V., Dougherty, S., Henderson, R., Ha, C. C., Oakes, M. M., & Bosworth, H. B. (2018). The new landscape of medication adherence improvement: Where population health science meets precision medicine. *Patient Preference and Adherence, 12*, 1225. https://doi.org/10.2147/PPA.S165404

6

Retirement Benefits

It is widely discussed in the financial pages of media outlets and financial advice columns that Americans do not save enough for retirement. A common view of what constitutes "enough" is a nest egg sufficient to allow a person to roughly maintain their standard of living after retirement—or at least avoid a drastic reduction. But meeting even modest retirement goals requires planning. To maintain even a roughly equal standard of living during retirement, a family with an income over $25,000 should be saving about 13 percent of their income (factoring in expected social security benefits); the challenge is stiffer for higher-income families (Bernheim et al., 2000).

Average savings rates for U.S. households are far below this level: the average is 7–8 percent. According to the Federal Reserve Bank, approximately one-fourth of adults who have not yet retired have no retirement savings, and just over half of nonretired adults assess their savings as being on track (Federal Reserve, 2022). White adults are more likely than Black or Hispanic adults to have some retirement savings and to regard their savings as on track. While older adults have the greatest savings, the group with the most savings (ages 65–74) had only a median of $164,000 in retirement savings in 2019, and people ages 45–54 had only a median of $100,000 (Federal Reserve, 2021). It has been estimated that only about half of U.S. households can expect to sustain their standard of living after retirement (Osterland, 2022).

The failure to save adequately for retirement has been ascribed to many of the behavioral factors discussed in Chapter 3, particularly limited attention, cognitive barriers, present bias, and inaccurate beliefs. Limited attention and cognitive barriers lead people to devote inadequate time to important financial decisions and limit their understanding of the ramifications of their choices. Present bias leads people to give insufficient weight to the future implications of current decisions about financial matters. Low levels of financial literacy in the general population exacerbate the effects of cognitive barriers and limited attention, and lead to inaccurate beliefs about the importance of saving (Lusardi & Mitchell, 2014).

Employers play a critical role in most people's retirement planning, and over the last several decades most U.S. employers who offer retirement benefits have moved from defined benefit plans to defined contribution plans. Under a defined benefit plan, a company or firm combines funds deducted from employee paychecks with company-contributed funds in an account that can grow and eventually pay a specific dollar amount per month or year to retired employees. In general, such plans can yield a payout roughly equal to the individual's salary, if the company-funded portion is sufficient. These plans have tax advantages both to workers and their employers and can provide workers with significant nest eggs. A worker with a salary of $50,000 who devotes six percent of their salary to a plan saves $3,000 in post-tax income and therefore saves that amount times their marginal tax rate (e.g., a 10 percent gain if they are in a 10 percent tax bracket). More important, if their employer matches that contribution at, say, a 50 percent rate, then the $3,000 saving turns into a $4,500 saving, equivalent to a 50 percent rate of return on top of the 10 percent tax gain. These are enormous rates of return for any form of savings.

However, the large majority of companies today have shifted to defined contribution plans, in which workers decide how much will be deducted from their paychecks, and the firm matches that deduction, according to a defined ratio. These plans are optional, and workers are not required to join them. In traditional economic models of financial decision making, it is assumed that people who are offered alternative retirement plans by their employers will rationally evaluate the financial advantages of those alternatives. That is, they will consider how much they want to contribute to savings plans (sacrificing current spending power), as well as the after-tax rate of return on any savings plans they are offered (which determines how much they will have to spend later). In making these calculations, workers would ideally take into account their particular retirement needs, the riskiness of their future income profiles, uncertain life expectancy, and other factors. This assumption has been shown to have limitations.

AUTOMATIC ENROLLMENT

Research conducted in the last two decades has demonstrated that behavioral factors not accounted for in the traditional economic model strongly affect people's decisions about enrolling in pension plans. A 2001 study identified striking contradictions to the traditional economic model and was followed by a significant body of work that eventually influenced government policy regarding retirement savings (Madrian & Shea, 2001). The authors studied choices by employees who were offered the option to enroll in an advantageous company 401(k) plan that guaranteed a good rate of return, especially when tax savings were included in the calculation. The offered plan also included a company match for each dollar the employees contributed (up to a maximum), which strengthened the already strong case for investing in the plan. The company required employees to actively indicate that they wished to enroll in this attractive plan and to make payroll contributions to it: the "default option"—that is, the option that would apply if the worker took no action—was to not enroll. The company examined in the study then changed the architecture of the arrangement by making enrollment in the plan the default option—that is, employees had to actively indicate that they did not wish to enroll if that was their decision.

According to traditional economic assumptions, the difference in what is set as the default—to enroll in the new plan or not—should have no impact, or at least not more than a small impact, on the decisions of rational people who have carefully considered both plans. However, the authors found that making automatic enrollment the default dramatically increased employees' enrollment in the plan, from 49 percent to 86 percent. The default option in this case also designated a specific amount for payroll deductions—usually a small percentage, three percent, of wages—but employees could choose a lower or higher amount if they wished. The authors found that many chose the default level of the contribution, which often led to increased savings from that source as well. This was a clear sign that employees were devoting limited attention to their pension plan arrangements.

Numerous subsequent studies strongly confirmed these findings, showing major increases in participation in 401(k) plans (the most common defined contribution plans that employers offer) when the default was to enroll rather than to not enroll. These findings held across a wide variety of companies, types of plans offered, company matching policies, and other variables (Beshears et al., 2009, 2018). Indeed, an important aspect of this finding is the extent to which it has been replicated in different contexts, which confirms its validity. In addition, like many behaviorally inspired interventions, default approaches are quite inexpensive to implement, making them a particularly attractive policy option.

This research attracted significant public attention that led to provisions in the landmark Pension Protection Act of 2006, which formally allowed employers to change the default in their tax-preferred pension plans, codified the rules regarding the required characteristics of default plans to qualify for favorable tax treatment, provided employer protection from losses from the plans, and generally encouraged employers to adopt automatic default plans (Beshears et al., 2010). Legislation passed in 2019 allowed employers to set higher maximum default contribution rates, which research has shown has a powerful effect on levels of savings. Additional legislation in December 2022 extended automatic enrollment to a wider set of employers; relaxed the penalties for one-time emergency withdrawals; and, in a provision that particularly highlights behavioral economics, allowed employers to offer workers a "small gift" to enroll in their company's plan. Automatic enrollment has been described as "the most successful contribution of so-called behavioral economics to public policy" (Porter, 2016).

STRATEGIES TO REFINE AUTOMATIC ENROLLMENT

While automatic enrollment in tax-advantaged retirement plans has had demonstrable benefits for workers, a number of questions remain. One is about the size of contributions employees make to the company retirement plan, if they enroll in it, and how the money employees contribute is invested, which is also subject to employee choice. In the initial Madrian and Shea study (2001), the company's default plan was for employees to contribute three percent of their earnings to the plan and specified that those investments be invested in a money market fund. Yet, as noted above, 13 percent or more is needed to maintain a preretirement standard of living in retirement, and money market investments are well-known to have much lower long-run rates of return than investments in stocks and bonds. It is even possible that people who were presented with the traditional plan (in which enrollment had to be actively selected) might have chosen contribution rates higher than three percent, and investments in higher-return investment instruments, than those offered in the company's default plan.

One way to address this problem is simply to increase the percentage contribution in an employer's default plan. A study of the effects of raising the default contribution percentage from three percent to six percent showed that it increased saving and did not significantly reduce plan participation (Beshears et al., 2009). Another way that firms have addressed this issue has been to offer a three-way choice instead of a two-way choice: (1) the default option of enrollment with a fixed contribution percentage and investment allocation, (2) nonenrollment, or (3) enrollment with a different a contribution percentage and investment allocation (often called "personalized enrollment"). Offering this third alternative alongside the other two makes explicit the idea that employees may wish to actively think about their contribution percentage and their investment allocation: that is, it attempts to make them pay more attention to it and encourages them to do so.

To address the possible concern that employees may be reluctant to immediately jump to a relatively high contribution rate, an alternative known as autoescalation has been developed. In such a plan, contribution rates start off relatively low but rise automatically over time. A behaviorally inspired default plan that uses this approach is the Save More Tomorrow plan, pioneered by Benartzi & Thaler (2001). Employees that opt for this plan have their savings rate in a 401(k) plan increased by a fixed amount, say two percent each year, by default, up to a specified ceiling. This plan encourages people to save more over time without having to start saving more immediately, which is often a hurdle. Employees may opt out at any point. This type of plan addresses the behavioral trait of present bias (see Chapter 3). In its initial implementations this plan was very successful in raising savings rates of participants, and some features of this plan have been implemented nationwide.

A second issue is that people sometimes want to withdraw funds from a retirement plan for immediate consumption needs, despite the typically high penalties for early withdrawal. This is especially a concern with low-income earners who accept the default plan, with its minimum required contributions, but may later need cash to deal with temporary reductions in income or increases in expenses. This may not be a substantial problem. According to one study, only 0.3 percent of people enrolled in Vanguard plans withdrew for "hardship" reasons (i.e., the withdrawal was legally allowed but with penalties and tax due; Munnell & Webb, 2015). However, the cumulative impact for the people who made such withdrawals was an almost 25 percent reduction in the amount of money they had available when they retired. About 0.5 percent cashed out their plans when leaving their employer (this option is legally allowed), although many rolled over their balance to an individual retirement account.

Another study showed that workers with present bias often withdraw funds from their 401(k) plans when separating from their employers and also often changed their retirement assets into more liquid forms (Beshears et al., 2022b; see also Wang, Zhai, & Lynch, 2022). The researchers proposed dealing with the short-run liquidity constraint problem by establishing "rainy day" funds for employees, where automatic payroll deductions can go into a fund that is intended just for emergency withdrawals. There have also been proposals to direct employee contributions partially into more liquid buffer stock accounts, at least for initial contributions (Beshears et al., 2015b, 2020; John, 2015; Gruber, 2016; Mitchell & Lynne, 2017). Bhargava & Conell-Price (2022) have suggested that an alternative framing of such accounts as "serenity accounts" could result in greater participation.

A third issue is whether automatic enrollment plans lead employees to shift their savings from other employer plans that are less advantageous, without actually increasing the amount they are saving. This issue has not been thoroughly studied, but some evidence indicates that this may not be a significant issue, since employees' net savings increase, at least on average and in the aggregate. For example, one study looked at the savings effects when a group of workers accumulated sufficient years of service in their firms to become eligible for tax-favored 401(k) contributions (Gelber, 2011). The study found an increase in 401(k) balances and a statistically insignificant effect on the levels of other financial assets. This study seemed to confirm earlier work showing that savings incentives resulted in a net increase in retirement assets greater than reductions in other plans (Engen et al., 1994; Poterba, Venti, & Wise, 1995). Another study showed that automatic enrollment did not lead to an increase in borrowing, which might be expected if enrollment created financial distress (Beshears et al., 2022a).

Recently, researchers have applied other behavioral approaches to influence employees' choices for pension plans. One study showed that even when employers offer default plans, many people do not contribute to the plans at high-enough rates to sufficiently reduce financial insecurity during retirement (Bhargava et al., 2021). The authors found that employers can increase contribution rates by using behaviorally based design features that lead employees to choose "personalized plan options"—that is, options that are tailored to an individual's specific financial circumstances—instead of defaults. Such features include seemingly minor changes in the way the options are portrayed to employees, the language and words used, and even the color scheme of the choices. These types of changes in framing are closely related to the concept of reference dependence (see Chapter 3). Another example of personalized plan options was included in the Pension Protection Act of 2006, which allowed employers to automatically enroll employees in so-called target-date retirement funds, which make the asset allocation dependent on the individual's age and life expectancy.

Other work has shown the benefits of framing in the presentation of alternative retirement plans to employees, offering employees personalized retirement projections, and offering financial consultation in combination with defaults (Goda, Manchester, & Sojourner, 2014; Blumenstock, Callen, & Ghani, 2018; Beshears et al., 2021). A study of the role of incentives designed to induce employees to make larger contributions and to opt for personalized plans showed that personal recommendations designed to improve financial literacy and simplified enrollment procedures had limited impacts on employees' savings rates (Bhargava & Conell-Price, 2022). However, the authors found that small incentives designed to counter present bias were effective.

While this chapter has focused on behavioral issues in employer retirement plans, there is a larger literature on retirement savings in general that addresses the effects of behavioral interventions on savings at older ages. This work includes studies of the effects of financial education interventions on retirement savings (Fernandes, Lynch, & Netemeyer, 2014; Kaiser et al., 2022), the effects of providing peer information on individual retirement decisions (Beshears et al., 2015a), interventions to encourage retirees not to draw down their assets too quickly (Shu & Shu, 2018), and many others. This literature shows the wide applicability of behaviorally motivated interventions to improve the financial well-being of older people.

FINDINGS

A substantial body of research has examined the role of defaults and other factors in the retirement savings decisions of workers. This research has demonstrated that behavioral factors play a key role in people's decisions about a matter that had previously seemed to be a straightforward case for traditional economic analysis, in which logic alone would lead a rational actor to take advantage of an offered benefit. We highlight some key findings from this work.

- In making decisions about retirement savings benefits, people are strongly influenced by behavioral factors: limited attention and cognition; inaccurate beliefs; present bias; and, to a slightly lesser degree, reference dependence.
- The use of default designs by employers has been shown to have a major impact on saving for retirement, and there is little evidence of significant downsides for employees.
- Default designs have been shown to have those positive effects across a wide variety of settings, making them one of the behavioral designs with the largest generalizability.
- Other characteristics of plans, including framing, wording, and visuals, have also been shown to affect workers' choice of plan and have the potential to at least modestly increase retirement assets.

To build on the success that has already been achieved in boosting retirement savings, it will be useful to have additional evidence on behaviorally based tools for increasing saving to levels that will better meet people's actual retirement needs. Specifically, research is needed to address:

- ways to encourage employees to pay more attention to the exact contribution rate and form of investment in their retirement plans to allow employees to make more personalized choices rather than just accepting the default rate and form;
- methods of developing rainy day funds and other forms of liquid assets that allow workers to deal with short-term needs instead of withdrawing funds from their retirement plans; and
- ways to encourage employees who separate from their firms, who are allowed to roll over their retirement funds, to continue to enroll in plans with advantageous rates of return.

REFERENCES

Benartzi, S., & Thaler, R. H. (2001). Naive diversification strategies in defined contribution saving plans. *American Economic Review*, *91*(1), 79–98. https://doi.org/10.1257/aer.91.1.79

Bernheim, B. D., Forni, L., Gokhale, J., & Kotlikoff, L. J. (2000). *An economic approach to setting retirement saving goals.* Working Paper 483. Wharton Pension Research Council. https://repository.upenn.edu/prc_papers/483

Beshears, J., Choi, J. J., Laibson, D., & Madrian, B. C. (2009). The importance of default options for retirement saving outcomes: Evidence from the United States. *Social security policy in a changing environment*, 167–195. University of Chicago Press. http://www.nber.org/chapters/c4539

———. (2010). The impact of employer matching on savings plan participation under automatic enrollment. *Research findings in the economics of aging*, 311–327. University of Chicago Press. http://www.nber.org/chapters/c8208

———. (2018). *Potential vs. realized savings under automatic enrollment.* TIAA Institute. https://origin-www.tiaainstitute.org/sites/default/files/presentations/2018-07/Potential%20vs%20Realized%20Savings_Beshears_July%202018.pdf

Beshears, J., Choi, J. J., Laibson, D., Madrian, B. C., & Milkman, K. (2015a). The effect of providing peer information on retirement savings decisions. *The Journal of Finance*, *70*(3), 1161–1201. https://doi.org/10.1111/jofi.12258

Beshears, J., Choi, J. J., Harris, C., Laibson, D., Madrian, B., & Sakong, J. (2015b). *Self-control and commitment: Can decreasing the liquidity of a savings account increase deposits?* NBER Working Paper 21474. National Bureau of Economic Research.

Beshears, J., Choi, J. J., Iwry, M., John, D., Laibson, D., & Madrian, B. (2020). Building emergency savings through employer-sponsored rainy-day savings accounts. *Tax policy and the economy*, *34*. National Bureau of Economic Research.

Beshears, J., Dai, H., Milkman, K. L., & Benartzi, S. (2021). Using fresh starts to nudge increased retirement savings. *Organizational Behavior and Human Decision Processes*, *167*, 72–87. https://doi.org/10.1016/j.obhdp.2021.06.005

Beshears, J., Choi, J. J., Laibson, D., Madrian, B. C., & Skimmyhorn, W. L. (2022a). Borrowing to save? The impact of automatic enrollment on debt. *Journal of Finance*, *77*(1), 403-447.

Beshears, J., Choi, J., Laibson, D., & Maxted, P. (2022b, May). Present bias causes and then dissipates auto-enrollment savings effects. *AEA Papers and Proceedings*, *112*, 136–141. https://doi.org/10.1257/pandp.20221020

Bhargava, S., & Conell-Price, L. (2022). *Serenity now, save later? Evidence on retirement savings puzzles from a 401(k) field experiment.* SSRN. https://dx.doi.org/10.2139/ssrn.4056407

Bhargava, S., Conell-Price, L., Mason, R., & Benartzi, S. (2021). *Save(d) by design.* SSRN. http://dx.doi.org/10.2139/ssrn.3237820

Blumenstock, J., Callen, M., & Ghani, T. (2018). Why do defaults affect behavior? Experimental evidence from Afghanistan. *American Economic Review*, *108* (10), 2868–2901. https://doi.org/10.1257/aer.20171676

Engen, E. M., Gale, W. G., Scholz, J. K., Bernheim, B. D., & Slemrod, J. (1994). Do saving incentives work? *Brookings Papers on Economic Activity*, *1994*(1), 85–180. https://doi.org/10.2307/2534631

Federal Reserve. (2021). *Survey of consumer finances, 1989–2019.* https://www.federalreserve.gov/econres/scf/dataviz/scf/chart/#series:Retirement_Accounts;demographic:agecl;population:1,2,3,4,5,6;units:median;range:1989,2019

———. (2022). *Economic well-being of U.S. households in 2021.* Board of Governors to the Federal Reserve System. https://www.federalreserve.gov/publications/files/2021-report-economic-well-being-us-households-202205.pdf

Fernandes, D., Lynch, J. G., & Netemeyer, R. G. (2014). Financial literacy, financial education, and downstream financial behaviors. *Management Science, 60*(8), 1861–1883. https://doi.org/10.1287/mnsc.2013.1849

Gelber, A. M. (2011). How do 401(k)s affect saving? Evidence from changes in 401(k) eligibility. *American Economic Journal: Economic Policy, 3*(4), 103–122. https://doi.org/10.1257/pol.3.4.103

Goda, G. S., Manchester, C. F., & Sojourner, A. J. (2014). What will my account really be worth? Experimental evidence on how retirement income projections affect saving. *Journal of Public Economics, 119,* 80–92. https://doi.org/10.1016/j.jpubeco.2014.08.005

Gruber, J. (2016). *Security accounts as short term social insurance and long term savings.* Future of Work Initiative. Aspen Institute.

John, D. (2015). *Adding automatic emergency savings to retirement savings plans.* AARP. https://blog.aarp.org/thinking-policy/making-retirement-saving-even-more-valuable-by-adding-automatic-emergency-savings

Kaiser, T., Lusardi, A., Menkhoff, L., & Urban, C. (2022). Financial education affects financial knowledge and downstream behaviors. *Journal of Financial Economics, 145,* 255–272. https://doi.org/10.1016/j.jfineco.2021.09.022

Lusardi, A., & Mitchell, O. S. (2014). The economic importance of financial literacy: Theory and evidence. *Journal of Economic Literature, 52*(1), 5–44. https://dx.doi.org/10.1257/jel.52.1.5

Madrian, B. C., & Shea, D. F. (2001). The power of suggestion: Inertia in 401(k) participation and savings behavior. *The Quarterly Journal of Economics, 116*(4), 1149–1187. https://doi.org/10.1162/003355301753265543

Mitchell, D. S., & Lynne, G. (2017). *Driving retirement innovation: Can sidecar accounts meet consumers' short- and long-term financial needs?* Issue Brief No. 13. Aspen Institute.

Munnell, A., & Webb, A. (2015). *The impact of leakages from 401(k)s and IRAs.* Paper 15-2. Center for Retirement Research at Boston College. https://dx.doi.org/10.2139/ssrn.2559812

Osterland, A. (2022, April 11). *Are you saving enough for retirement? Odds are, probably not.* CNBC. https://www.cnbc.com/2022/04/11/are-you-saving-enough-for-retirement-odds-are-probably-not.html

Porter, E. (2016, February 24). Nudges aren't enough for problems like retirement savings. *New York Times,* Section B, 1.

Poterba, J. M., Venti, S. F., & Wise, D. A. (1995). Do 401(k) contributions crowd out other personal saving? *Journal of Public Economics, 58*(1), 1–32. https://doi.org/10.1016/0047-2727(94)01462-W

Shu, S. B., & Shu, S. D. (2018). The psychology of decumulation decisions during retirement. *Policy Insights from the Behavioral and Brain Sciences,* 1–8. https://doi.org/10.1177/2372732218790034

Wang, Y., Zhai, M., & Lynch, J. G. (2022). Cashing out retirement savings at job separation. *Marketing Science,* 1–25. https://doi.org/10.1287/mksc.2022.1404

7

Social Safety Net Benefits

In 2021, 37.9 million people, or 11.6 percent of the U.S. population, lived in poverty, defined as having an income of less than $27,740 for a family of four or $13,788 for an individual.[1] It has been estimated that the poverty rate would be twice as high in the absence of the government's social safety net programs; by one estimate these programs kept 37 million people out of poverty in 2019 (Trisi & Saenz, 2019; Fox & Burns, 2021). The primary safety net programs are the Supplemental Nutrition Assistance Program (SNAP, also known as food stamps); subsidized housing programs; the Medicaid program (which provides health insurance to the poor); the Temporary Assistance to Needy Families (TANF) program (which provides cash assistance for low-income families with children, primarily those with a single parent); and a variety of subsidized housing programs. The federal government also provides major assistance through income tax programs, particularly the Earned Income Tax Credit (EITC), which provides for significant tax credits to low-income families with earnings, with most support going to families with children. The government spent about $261 billion on the nonhealth safety net programs in 2018 and an additional $596 billion on Medicaid.

---

[1]The government defines the poverty line as the minimum income needed to purchase the basic necessities of life.

LOW PARTICIPATION

A long-standing puzzle for policy makers and researchers has been that not all individuals and families who appear to be eligible to receive benefits apply for them. Calculations of eligibility are based on household surveys of the population that collect information on the variables used by the government to determine eligibility, so there is some degree of error in estimates of how many people are eligible for a given program. Nevertheless, the take-up rate among eligible families in safety net programs—the estimated percent of eligible families who actually receive benefits—is in many cases so low that small errors in the estimation of who is eligible cannot plausibly explain the gap.

Not only are take-up rates low in general, research has shown that sometimes those most in need are the least likely to participate (Falk, 2017). However, these take-up rates are not very different from those in other industrialized countries, where take-up rates vary widely both across and within countries for different programs (Ko & Moffitt, 2022). The take-up rates are different among the programs and for different reasons.

SNAP

Take-up rates for SNAP are relatively high (about 82%); however, the 16 percent who are estimated to be eligible to receive benefits from the program but do not receive them constitutes seven million individuals (U.S. Department of Agriculture, 2022).

Medicaid

Take-up rates among families eligible for Medicaid are less than 50 percent for adults and about 65 percent for children (Decker, Abdus, & Lipton, 2022). Since only people who do not have other health insurance coverage are eligible for Medicaid, these take-up rates imply that millions of low-income families do not have any health insurance.

Subsidized Housing

Only about 21 percent of eligible families are estimated to receive housing subsidies for which they are eligible. However, this is largely because housing agencies offer only a fixed number of public housing units and housing vouchers, and demand far exceeds the supply; there are long waiting lists for these programs, sometimes as long as five years (Kingsley, 2017). The low rate in subsidized housing is therefore explainable.

TANF

Only about 28 percent of families financially eligible for the TANF program receive benefits (Falk, 2017). To some extent this is because benefits are very low, so that even small barriers to application are likely to make applying not worth it, but there are other reasons as well, noted below.

EITC

The EITC is somewhat different from the other programs because receipt of the credit requires a household to file a tax return, and not all households do so. Low-income households often do not file returns because their incomes are too low to incur any significant tax liability, but many would be eligible for a tax credit if they did. The vast majority of those who file taxes and are eligible for a credit do request and receive the credit. Overall, it has been estimated that 77 percent of all families eligible for the EITC file their taxes and request a credit (Jones, 2013). But the 23 percent who do not constitute a major fraction of the low-income population, many of whom would be lifted out of poverty by the additional income.

POSSIBLE EXPLANATIONS FOR LOW PARTICIPATION

Traditional economic models would predict that all eligible individuals should be interested in participating in these programs because doing so would increase their level of economic resources, and that participation rates would be very high for people who have few resources in the absence of the available government assistance. A number of hypotheses from behavioral economics have been suggested for low take-up rates, including psychological predispositions, people's ability to acquire and process information, perceptions of perceived benefits that do not reflect actual ones, and people's ability to cope with the often onerous bureaucratic requirements. Although bureaucratic requirements may be accurately perceived and hence consistent with the traditional economic model, several behavioral factors may affect participation. Those factors include high demands on attention and cognitive load, the framing of offers to apply, and the context in which those offers are made. Present bias and the failure to recognize the long-run benefits of making an effort to overcome current barriers to participation are also present (see Chapter 3).

One factor that is not recognized in traditional economic analysis might be characterized as psychological dispositions. The most prominent finding from research is that many low-income families feel stigmatized by being a "welfare" recipient: they have internalized what they see as society's stereotyped characterization and negative perceptions of welfare recipients

(Moffitt, 1983; Stuber & Kronebusch, 2004; Stuber & Schlesinger, 2006). These negative psychological dispositions, it has been suggested, may be especially significant when very few other families in the geographic area are receiving government benefits. Thus, social norms operate against receiving assistance (Besley & Coate, 1992; Lindbeck, Nyberg, & Weibull, 1999).

In addition, many eligible individuals are not aware of their eligibility because they do not have access to, or know how to process, information about eligibility (this is an example of limited attention and cognitive limitations). For example, a randomized controlled trial conducted in Pittsburgh showed that offering information to families eligible for SNAP who were not participating increased the participation rate from 62 percent to 81 percent (Daponte, Sanders, & Taylor, 1999). A positive effect was also shown in a randomized controlled trial in which information about how to apply for SNAP was offered to a group of nonparticipating but eligible 60-year-old people who were receiving Medicaid, a five percentage point gain (Finkelstein & Notowidigdo, 2019). Even larger effects (a 12 percentage point gain) resulted if the individuals were offered actual assistance in the application process. However, the study also showed that those who were induced to apply were the less needy individuals among all nonparticipating eligible individuals. This finding suggests that overcoming barriers to participation may be most difficult with the most needy populations, an issue we return to below.

The application requirements for most programs require significant effort as a result of what Herd & Moynihan (2018) call "administrative burden" (see Chapter 13). Travel time to agencies is a problem, especially when a job constrains the time available, and that travel may also involve monetary costs. But even more burdensome are the time and paperwork requirements needed to establish eligibility, which may entail submission of pay stubs, verification of assets and bank balances, reports and verification of the composition of the family and who pays for what, documentation of child care costs and rent, and many other items. While these rules and their consequent compliance burden may stem from an effort to determine eligibility as accurately as possible and to prevent fraud by requiring documentation of income and assets, research on low-income people has shown that these administrative burdens loom large in discouraging application, especially because behavioral factors, such as the cognitive barriers, are particularly prevalent among low-income people (Mullainathan & Shafir, 2013). The problem can be particularly severe for applicants with low levels of education and literacy, who may have difficulty understanding and complying with relatively complex tasks.

There is a significant body of evidence that documents these barriers (e.g., Kleven & Kopczuk, 2011). For example, one study showed that jurisdictions in the United States that offered electronic tax filing had levels of

EITC take-up about one percentage point higher than those that required traditional paper copies of tax returns (Kopczuk & Pop-Eleches, 2007). Another has shown that reductions in the burdens of applying for Medicaid in one state increased participation by about 1,371 enrollees per month (Herd et al., 2013). Geographic access to clinics for the Special Supplemental Nutrition Program for Women, Infants, and Children has been found to increase benefit take-up by six percent (Rossin-Slater, 2013).

A program offering benefits for children of low-income parents had positive effects on take-up if defaults for opt-in were used, regular monthly checks were disbursed, predictable notifications for needed actions with low levels of hassle and compliance effort were used, and easy-to-use debit cards were issued. We note, however, that opt-in defaults are rarely possible for social safety net programs, for which benefits generally are not paid without an explicit opt-in (Gennetian et al., 2013). Bertrand, Mullainathan, and Shafir, (2006) describe the same informational and hassle factors referred to previously in affecting benefit take-up, along with procrastination: they found that offering moving assistance to new recipients of housing vouchers, coupled with landlord outreach and cash payments, increased moving to high-opportunity areas by 23 percentage points. The study also found that only providing information had very little effect, contrary to some of the other interventions discussed above for safety net programs (Bertrand, Mullainathan, & Shafir, 2006).

Further evidence of administrative barriers comes from research on SNAP. In the 2000s, the federal government allowed states to adopt policies to reduce application costs, including online application and management, electronic debit cards, simplified reporting, and longer recertification intervals. Cross-state comparisons show that these policies significantly increased participation, with a 37 percent increase over a 16-year period (Ganong & Liebman, 2018; Dickert-Conlin et al., 2021). The introduction of an online management program in one state also reduced program exit rates (Gray, 2019).

Considerable research has also examined recertification. One study showed that large numbers of eligible families did not recertify for the SNAP program because of the paperwork burdens involved in recertification, while another study showed that longer recertification intervals increased SNAP participation by 11 percentage points (Ribar, Edelhoch, & Liu, 2008; Gray, 2019; Bergman et al., 2023). And another study showed that individuals who were notified of the need for recertification in SNAP later than others were 22 percent less likely to reenroll than those who received the earlier notification. This study also showed that people who did not reenroll were as needy as the average participant, contrary to the suggestion that less needy individuals are less likely to reenroll (Homonoff & Somerville, 2021). The authors suggested that inattention and lack of awareness of the time requirements may be responsible for the results.

Some research has shown that administrative burdens lead those who are most in need not to apply, as might be expected on the basis of the theoretical work discussed in Chapter 3. For example, although the fraction of eligible families who participate in TANF has significantly increased over time, from 18 percent in 1996 to 72 percent in 2012, the trend has been that those in greatest need—people who are not working, are without earnings, and have the lowest incomes—have become an increasingly large percentage of those not participating (Falk, 2017).

For Medicaid, evidence that the neediest families are discouraged by the program's paperwork requirements has also been documented in detail (Heinrich et al., 2022). One study showed that Medicaid take-up is about 25 percentage points lower for childless low-income families than for higher-income families (Kenney et al., 2012). In contrast, for SNAP, there were no differences in terms of potential earnings between eligible families who did not recertify for the program and those who did (Gray, 2019).[2]

INTERVENTIONS

There are a number of studies of interventions that take their cue directly from behavioral economics. Many are randomized controlled trials that test some type of nudge, such as a study showing that providing SNAP recipients a reminder text or a text plus a telephone call increased the likelihood of recertification by five percent, especially for people with relatively less education (Lopoo, Heflin, & Boskovski, 2020).

A study that directly addressed psychological dispositions related to stigma tested several interventions in which those eligible for the EITC or a government stimulus check were invited to apply using language expressing individuals' "ownership" of the benefit (as opposed to its perception as a handout; De La Rosa et al., 2021). The study showed positive effects of from 20 percent to 128 percent on decisions to visit the program website.[3] Another source of evidence comes from a project of the Manpower Demonstration Research Corporation, funded by the Department of Health and Human Services, to test ways to encourage take-up in partnership with state social program administrators. Called the Behavioral Interventions to Advance Self-Sufficiency project, it involved 15 state and local agencies concerned with child support, child care, and work support programs that involved more than 100,000 clients. The behavioral interventions tested involved an initial phase of identifying bottlenecks and barriers in the

---

[2]The Office of Management and Budget has recognized this issue and recently issued a memo to all federal agencies on how to improve access to public benefit programs by reducing administrative burden: see https://www.whitehouse.gov/wp-content/uploads/2022/04/M-22-10.pdf

[3]The study did not collect data on actual applications.

application process, followed by a search for low-cost and inexpensive ways to reduce those bottlenecks and barriers by simplifying forms, clarifying forms and instructions in simpler language, using simple postcard reminders for appointment and form requirements, and a number of similar approaches. The results were generally successful both in application outcomes, with effect sizes of from three to five percentage points (and some larger), and in terms of giving program administrators tools to analyze problems in their own programs and to understand how to address those problems in a systematic fashion.[4]

A number of researchers have examined ways to increase participation in EITC, primarily focused on some type of nudge. The results from these studies are mixed. For example, one study showed a positive effect of 8–9 percentage points in response to a variety of letters mailed to seemingly eligible households that had not filed for the credit. However, in similar studies, postcard-style mailings to larger samples of eligible households yielded positive but very small effects (1% or less; Bhargava & Manoli, 2015; Guyton et al., 2017; Goldin, Homonoff, & Meckel, 2022). A possible reason for the discrepant findings could be that the first study tested the intervention only on families who had filed taxes at least once before and hence were in the administrative data system, while the second two studies tested the intervention on a larger sample of households, including those who had never filed taxes (Linos et al., 2022).

Other studies show larger effects for nudges that were tested on families who had already had some contact with the government than for nudges that were tested on more general populations (Linos et al., 2022). When varied types of nudges were tested on samples of families who had not had contact with the government, take-up of the EITC did not increase. These results suggest that the barriers for low-income households that do not file returns are so substantial that even well-designed low-touch nudges will not be effective. Consistent with the hypothesis that more than simple nudges are needed to increase program take-up by significant amounts, a study by Bergman et al. (2023) showed that providing information to families eligible for a housing subsidy to move to a better neighborhood had little effect on take-up, but a more substantial intervention that assisted families in searching for new housing had a very large effect. The cost of the more substantial intervention, approximately $2,600 per family, while far smaller than the benefits of the intervention to the families, was much greater than the cost of a simple informational or similar nudge.

An issue with many interventions designed to reach those who might be eligible for a program but are not participating is the lack of a nationwide

---

[4] See https://www.acf.hhs.gov/opre/project/behavioral-interventions-advance-self-sufficiency-bias-2010-2016

administrative database that has contact information for all, or at least most, of the low-income population. Many other industrialized countries have such administrative databases and use them to contact eligible nonparticipants, particularly the most disadvantaged individuals and families (Ko & Moffitt, 2022). Many of the most disadvantaged families and individuals in the United States are not in any administrative data system, which makes them difficult to reach with many interventions. It is worth noting in this context that a default opt-in, such as the approach that has been so successful in increasing retirement savings (see Chapter 6), is not a realistic solution for program take-up. It is not currently feasible to automatically enroll families in social safety net programs and require them to actively opt out. In addition, establishing eligibility requires that income and other variables be checked by the government, and this necessarily requires that potential recipients voluntarily and actively participate.

FINDINGS

There is a substantial body of high-quality evidence about low rates of participation in social safety net programs and the relatively high rates of eligible families who do not receive benefits for which they are entitled (ranging from 16 to 72% of eligible people for different programs). Several findings about the role of behavioral principles in this problem stand out:

- Because these programs are aimed at low-income families, the problem of cognitive barriers is particularly relevant: lower-than-average levels of education and literacy are common for this population, yet the administrative complexity of applying for the programs and continuing to receive benefits is significant.
- Low-income individuals and families often cope with significant daily life challenges, so limited attention is a significant factor for this population.
- Because of the challenges faced by this population in daily life, they may not have the attention necessary to accurately perceive the future benefits of program application, resulting in a form of present bias.
- Many eligible individuals and families lack information about complex program requirements, and low levels of education and literacy impede their capacity to acquire the information they need to accurately estimate how likely they are to receive benefits.
- At least some individuals and families perceive social stigma associated with participating in social safety net programs; this reflects the importance of social norms in their decision-making processes.

- Many of the behavioral barriers identified in the literature have particularly strong effects for the lowest-income and most disadvantaged members of the low-income population, which means they are often least likely to participate in programs for which they are eligible.

In the realm of interventions to address incomplete take-up, the research has yielded a few findings:

- The evidence on the effectiveness of low-cost nudges to encourage participation is mixed, with some interventions showing modest effects on take-up but others showing no significant effect or any effect at all unless the study population includes households that have already participated in the program in the past.
- A few costly large-scale interventions, particularly those implemented by the U.S. Department of Agriculture for SNAP, appear to have had positive effects on take-up with interventions that provided additional information, simplified application forms, and otherwise reduced the administrative burden of applying but were more costly. Interventions that assist families directly are also more expensive than simple nudges but may have large payoffs.

More research is needed on both the behavioral factors that discourage take-up of social safety net programs and the most effective interventions to increase take-up.

- The importance of stigma and social norms, relative to other factors such as information and administrative burden, needs more study.
- As noted above, many of the interventions in this area have increased participation by low-income families not receiving benefits for which they are eligible. Nevertheless, most studies have not attempted to identify whether take-up increases only for the somewhat better-off families in the low-income population or also for the most needy, worse-off families.
- Additional evidence on nudges is needed to better understand how effectiveness depends on the nature of the study population and contextual factors.
- Some research has suggested that interventions that provide more direct assistance with applying for benefits, rather than simple informational or framing nudges, have a greater effect, but too few tests of those types of interventions have been conducted to yield a clear finding.

- More research is needed on how administrative burden in program application can be reduced while maintaining the need for accurate determination of eligibility to prevent errors and fraud.

REFERENCES

Bergman, P., Chetty, R., DeLuca, S., Hendren, N., Katz, L. F, & Palmer, P. (2023). *Creating moves to opportunity: Experimental evidence on barriers to neighborhood choice*. National Bureau of Economic Research. https://doi.org/10.3386/w26164

Bertrand, M., Mullainathan, S., & Shafir, E. (2006). Behavioral economics and marketing in aid of decision making among the poor. *Journal of Public Policy & Marketing*, 25(1), 8–23. https://doi.org/10.1509/jppm.25.1.8

Besley, T., & Coate, S. (1992). Workfare versus welfare: Incentive arguments for work requirements in poverty-alleviation programs. *The American Economic Review*, 82(1), 249–261. http://www.jstor.org/stable/2117613

Bhargava, S., & Manoli, D. (2015). Psychological frictions and the incomplete take-up of social benefits: Evidence from an IRS field experiment. *American Economic Review*, 105(11), 3489–3529. https://doi.org/10.1257/aer.20121493

Daponte, B. O., Sanders, S., & Taylor, L. (1999). Why do low-income households not use food stamps? Evidence from an experiment. *Journal of Human Resources*, 34(3), 612–628. https://doi.org/10.2307/146382

Decker, S. L., Abdus, S., & Lipton, B. J. (2022). Eligibility for and enrollment in Medicaid among nonelderly adults after implementation of the Affordable Care Act. *Medical Care Research and Review*, 79(1), 125–132. https://doi.org/10.1177/1077558721996851

De La Rosa, W., Sharma, E., Tully, S., Gianella, E., & Rino, G. (2021). Psychological ownership as an intervention: Addressing the government benefits participation gap. *NA—Advances in Consumer Research*, 318–319. Association for Consumer Research. http://www.acrwebsite.org/volumes/3000530/volumes/v49/NA-49

Dickert-Conlin, S., Fitzpatrick, K., Stacy, B., & Tiehen, L. (2021). The downs and ups of the SNAP caseload: What matters? *Applied Economic Perspectives and Policy*, 43(3), 1026–1050. https://doi.org/10.1002/aepp.13076

Falk, G. (2017). *The Temporary Assistance for Needy Families (TANF) block grant: Subsidized employment demonstration proposal: In brief*. Cornell University. https://hdl.handle.net/1813/79208

Finkelstein, A., & Notowidigdo, M. J. (2019). Take-up and targeting: Experimental evidence from SNAP. *The Quarterly Journal of Economics*, 134(3), 1505–1556. https://doi.org/10.1093/qje/qjz013

Fox, L., & Burns, K. (2021). *The supplemental poverty measure: 2020*. Current population reports. U.S. Census Bureau. https://www.census.gov/content/dam/Census/library/publications/2021/demo/p60-275.pdf

Ganong, P., & Liebman, J. B. (2018). The decline, rebound, and further rise in SNAP enrollment: Disentangling business cycle fluctuations and policy changes. *American Economic Journal: Economic Policy*, 10(4), 153–176. https://doi.org/10.1257/pol.20140016

Gennetian, L. A., Ludwig, J., McDade, T., & Sanbonmatsu, L. (2013). Why concentrated poverty matters. *Pathways Spring*, 10–13. SSRN. https://ssrn.com/abstract=2326579

Goldin, J., Homonoff, T., & Meckel, K. (2022). Issuance and incidence: SNAP benefit cycles and grocery prices. *American Economic Journal: Economic Policy*, 14(1), 152–178. https://10.1257/pol.20190777

Gray, C. (2019). Leaving benefits on the table: Evidence from SNAP. *Journal of Public Economics*, 179, 104054. https://doi.org/10.1016/j.jpubeco.2019.104054

Guyton, J., Langetieg, P., Manoli, D., Payne, M., Schafer, B., & Sebastiani, M. (2017). Reminders and recidivism: Using administrative data to characterize nonfilers and conduct EITC outreach. *American Economic Review*, 107(5), 471–475. https://doi.org/10.1257/aer.p20171062

Heinrich, C. J., Camacho, S., Henderson, S. C., Hernandez, M., & Joshi, E. (2022). Consequences of administrative burden for social safety nets that support the healthy development of children. *Journal of Policy Analysis and Management*, 41(1), 11–44.

Herd, P., DeLeire, T., Harvey, H., & Moynihan, D. P. (2013). Shifting administrative burden to the state: The case of Medicaid take-up. *Public Administration Review*, 73(Suppl_1), S69–S81. https://doi.org/10.1111/puar.12114

Herd, P., & Moynihan, D. P. (2018). *Administrative burden: Policymaking by other means.* Russell Sage Foundation.

Homonoff, T., & Somerville, J. (2021). Program recertification costs: Evidence from SNAP. *American Economic Journal: Economic Policy*, 13(4), 271–298. https://doi.org/10.1257/pol.20190272

Jones, M. R. (2013). *The EITC and labor supply: Evidence from a regression kink design.* Center for Administrative Records Research and Applications. U.S. Census Bureau.

Kenney, G. M., Lynch, V., Haley, J., & Huntress, M. (2012). Variation in Medicaid eligibility and participation among adults: Implications for the Affordable Care Act. *INQUIRY: The Journal of Health Care Organization, Provision, and Financing*, 49(3), 231–253. https://doi.org/10.5034/inquiryjrnl_49.03.08

Kingsley, G. T. (2017). *Trends in housing problems and federal housing assistance.* Urban Institute. https://www.urban.org/sites/default/files/publication/94146/trends-in-housing-problems-and-federal-housing-assistance.pdf

Kleven, H. J., & Kopczuk, W. (2011). Transfer program complexity and the take-up of social benefits. *American Economic Journal: Economic Policy*, 3(1), 54–90. https://doi.org/10.1257/pol.3.1.54

Ko, W., & Moffitt, R. A. (2022). *Take-up of social benefits.* NBER Working Paper 30148. National Bureau of Economic Research. https://doi.org/10.3386/w30148

Kopczuk, W., & Pop-Eleches, C. (2007). Electronic filing, tax preparers and participation in the Earned Income Tax Credit. *Journal of Public Economics*, 91(7–8), 1351–1367. https://doi.org/10.1016/j.jpubeco.2006.11.003

Lindbeck, A., Nyberg, S., & Weibull, J. W. (1999). Social norms and economic incentives in the welfare state. *The Quarterly Journal of Economics*, 114(1), 1–35. https://doi.org/10.1162/003355399555936

Linos, E., Prohofsky, A., Ramesh, A., Rothstein, J., & Unrath, M. (2022). Can nudges increase take-up of the EITC? Evidence from multiple field experiments. *American Economic Journal: Economic Policy*, 14(4), 432–452. https://doi.org/10.1257/pol.20200603

Lopoo, L. M., Heflin, C., & Boskovski, J. (2020). Testing behavioral interventions designed to improve on-time SNAP recertification. *Journal of Behavioral Public Administration*, 3(2). https://doi.org/10.30636/jbpa.32.183

Moffitt, R. (1983). An economic model of welfare stigma. *The American Economic Review*, 73(5), 1023–1035. https://www.jstor.org/stable/1814669

Mullainathan, S., & Shafir, E. (2013). *Scarcity: Why having too little means so much.* Macmillan.

Ribar, D. C., Edelhoch, M., & Liu, Q. (2008). Watching the clocks: The role of food stamp recertification and TANF time limits in caseload dynamics. *Journal of Human Resources*, 43(1), 208–238. https://doi.org/10.3368/jhr.43.1.208

Rossin-Slater, M. (2013). WIC in your neighborhood: New evidence on the impacts of geographic access to clinics. *Journal of Public Economics*, 102, 51–69. https://doi.org/10.1016/j.jpubeco.2013.03.009

Stuber, J., & Kronebusch, K. (2004). Stigma and other determinants of participation in TANF and Medicaid. *Journal of Policy Analysis and Management, 23*(3), 509–530. https://doi.org/10.1002/pam.20024

Stuber, J., & Schlesinger, M. (2006). Sources of stigma for means-tested government programs. *Social Science & Medicine, 63*(4), 933–945. https://doi.org/10.1016/j.socscimed.2006.01.012

Trisi, D., & Saenz, M. (2019, November 26). *Economic security programs cut poverty nearly in half over last 50 years*. Center on Budget and Policy Priorities. https://www.cbpp.org/sites/default/files/atoms/files/9-14-18pov.pdf

U.S. Department of Agriculture. (2022). *Trends in USDA Supplemental Nutrition Assistance Program participation rates: Fiscal year 2016 to fiscal year 2019*. https://fns-prod.azureedge.us/sites/default/files/resource-files/Trends2016-2019.pdf

8

Climate Change

Problems associated with global climate change are largely the result of human behavior that is intricately embedded in people's daily lives and entwined with societal and cultural norms (Constantino et al., 2022). Thus, mitigating and adapting to climate change requires changing human behavior and practices and sustaining those changes. Changes at the societal level, such as in infrastructure, manufacturing, and technological improvements, have an obvious role, and recent work suggests that behavioral interventions may be effective in increasing commitment to large-scale structural upgrades. However, this work is new and such approaches have not yet been deployed in practice (Forster, Kunreuther, & Weber, 2021). But changes at the individual, household, and business levels that are less expensive and can be implemented more quickly and easily also have a significant role to play. The 2022 report of the Intergovernmental Panel on Climate Change (International Panel on Climate Change, 2022) indicates that changes in food consumption, shifts to more sustainable use of consumer goods, reduced energy consumption, and other behavioral and lifestyle changes could play an important role in reducing emissions that contribute to climate change. Government regulators might affect those decisions through such actions as, for example, requiring changes in the pricing of products and services and how this pricing information is communicated to customers.

The changes that could be made at the individual and household levels that have the greatest potential impact on climate health include consuming less energy at the household level (heating, cooling, appliance use) and consuming less energy for transportation (airplane, automobile, and truck consumption).¹ Residential energy consumption accounts for approximately 20 percent of greenhouse gas emissions in the United States, and transportation (including transportation of goods) accounts for 25 percent of global greenhouse gas emissions (Goldstein, Gounaridis, & Newell, 2020; Ritchie, 2020).

Behavioral economists have studied decisions and behaviors related to activities with an impact on global climate change in a variety of contexts. The committee explored the challenges of influencing individual decision making related to climate in general and reviewed research in three sectors that account for substantial greenhouse gas emissions: energy use and efficiency, transportation, and land use. We also considered what this research suggests about how behavioral principles operate in these contexts. Before considering those sectors we first discuss the general issue of behavioral economic concepts in the domain of climate change.

DIFFICULTIES IN APPLYING BEHAVIORAL PRINCIPLES TO CLIMATE GOALS

There are numerous challenges in using behavioral economic concepts to address climate change. Some of the challenges that apply in many contexts are externalities—that is, the consequences or benefits that accrue to parties not directly involved—that are factored into traditional economic models, as well as anomalies that lead to behavior that is inconsistent with the traditional models. For example, there is a large temporal distance between the actions that might benefit the climate and their consequences, so decision makers may not easily perceive the effects of their actions. This distance can reinforce people's doubts about the scientific information and arguments they hear. The negative effects of climate change are also felt more acutely in some locations and by some groups of people than others. For instance, people living along coasts, in drought-prone areas, and those with fewer financial resources or members of groups that have been historically disadvantaged are generally most vulnerable to risks associated with climate change, such as polluted air.²

It is also true that there is significant uncertainty about the precise effects climate change will have by region and especially over longer time frames. Such uncertainty is inherent in the modeling on which climate scientists rely,

---

[1] The committee benefited from a workshop presentation on applications of behavioral economics to climate change by Åsa Löfgren (https://www.nationalacademies.org/event/07-18-2022/workshop-on-behavioral-economics-exploring-applications-and-research-methods) and a paper the committee commissioned on this subject (Messer, Ganguly, & Xie, 2022).

[2] See *Reports & Resources*, Global Change Research Program (https://www.globalchange.gov/browse).

but it is not easy for nonspecialists to assess the probabilities—particularly to understand the lower-probability but most disastrous possible outcomes. Making an individual or household decision based on complex probabilities is a difficult task. There is also significant ambiguity about the potential benefits of proposed adaptation and mitigation strategies. In general, the costs of changing behavior to reduce the risks of climate change are borne in the short term while the benefits are accrued in the medium and long terms. Neither people considering their own circumstances nor policy makers weighing competing political interests are likely to focus on long-term consequences. Furthermore, many of the benefits of preventing and mitigating climate change do not accrue to the people making the changes.

In addition, calculations about the climate effects of many behaviors and choices change as new information is accumulated and factored into modeling, and most people are well aware that there are many things scientists do not know. In the face of such uncertainty, people tend to envision changes in climate that more closely resemble their lived experience (a status quo bias) rather than envisioning a radically different climate. Finally, many of the behaviors in question are deeply embedded in people's livelihoods, their current homes and possessions, and long-standing habits and beliefs. With all of these pressures, it is not surprising that changing behaviors related to climate is difficult.

The committee commissioned a paper that explored the research on policy interventions to change behaviors in several sectors that emit large amounts of greenhouse gases.[3] The authors focused on the ratio of cost to benefit, the credibility of the evidence for interventions, and the durability of the effects. Drawing on this paper and the committee's review of other sources, this chapter discusses three domains for which the results appear to offer the most valuable information about the committee's core behavioral principles (see Chapter 3): energy use and efficiency, transportation, and land use decisions.

ENERGY USE AND EFFICIENCY

Most of the energy-related carbon dioxide emissions in the United States come from the transportation and electric power sectors, and as noted above, residential energy use contributes about 20 percent of overall carbon emissions (Goldstein, Gounaridis, & Newell, 2020). Changing individual behavior has the potential to be a faster and less expensive approach to reducing emissions than development of energy-efficient

---

[3]For a discussion of other areas and a detailed description of their search methods and selection criteria, see Messer, Ganguly, & Xie (2022).

technologies or policy approaches, such as cap-and-trade systems or a carbon tax (Vandenbergh, Barkenbus, & Gilligan, 2007; Dietz et al., 2009).

Energy efficiency can be increased by means of relatively costly, but comparatively long-lasting, one-shot decisions, such as replacing old appliances and other durable goods with new, energy-efficient ones and purchasing renewable energy. People can also reduce their consumption through frequently made decisions (using less energy at home). Policies that incorporate market-based solutions (such as subsidies and price increases) that specifically target behavioral interventions can create incentives for both kinds of decisions.[4] We consider several of the committee's core principles in this domain: limited attention and cognition, social preferences and norms, and present bias and reference dependence.

Limited Attention and Cognition

Messer, Ganguly, & Xie (2022) found a number of studies of interventions that primarily target users' limited attention and cognition (Allcott, 2011a; Shawhan et al., 2011; Gilbert & Graff Zivin, 2014; Ito, 2014; Jessoe & Rapson, 2014, 2015; Harding & Lamarche, 2016; Martin & Rivers, 2018; Burkhardt, Gillingham, & Kopalle, 2019; Carlsson, Jaime, & Villegas, 2021; Jessoe et al., 2021).[5] The wholesale cost of electricity is in constant flux as prices respond to varying patterns of usage. However, consumers generally pay flat or tiered rates that do not reflect wholesale prices at the time of consumption. Dynamic pricing structures (also called peak-load pricing and real-time pricing), rewards, and provision of information can all give customers incentives to use less energy at peak times. Messer, Ganguly, & Xie (2022) reviewed studies of the effects of these approaches on residential electricity use. The studies, which included large-scale field experiments, quasi-experiments, and natural experiments to identify causal effects, involved large sample sizes (mostly above 10,000 households).

The evidence regarding dynamic pricing structures is mixed. There was some evidence that real-time and peak-load pricing encouraged energy conservation during peak periods and that reductions continued after peak hours ended. Other studies, however, showed that customers responded only to price decreases, paid infrequent attention to pricing changes, and were more responsive to changes in average prices than marginal changes. Researchers noted the heavy cognitive burden of understanding utility pricing and how to track it; some studies focused on ways to provide

---

[4]For an extensive review of the empirical literature on behavioral interventions that target household energy demand, see Composto & Weber (2022).

[5]We summarize key findings from the detailed description of the research in each area provided by Messer, Ganguly, & Xie (2022); for more detailed information, see the full paper.

information and real-time feedback that could increase the salience of pricing for customers. Even monthly electric bills that provide specific information about patterns of usage have been shown to help households reduce consumption.

Technologies—such as smart meters, smart thermostats, in-home displays of usage, and apps that could report usage on smartphones—encourage consumers to respond to temporary price increases, though responses in the research appeared to vary with demographic characteristics and weather patterns (Jessoe & Rapson, 2014). In-home displays that provide updates about appliances' energy consumption appeared to help people form energy-conserving habits (Martin & Rivers, 2018), but other researchers suggest that there is little evidence that use of smart thermostats reduces energy consumption (Brandon et al., 2022). Although the studies indicate that providing information is an important feature of dynamic pricing approaches, the research did not make clear how behavioral factors may limit their effectiveness or how to better target the information provided.

Social Preferences and Norms

Moral suasion (informing people of desirable behaviors) and appealing to social norms and social comparisons are among the most used and studied behaviorally based interventions to encourage energy conservation (Carlsson et al., 2021a). Messer, Ganguly, & Xie (2022) identified numerous studies that examined treatment and persistent effects of moral suasion on reductions in residential energy use (Allcott & Mullainathan, 2010; Allcott, 2011b; Bollinger & Gillingham, 2012; Allcott & Rogers, 2014; Delmas & Lessem, 2014; Fowlie, Greenstone, & Wolfram, 2015, 2018; Graziano & Gillingham, 2015; Toledo, 2016; Brandon et al., 2017; Sudarshan, 2017; Ito, Ida, & Tanaka, 2018; Kraft-Todd et al., 2018; Allcott & Kessler, 2019; Holladay et al., 2019; Bollinger, Gillingham, & Ovaere, 2020; Myers & Souza, 2020; Bonan et al., 2021; Carlsson, Jaime, & Villegas, 2021; Carlsson et al., 2021a; Jessoe et al., 2021; Bollinger et al., 2022); they discussed several that used field experiments to represent the state of findings in this domain.

One study, which the authors identified as seminal, showed that consumers who viewed comparisons of their own electricity use to that of a neighbor reduced their consumption of electricity—and that this social-comparison intervention was cost-effective, though the effect sizes were modest (Alcott, 2011b). Subsequent work confirmed these findings and showed that they tended to persist but pointed to the importance of follow-up nudging. In addition, effects varied by setting and population. Other work on social norms and moral suasion has shown that results vary by type of energy user. Approaches tested have included invoking injunctive norms—appealing to perceived moral or social standards, for example, using smiling and frowning faces to show neighbor comparisons in energy use—providing real-time feedback on energy use by appliances, and making such information public. People whose energy use is close to the median in a particular context appear to be most responsive to such strategies.

Similarly, field experiments and quasi-experiments, as well as observational studies, have shown that peer effects and provision of information about social norms affect households' adoption of solar panels. This work suggests that the effects are strongest when neighboring solar panels are visible from the street and when they are numerous. Other work has suggested that prosocial information about solar energy and appeals to self-interest can reinforce the effects of peer influence.

Looking across the work, it appears that moral and social interventions, such as providing real-time feedback, and social comparisons, such as providing information, particularly about what peers do, are effective in convincing households to reduce their energy use, at least modestly, and that the effects persist.

Present Bias and Reference Dependence

Because energy is not paid for at the time it is consumed, consumers often fail to track the relationship between immediate energy consumption and delayed payments: in placing more weight on a present desire to use energy than the cost they will eventually pay, consumers demonstrate present bias. The studies identified by Messer, Ganguly, & Xie (2022) that examined interventions that address present bias suggest that electricity use can be inexpensively addressed using such interventions as making dynamic electricity pricing a default choice, albeit with modest effect sizes (Harding & Hsaiw, 2014; Allcott & Taubinsky, 2015; Palmer & Walls, 2015; Allcott & Greenstone, 2017; Gillingham, Keyes, & Palmer, 2018; De Groote & Verboven, 2019; Holladay et al., 2019; Tsvetanov, 2019; Liao, 2020; Wang, Ida, & Shimada, 2020; Fowlie et al., 2021; Werthschulte & Löschel, 2021; Boogen et al., 2022; Fraser, 2022; Giandomenico, Papineau, & Rivers, 2022). Other work suggests that consumers seesaw between conservation and overconsumption month after month in response to the billing cycle, a phenomenon that is not easily addressed with changes in billing methods (Gilbert & Graff Zivin, 2014).

Researchers have measured the effects of present bias on energy use using surveys and experiments to test such approaches as goal setting to increase awareness of, and counteract, overconsumption. Among the findings were that consumers may be more responsive to awareness of their own successes and failures in achieving their goals than to financial incentives. Other work examined default options in a program involving time-based dynamic electricity pricing and showed that when the default for participation was to opt in, most consumers did not opt out and did reduce their electricity use in response to higher prices during peak times.

TRANSPORTATION

Greenhouse gas emissions could be reduced by 40–70 percent if people in developed countries reduced their air travel; made "green" lifestyle choices; and chose to walk, cycle, and use electric transportation, according to estimates by the International Panel on Climate Change (2022). Behavioral interventions can address the effects on decision making about big purchases, such as buying hybrid and electric vehicles, as well as habits, such as opting for public transportation, replacing individual car trips with carpooling, and planning trips more efficiently. This section considers four of the committee's core principles in this domain: limited attention and cognition and present bias, reference dependence, and social preferences and norms.

Limited Attention and Cognition and Present Bias

Limited attention and cognition are especially relevant in decisions about vehicle purchases. Traditional economic models are based on the assumption that consumers correctly value future operating costs when assessing the tradeoffs between the cost of a vehicle and the expected costs. However, behavioral economists have shown that consumers frequently underestimate the savings they would realize with an energy-efficient vehicle when choosing between that option and a less fuel-efficient one and that car buyers typically calculate fuel savings without considering the present discounted value of future fuel costs (Gillingham & Palmer, 2014).

The studies identified in the paper commissioned for the committee provide mixed evidence about the factors that influence consumers' thinking about this tradeoff (Turrentine & Kurani, 2007; Gillingham & Palmer, 2014; Matthews et al., 2017; Alcott & Knittel, 2019; DellaValle & Zubaryeva, 2019; Gillingham, Houde, & van Benthem, 2021; Huse & Koptyug, 2022). Some work has shown that drawing consumers' attention to future operating costs, including for both fuel and taxes—increasing their salience—does affect their valuation and decisions. However, experimental evidence has not shown effects from providing individually tailored fuel cost information to consumers. Researchers have suggested that the way interventions are provided (e.g., timing) and the presence (or lack) of associated behavioral interventions may account for variation in results. For example, one study showed that making future cost savings salient for consumers significantly changed their choices only for people who strongly valued future benefits, preferred large vehicles, and self-identified as proenvironmental. The reviewed studies also showed that point-of-purchase interventions are important when promoting sales of electric vehicles.

Reference Dependence

Consumers can directly reduce their carbon footprints by opting to use public transportation for daily commutes and other long-distance trips, carpooling, or planning trips more efficiently. Established habits are a key barrier to such decisions, and strategies for addressing this include asking people to make visible personal commitments and personalized trip plans (Chen & Chao, 2011; Verplanken & Roy, 2016). Providing monetary incentives, such as free try-out periods for particular modes of public transportation, can also be an effective intervention (Matthies, Klöckner, & Preißner, 2006). Targeting commuters who are moving to a different home or town by providing information about the bus system, suggesting personalized travel plans for shopping, and providing free one-day bus tickets may also be effective (Bamberg, 2006; Fujii & Taniguchi, 2006). However, in contrast to the findings on electricity use, one study showed that social norm–based nudges were not effective at changing people's use of public transit to save on transportation costs (Gravert & Collentine, 2021).

Social Preferences and Norms

Many people associate driving with autonomy, which means that carpooling is not a natural preference for them. Moreover, both personal identities and cultures are associated with car travel, and age and gender affect willingness to use carpools. For example, some older people may prefer the convenience of being picked up by a private car but place a high value on the condition of carpool vehicles, while women may be more likely to avoid carpools because of safety concerns. Thus, in addition to addressing habits, interventions to encourage the use of public transportation and carpools have also addressed consumer heterogeneity and linked social identities (Root & Schintler, 2003; Matthies, Klöckner, & Preißner, 2006; Beale & Bonsall, 2007; Eriksson, Garvill, & Nordlund, 2008; Hörlén et al., 2008; Bolderdijk et al., 2013; Yeomans & Herberich, 2014; Kormos, Gifford, & Brown, 2015; Kristal & Whillans, 2020). However, as noted above, another study found that social norm–based nudges were not effective at changing people's usage of public transit (Gravert & Collentine, 2021). Mixed or null results for such interventions as letters, emails, noncash incentives, and personalized travel plans point to the difficulty of changing commuter behavior and the need to consider other factors.

Emphasizing social norms appears to be most effective if they are targeted to particular groups, such as people who are already intending to reduce their car use. For example, a campaign by municipal officials in Sweden that used the slogan "No ridiculous car trips" asked residents to submit written accounts of times they had driven unnecessarily, and gave small gifts to people who bicycled. In another study, marketing nudges motivated people to take the bus by removing misconceptions about the bus system, but only for certain groups of people. Marketing nudges are messages designed to encourage people to engage in certain behaviors by extolling the features of that activity, such as, in this case, by pointing out the appealing aspects of traveling by bus, as opposed to encouraging people to take the bus to benefit the planet. Combining that approach with a separate message that conceded that cars are convenient for some trips while buses should be the preferred alternative for others broadened the impact of the marketing. Similarly, targeting both the relatively short trips related to work more typical for men separately from the "trip chains" required for caretaking that involve several stops, often taken by women, is another example.

LAND USE DECISIONS

Climate change poses a severe threat to agricultural productivity, which is affected by variability in weather, rising temperatures, flooding and other natural disasters, and invasive pests. At the same time, agriculture contributes 19–20 percent of total greenhouse gas emissions worldwide (World Bank, 2021). Behavioral economists have explored decision making about land by both individual farmers and agricultural cooperatives. We discuss two of the committee's core principles for this domain: limited attention and cognition and social preferences and norms.

Limited Attention and Cognition

Agricultural conservation programs that encourage landowners to prevent soil erosion, protect drinking water, or preserve and restore forestland have been plagued by low adoption rates in part because of complexity associated with completing paperwork and navigating the enrollment requirements of federal programs.[6] Thus, making programs salient and simple is a logical intervention target. Researchers have found that even simple interventions such as changing default enrollment and sending reminders about available programs to farmers have increased their participation (Higgins et al., 2017; Palm-Forster & Messer, 2021). However, another study of reminder letters has shown that they are effective only for well-informed

---

[6]For information about such programs, see https://www.fsa.usda.gov/programs-and-services/conservation-programs/index

groups and for farmers whose contracts were expiring (Wallander et al., 2018).

Social Preferences and Norms

Messer, Ganguly, & Xie (2022) identified numerous studies showing that messaging related to social norms and preferences has been instrumental in nudging producers to adopt climate-smart practices (Wossen et al., 2013; Kwayu, Sallu, & Paavola, 2014; Czap et al., 2015, 2019; Kuhfuss et al., 2016; Lynne et al., 2016; Wallander et al., 2018; Dessart, Barreiro-Hurlé, & van Bavel, 2019; Bujold, Williamson, & Thulin, 2020; Butler et al., 2020; Le Coent, Préget, & Thoyer, 2021; Palm-Forster & Messer, 2021; Wu, Palm-Forster, & Messer, 2021; Banerjee, 2022; Palm-Forster et al., 2022; Rommel et al., 2022). For example, ego nudges—messages that appeal to individuals' desire for public engagement or recognition—in road signs that identified participants in conservation programs were effective in motivating farmers and other agricultural producers to follow through with practices they agreed to adopt because they viewed their decisions as consistent with their self-images and identities. Similarly, empathy nudges are effective in promoting proenvironmental decisions.[7]

Among the evidence from this work is the finding that producers are particularly responsive to nudges informing them about other farmers who have already adopted climate-smart practices and programs in which participation is already high. However, social norm strategies can backfire when only a small number of farmers have already adopted desired practices. There is also evidence that the messenger who delivers a norm-based nudge matters: producers were more likely to act when they received positive information from individuals they viewed as similar to themselves. Social networks can be used to send credible signals about proenvironmental stewardship actions producers are taking (e.g., certification and verification programs).

FINDINGS

The work in the domains of energy use and efficiency, transportation, and land use demonstrates the importance of addressing behavioral factors that influence decision making. Studies in all three domains have addressed limited attention and cognition and appeals to social norms; present bias and reference dependence have also been considered in the domains of

---

[7]Empathy nudges are designed to appeal to specific behavioral factors, such as one's sense of self (ego) or the potential to feel empathy.

energy use and transportation. This work demonstrates several important key points:

- Providing customers with information that is carefully targeted to their concerns can address present bias and limited attention and cognition to encourage energy conservation, climate-friendly transportation decisions, and engagement in land conservation programs.
- Nudges related to social norms and preferences—if carefully targeted to specific populations—showed modest effects for encouraging energy conservation, climate-friendly transportation choices, and land use decisions. Since these are low-cost interventions, they still often have a high return (despite modest effect sizes).

Studies across contexts of interventions that address different behavioral obstacles (based on different key principles) highlight the degree to which effects vary by context, population, and goal: they point to the importance of targeting interventions to specific populations and to specific points of decision making. For low-cost interventions, this careful focus may be less important since achieving results for some portion of those who experience the intervention may be a reasonable outcome. Moreover, in many cases, such as the messaging about use of public transportation, there would be little downside to incorporating multiple tailored messages into a nudge program. The results of a meta-analysis supported the value of studying packages of interventions rather than single ones in isolation (Khanna et al., 2021).

Most of the behavioral economic research that the committee found in its search (including the commissioned paper, workshop presentation, and our own investigations) showed comparatively small effect sizes. Meta-analyses of effects of behavioral interventions showed varied results and a lack of evidence of long-run effects (Nisa et al., 2019; Carlsson et al., 2021b; Khanna et al., 2021). We note, however, that these results look modest in part because of the magnitude of the overall problem. It would be necessary to reduce emissions by more than 50 percent, for example, just to reach a target of limiting global warming to an increase of 1.5 degrees. However, the behavioral interventions that have been studied are generally low in cost and easy to implement. Individual-level decisions related to energy consumption, transportation, and land use may seem minor in the face of so vast and complex a challenge as global climate change, but interventions can be targeted to specific populations and to specific points of decision making, and thus address significant behavioral obstacles that affect individual decision making.

Addressing the problem of climate change fundamentally requires policies to address externalities and coordinate across multiple actors. While these tools fit squarely in the traditional economics toolkit, they require significant changes in the behavior of a range of actors. Those behavioral changes and the policies designed to induce them will be shaped by the core behavioral principles discussed in this report. Taken together, an array of comparatively low-cost, low-effort measures could make a very important contribution to the problem of climate change if applied in a sustained way across multiple sectors.

REFERENCES

Allcott, H. (2011a). Rethinking real-time electricity pricing. *Resource and Energy Economics*, 33, 820–842. https://doi.org/10.1016/j.reseneeco.2011.06.003

———. (2011b). Social norms and energy conservation. *Journal of Public Economics*, 95(9–10), 1082–1095. https://doi.org/10.1016/j.jpubeco.2011.03.003

Allcott, H., & Greenstone, M. (2017). *Measuring the welfare effects of residential energy efficiency programs*. NBER Working Paper 23386. National Bureau of Economic Research. https://doi.org/10.3386/w23386

Allcott, H., & Kessler, J. B. (2019). The welfare effects of nudges: A case study of energy use social comparisons. *American Economic Journal: Applied Economics*, 11, 236–276. https://doi.org/10.1257/app.20170328

Allcott, H., & Knittel, C. (2019). Are consumers poorly informed about fuel economy? Evidence from two experiments. *American Economic Journal: Economic Policy*, 11, 1–37. https://doi.org/10.1257/pol.20170019

Allcott, H., & Mullainathan, S. (2010). Behavior and energy policy. *Science*, 327, 1204–1205. https://doi.org/10.1126/science.1180775

Allcott, H., & Rogers, T. (2014). The short-run and long-run effects of behavioral interventions: Experimental evidence from energy conservation. *American Economic Review*, 104, 3003–3037. https://doi.org/10.1257/aer.104.10.3003

Allcott, H., & Taubinsky, D. (2015). Evaluating behaviorally motivated policy: Experimental evidence from the lightbulb market. *American Economic Review*, 105, 2501–2538. https://doi.org/10.1257/aer.20131564

Bamberg, S. (2006). Is a residential relocation a good opportunity to change people's travel behavior? Results from a theory-driven intervention study. *Environment and Behavior*, 38, 820–840. https://doi.org/10.1177/0013916505285091

Banerjee, S. (2022). Use of experimental economics in policy design and evaluation: An application to water resources and other environmental domains. *Oxford Research Encyclopedia of Environmental Science*. https://doi.org/10.1093/acrefore/9780199389414.013.764

Beale, J. R., & Bonsall, P. W. (2007). Marketing in the bus industry: A psychological interpretation of some attitudinal and behavioural outcomes. *Transportation Research Part F: Traffic Psychology and Behaviour*, 10, 271–287. https://doi.org/10.1016/j.trf.2006.11.001

Bolderdijk, J. W., Steg, L., Geller, E. S., Lehman, P. K., & Postmes, T. (2013). Comparing the effectiveness of monetary versus moral motives in environmental campaigning. *Nature Climate Change*, 3, 413–416. https://doi.org/10.1038/nclimate1767

Bollinger, B., & Gillingham, K. (2012). Peer effects in the diffusion of solar photovoltaic panels. *Marketing Science*, 31, 900–912. https://doi.org/10.1287/mksc.1120.0727

Bollinger, B., Gillingham, K. T., & Ovaere, M. (2020). Field experimental evidence shows that self-interest attracts more sunlight. *Proceedings of the National Academy of Sciences*, 117, 20503–20510. https://doi.org/10.1073/pnas.2004428117

Bollinger, B., Gillingham, K., Kirkpatrick, A. J., & Sexton, S. (2022). Visibility and peer influence in durable good adoption. *Marketing Science*, *41*, 453–476. https://doi.org/10.1287/mksc.2021.1306

Bonan, J., Cattaneo, C., d'Adda, G., & Tavoni, M. (2021). Can social information programs be more effective? The role of environmental identity for energy conservation. *Journal of Environmental Economics and Management*, *108*, 102467. https://doi.org/10.1016/j.jeem.2021.102467

Boogen, N., Daminato, C., Filippini, M., & Obrist, A. (2022). Can information about energy costs affect consumers' choices? Evidence from a field experiment. *Journal of Economic Behavior & Organization*, *196*, 568–588. https://doi.org/10.1016/j.jebo.2022.02.014

Brandon, A., Ferraro, P. J., List, J. A., Metcalfe, R. D., Price, M. K., & Rundhammer, F. (2017). *Do the effects of nudges persist? Theory and Evidence from 38 natural field experiments*. NBER Working Paper 23277. National Bureau of Economic Research. https://doi.org/10.3386/w23277

Brandon, A., Clapp, C. M., List, J. A., Metcalfe, R. D., & Price, M. (2022). *The human perils of scaling smart technologies: Evidence from field experiments*. NBER Working Paper 30482. National Bureau of Economic Research. https://doi.org/10.3386/w30482

Bujold, P., Williamson, K., & Thulin, E. (2020). *The science of changing behavior for environmental outcomes: A literature review*. Rare Center for Behavior & the Environment and the Scientific and Technical Advisory Panel to the Global Environment Facility. https://behavior.rare.org/literature-review/

Burkhardt, J., Gillingham, K., & Kopalle, P. K. (2019). *Experimental evidence on the effect of information and pricing on residential electricity consumption*. NBER Working Paper 25576. National Bureau of Economic Research. https://doi.org/10.3386/w25576

Butler, J. M., Fooks, J. R., Messer, K. D., & Palm-Forster, L.H. (2020). Addressing social dilemmas with mascots, information, and graphics. *Economic Inquiry*, *58*, 150–168. https://doi.org/10.1111/ecin.12783

Carlsson, F., Jaime, M., & Villegas, C. (2021). Behavioral spillover effects from a social information campaign. *Journal of Environmental Economics and Management*, *109*, 102325. https://doi.org/10.1016/j.jeem.2020.102325

Carlsson, F., Gravert, C., Johansson-Stenman, O., & Kurz, V. (2021a). The use of green nudges as an environmental policy instrument. *Review of Environmental Economics and Policy*, *15*, 216–237. https://doi.org/10.1086/715524

Carlsson, F., Kataria, M., Krupnick, A., Lampi, E., Löfgren, Å., Qin, P., Sterner, T., & Yang, X. (2021b). The climate decade: Changing attitudes on three continents. *Journal of Environmental Economics and Management*, *107*, 102426. https://doi.org/10.1016/j.jeem.2021.102426

Chen, C. F., & Chao, W. H. (2011). Habitual or reasoned? Using the theory of planned behavior, technology acceptance model, and habit to examine switching intentions toward public transit. *Transportation Research Part F: Traffic Psychology and Behaviour*, *14*, 128–137. https://doi.org/10.1016/j.trf.2010.11.006

Composto, J. W., & Weber, E. U. (2022). Effectiveness of behavioural interventions to reduce household energy demand: A scoping review. *Environmental Research Letters*, *17*(6). https://doi.org/10.1088/1748-9326/ac71b8

Constantino, S. M., Sparkman, G., Kraft-Todd, G. T., Bicchieri, C., Centola, D., Shell-Duncan, B., Vogt, S., & Weber, E. U. (2022). Scaling up change: A critical review and practical guide to harnessing social norms for climate action. *Psychological Science in the Public Interest*, *23*(2), 50–97. https://doi.org/10.1177/15291006221105279

Czap, N. V., Czap, H. J., Lynne, G. D., & Burbach, M. E. (2015). Walk in my shoes: Nudging for empathy conservation. *Ecological Economics*, *118*, 147–158. https://doi.org/10.1016/j.ecolecon.2015.07.010

Czap, N. V., Czap, H. J., Banerjee, S., & Burbach, M. E. (2019). Encouraging farmers' participation in the Conservation Stewardship Program: A field experiment. *Ecological Economics, 161*, 130–143. https://doi.org/10.1016/j.ecolecon.2019.03.010

De Groote, O., & Verboven, F. (2019). Subsidies and time discounting in new technology adoption: Evidence from solar photovoltaic systems. *American Economic Review, 109*, 2137–2172. https://doi.org/10.1257/aer.20161343

DellaValle, N., & Zubaryeva, A. (2019). Can we hope for a collective shift in electric vehicle adoption? Testing salience and norm-based interventions in South Tyrol, Italy. *Energy Research & Social Science, 55*, 46–61. https://doi.org/10.1016/j.erss.2019.05.005

Delmas, M. A., & Lessem, N. (2014). Saving power to conserve your reputation? The effectiveness of private versus public information. *Journal of Environmental Economics and Management, 67*, 353–370. https://doi.org/10.1016/j.jeem.2013.12.009

Dessart, F. J., Barreiro-Hurlé, J., & van Bavel, R. (2019). Behavioural factors affecting the adoption of sustainable farming practices: A policy-oriented review. *European Review of Agricultural Economics, 46*, 417–471. https://doi.org/10.1093/erae/jbz019

Dietz, T., Gardner, G. T., Gilligan, J., Stern, P. C., & Vandenbergh, M. P. (2009). Household actions can provide a behavioral wedge to rapidly reduce US carbon emissions. *Proceedings of the National Academy of Sciences, 106*(44), 18452–18456. https://doi.org/10.1073/pnas.0908738106

Eriksson, L., Garvill, J., & Nordlund, A. M. (2008). Interrupting habitual car use: The importance of car habit strength and moral motivation for personal car use reduction. *Transportation Research Part F: Traffic Psychology and Behaviour, 11*, 10–23. https://doi.org/10.1016/j.trf.2007.05.004

Forster, H. A., Kunreuther, H., & Weber, E. U. (2021). Planet or pocketbook? Environmental motives complement financial motives for energy efficiency across the political spectrum in the United States. *Energy Research & Social Science, 74*, 101938. https://doi.org/10.1016/j.erss.2021.101938

Fowlie, M., Greenstone, M., & Wolfram, C. (2015). Are the non-monetary costs of energy efficiency investments large? Understanding low take-up of a free energy efficiency program. *American Economic Review, 105*, 201–204. https://doi.org/10.1257/aer.p20151011

———. (2018). Do energy efficiency investments deliver? Evidence from the Weatherization Assistance Program. *The Quarterly Journal of Economics, 133*(3), 1597–1644. https://doi.org/10.1093/qje/qjy005

Fowlie, M., Wolfram, C., Baylis, P., Spurlock, C. A., Todd-Blick, A., & Cappers, P. (2021). Default effects and follow-on behaviour: Evidence from an electricity pricing program. *The Review of Economic Studies, 88*(6), 2886–2934. https://doi.org/10.1093/restud/rdab018

Fraser, A. (2022). Success, failure, and information: How households respond to energy conservation goals. *Journal of the Association of Environmental and Resource Economists, 10*(1). https://doi.org/10.1086/721094

Fujii, S., & Taniguchi, A. (2006). Determinants of the effectiveness of travel feedback programs—A review of communicative mobility management measures for changing travel behaviour in Japan. *Transport Policy, 13*, 339–348. https://doi.org/10.1016/j.tranpol.2005.12.007

Giandomenico, L., Papineau, M., & Rivers, N. (2022). A systemic review of energy efficiency home retrofit evaluation studies. *Annual Review of Resource Economics, 14*(1), 689–708. https://doi.org/10.1146/annurev-resource-111920-124353

Gilbert, B., & Graff Zivin, J. (2014). Dynamic salience with intermittent billing: Evidence from smart electricity meters. *Journal of Economic Behavior & Organization, 107*, 176–190. https://doi.org/10.1016/j.jebo.2014.03.011

Gillingham, K., & Palmer, K. (2014). Bridging the energy efficiency gap: Policy insights from economic theory and empirical evidence. *Review of Environmental Economics and Policy, 8*, 18–38. https://doi.org/10.1093/reep/ret021

Gillingham, K., Keyes, A., & Palmer, K. (2018). Advances in evaluating energy efficiency policies and programs. *Annual Review of Resource Economics*, *10*(1), 511–532.

Gillingham, K., Houde, S., & van Benthem, A. (2021). Consumer myopia in vehicle purchases: Evidence from a natural experiment. *American Economic Journal: Economic Policy*, *13*(3), 1–33. https://doi.org/10.1257/pol.20200322

Goldstein, B., Gounaridis, D., & Newell, J. P. (2020). The carbon footprint of household energy use in the United States. *Proceedings of the National Academy of Sciences*, *117*(32), 19122–19130. https://doi.org/10.1073/pnas.1922205117

Gravert, C., & Collentine, L. O. (2021). When nudges aren't enough: Norms, incentives and habit formation in public transport usage. *Journal of Economic Behavior & Organization*, *190*, 1–4.

Graziano, M., & Gillingham, K. (2015). Spatial patterns of solar photovoltaic system adoption: The influence of neighbors and the built environment. *Journal of Economic Geography*, *15*, 815–839. https://doi.org/10.1093/jeg/lbu036

Harding, M., & Hsiaw, A. (2014). Goal setting and energy conservation. *Journal of Economic Behavior & Organization*, *107*, 209–227. https://doi.org/10.1016/j.jebo.2014.04.012

Harding, M., & Lamarche, C. (2016). Empowering consumers through data and smart technology: Experimental evidence on the consequences of time-of-use electricity pricing policies. *Journal of Policy Analysis and Management*, *35*, 906–931. https://doi.org/10.1002/pam.21928

Higgins, N., Hellerstein, D., Wallander, S., & Lynch, L. (Eds.). (2017). *Economic experiments for policy analysis and program design: A guide for agricultural decision makers*. Economic Research Report 236. Economic Research Service, U.S. Department of Agriculture.

Holladay, S., LaRiviere, J., Novgorodsky, D., & Price, M. (2019). Prices versus nudges: What matters for search versus purchase of energy investments? *Journal of Public Economics*, *172*, 151–173. https://doi.org/10.1016/j.jpubeco.2018.12.004

Hörlén, A., Forslund, S., Nilsson, P., & Jönsson, L. (2008). *Civitas SMILE: Utvärderingsrapport Inga löjliga bilresor*. http://www.abcmultimodal.eu/evaluation-no-ridiculous-car-trips.html

Huse, C., & Koptyug, N. (2022). Salience and policy instruments: Evidence from the auto market. *Journal of the Association of Environmental and Resource Economists*, *9*, 345–382. https://doi.org/10.1086/716878

International Panel on Climate Change. (2022). *Climate change 2022: Impacts, adaptation and vulnerability*. Contribution of Working Group II to the Sixth Assessment Report of the Intergovernmental Panel on Climate Change. Cambridge University Press. https://www.ipcc.ch/report/ar6/wg2

Ito, K. (2014). Do consumers respond to marginal or average price? Evidence from nonlinear electricity pricing. *American Economic Review*, *104*(2), 537–563. https://doi.org/10.1257/aer.104.2.537

Ito, K., Ida, T., & Tanaka, M. (2018). Moral suasion and economic incentives: Field experimental evidence from energy demand. *American Economic Journal: Economic Policy*, *10*, 240–267. https://doi.org/10.1257/pol.20160093

Jessoe, K., & Rapson, D. (2014). Knowledge is (less) power: Experimental evidence from residential energy use. *American Economic Review*, *104*, 1417–1438. https://doi.org/10.1257/aer.104.4.1417

———. (2015). Commercial and industrial demand response under mandatory time-of-use electricity pricing. *The Journal of Industrial Economics*, *63*, 397–421. https://doi.org/10.1111/joie.12082

Jessoe, K., Lade, G. E., Loge, F., & Spang, E. (2021). Spillovers from behavioral interventions: Experimental evidence from water and energy use. *Journal of the Association of Environmental and Resource Economists*, *8*, 315–346. https://doi.org/10.1086/711025

Khanna, T. M., Baiocchi, G., Callaghan, M., Creutzig, F., Guias, H., Haddaway, N. R., Hirth, L., Javaid, A., Koch, N., Laukemper, S., & Löschel, A. (2021). A multi-country meta-analysis on the role of behavioural change in reducing energy consumption and CO_2 emissions in residential buildings. *Nature Energy, 6(9)*, 925–932. https://doi.org/10.1038/s41560-021-00866-x

Kormos, C., Gifford, R., & Brown, E. (2015). The influence of descriptive social norm information on sustainable transportation behavior: A field experiment. *Environment and Behavior, 47*, 479–501. https://doi.org/10.1177/0013916513520416

Kraft-Todd, G. T., Bollinger, B., Gillingham, K., Lamp, S., & Rand, D. G. (2018). Credibility-enhancing displays promote the provision of non-normative public goods. *Nature, 563*, 245–248. https://doi.org/10.1038/s41586-018-0647-4

Kristal, A. S., & Whillans, A. V. (2020). What we can learn from five naturalistic field experiments that failed to shift commuter behaviour. *Nature Human Behavior, 4*, 169–176. https://doi.org/10.1038/s41562-019-0795-z

Kuhfuss, L., Préget, R., Thoyer, S., Hanley, N., Coent, P. L., & Désolé, M. (2016). Nudges, social norms, and permanence in agri-environmental schemes. *Land Economics, 92*, 641–655. https://doi.org/10.3368/le.92.4.641

Kwayu, E. J., Sallu, S. M., & Paavola, J. (2014). Farmer participation in the equitable payments for watershed services in Morogoro, Tanzania. *Ecosystem Services, 7*, 1–9. https://doi.org/10.1016/j.ecoser.2013.12.006

Le Coent, P., Préget, R., & Thoyer, S. (2021). Farmers follow the herd: A theoretical model on social norms and payments for environmental services. *Environmental and Resource Economics, 78*, 287–306. https://doi.org/10.1007/s10640-020-00532-y

Liao, Y. (2020). Weather and the decision to go solar: Evidence on costly cancellations. *Journal of the Association of Environmental and Resource Economists, 7*, 1–33. https://doi.org/10.1086/705592

Lynne, G. D., Czap, N. V., Czap, H. J., & Burbach, M. E. (2016). A theoretical foundation for empathy conservation: Toward avoiding the tragedy of the commons. *Review of Behavioral Economics, 3*, 243–279. https://doi.org/10.1561/105.00000052

Martin, S., & Rivers, N. (2018). Information provision, market incentives, and household electricity consumption: Evidence from a large-scale field deployment. *Journal of the Association of Environmental and Resource Economists, 5*, 207–231. https://doi.org/10.1086/694036

Matthews, L., Lynes, J., Riemer, M., Del Matto, T., & Cloet, N. (2017). Do we have a car for you? Encouraging the uptake of electric vehicles at point of sale. *Energy Policy, 100*, 79–88. https://doi.org/10.1016/j.enpol.2016.10.001

Matthies, E., Klöckner, C. A., & Preißner, C. L. (2006). Applying a modified moral decision making model to change habitual care use: How can commitment be effective? *Applied Psychology, 55*, 91–106. https://doi.org/10.1111/j.1464-0597.2006.00237.x

Messer, K., Ganguly, D., & Xie, L. (2022). *Applications of behavioral economics to climate change mitigation and adaptation.* Commissioned paper prepared for the Committee on Future Directions for Applying Behavioral Economics to Policy, National Academies of Sciences, Engineering, and Medicine. https://nap.nationalacademies.org/resource/26874/Applying_Behavioral_Economics_to_Climate_Change_Messer_Ganguly_Xie.pdf

Myers, E., & Souza, M. (2020). Social comparison nudges without monetary incentives: Evidence from home energy reports. *Journal of Environmental Economics and Management, 101*, 102315. https://doi.org/10.1016/j.jeem.2020.102315

Nisa, C. F., Bélanger, J. J., Schumpe, B. M., & Faller, D. G. (2019). Meta-analysis of randomised controlled trials testing behavioural interventions to promote household action on climate change. *Nature Communications, 10*(1), 1–13. https://doi.org/10.1038/s41467-019-12457-2

Palm-Forster, L. H., & Messer, K. D. (2021). Experimental and behavioral economics to inform agri-environmental programs and policies. *Handbook of agricultural economics, 5*, 4331–4406. Elsevier.

Palm-Forster, L. H., Griesinger, M., Butler, J. M., Fooks, J. R., & Messer, K. D. (2022). Stewardship signaling and use of social pressure to reduce nonpoint source pollution. *Land Economics, 98*(4), 618–638. https://doi.org/10.3368/le.98.4.041820-0056R1

Palmer, K., & Walls, M. (2015). Limited attention and the residential energy efficiency gap. *American Economic Review, 105*, 192–195. https://doi.org/10.1257/aer.p20151009

Ritchie, H. (2020). Cars, planes, trains: Where do CO_2 emissions from transport come from? *Our World in Data.* https://ourworldindata.org/co2-emissions-from-transport

Rommel, J., Schulze, C., Matzdorf, B., Sagebiel, J., & Wechner, V. (2022). Learning about German farmers' willingness to cooperate from public goods games and expert predictions. *Q Open*, qoac023. https://doi.org/10.1093/qopen/qoac023

Root, A., & Schintler, L. (2003). Gender, transportation, and the environment. *Handbook of transport and the environment*, 647–663. Emerald Group Publishing Limited.

Shawhan, D., Messer, K. D., Schulze, W. D., & Schuler, R. E. (2011). An experimental test of automatic mitigation of wholesale electricity prices. *International Journal of Industrial Organization, 29*(1), 46–53.

Sudarshan, A. (2017). Nudges in the marketplace: The response of household electricity consumption to information and monetary incentives. *Journal of Economic Behavior & Organization, 134*, 320–335. https://doi.org/10.1016/j.jebo.2016.12.015

Toledo, C. (2016). Do environmental messages work on the poor? Experimental evidence from Brazilian favelas. *Journal of the Association of Environmental and Resource Economists, 3*, 37–83. https://doi.org/10.1086/683803

Tsvetanov, T. (2019). When the carrot goes bad: The effect of solar rebate uncertainty. *Energy Economics, 81*, 886–898. https://doi.org/10.1016/j.eneco.2019.05.028

Turrentine, T. S., & Kurani, K. S. (2007). Car buyers and fuel economy? *Energy Policy, 35*, 1213–1223. https://doi.org/10.1016/j.enpol.2006.03.005

Vandenbergh, M. P., Barkenbus, J., & Gilligan, J. (2007). Individual carbon emissions: The low-hanging fruit. *University of California, Los Angeles Law Review, 55*, 1701. https://heinonline.org/HOL/P?h=hein.journals/uclalr55&i=1713

Verplanken, B., & Roy, D. (2016). Empowering interventions to promote sustainable lifestyles: Testing the habit discontinuity hypothesis in a field experiment. *Journal of Environmental Psychology, 45*, 127–134. https://doi.org/10.1016/j.jenvp.2015.11.008

Wallander, S., Bowman, M., Beeson, P., & Claassen, R. (2018, January 5–7). *Farmers and habits: The challenge of identifying the sources of persistence in tillage decisions* [Conference presentation 266307]. 2018 Allied Social Sciences Association Annual Meeting, Philadelphia, PA, United States.

Wang, W., Ida, T., & Shimada, H. (2020). Default effect versus active decision: Evidence from a field experiment in Los Alamos. *European Economic Review, 128*, 103498. https://doi.org/10.1016/j.euroecorev.2020.103498

Werthschulte, M., & Löschel, A. (2021). On the role of present bias and biased price beliefs in household energy consumption. *Journal of Environmental Economics and Management, 109*, 102500. https://doi.org/10.1016/j.jeem.2021.102500

World Bank. (2021). *Climate-smart agriculture.* https://www.worldbank.org/en/topic/climate-smart-agriculture

Wossen, T., Berger, T., Mequaninte, T., & Alamirew, B. (2013). Social network effects on the adoption of sustainable natural resource management practices in Ethiopia. *International Journal of Sustainable Development & World Ecology, 20*, 477–483. https://doi.org/10.1080/13504509.2013.856048

Wu, S., Palm-Forster, L. H., & Messer, K. D. (2021). Impact of peer comparisons and firm heterogeneity on nonpoint source water pollution: An experimental study. *Resource and Energy Economics, 63*, 101142. https://doi.org/10.1016/j.reseneeco.2019.101142

Yeomans, M., & Herberich, D. (2014). An experimental test of the effect of negative social norms on energy-efficient investments. *Journal of Economic Behavior & Organization, 108*, 187–197.

9

Education

The ongoing COVID-19 pandemic has both highlighted and exacerbated long-standing problems in public education. Scores on the National Assessment of Educational Progress released in October 2022, for example, showed the largest declines since 1990 in reading performance and a first-ever decrease in mathematics performance for nine-year-old students.[1] These and other declines in test performance have disproportionately affected low-income students, students from historically underserved groups, and English-language learners (Kuhfeld, Soland, & Lewis, 2022; Office for Civil Rights, 2022). But the urgency of addressing these negative effects of the pandemic comes in the context of decades of work to address persistent problems: to boost student achievement and attainment, reduce achievement gaps, and provide strong motivations for teachers and administrators to make choices that will benefit student learning.[2]

Behavioral economic interventions have the potential to address many of the factors that impede educational attainment and achievement, from students' motivations to bureaucratic challenges associated with securing admission and funding for postsecondary education. Researchers have begun to examine how behavioral economics successes in other domains could apply to challenges in K–12 and postsecondary education, and the volume of such research has increased in the past decade. Scholars have

---

[1] See *The Nation's Report Card*: https://www.nationsreportcard.gov/highlights/ltt/2022
[2] For data on achievement gaps and trends, see https://cepa.stanford.edu/educational-opportunity-monitoring-project/achievement-gaps/race/. For data on educational attainment, see https://nces.ed.gov/programs/raceindicators/indicator_rfa.asp

studied interventions targeting students, teachers, and parent–child interactions at the elementary, secondary, and postsecondary levels, although the quantity of studies varies considerably across these domains.

Thus far, those approaches to educational improvements have not borne substantial fruit (Levitt et al., 2016; Damgaard & Nielsen, 2018). This chapter focuses on the limited available research on parent–child interactions, access to postsecondary schooling, and ways to improve teacher performance, linking this literature to the five core principles.

PARENT–CHILD INTERACTIONS

Researchers have explored the use of nudges and rewards of various kinds to boost achievement among students at various stages of development, focusing on the behavioral factors that may influence parent–child interactions. Parents are clearly crucial teachers and role models in their children's lives. While they realize the importance of educational investments in their children, the potential impact of a particular event, such as reading to their child, can seem vague and remote, while the competing demands on their time, coupled with fatigue at the end of the day, are immediate and well understood (Lavecchia, Liu, & Oreopoulos, 2016).

To address the achievement of younger students and overcome parents' limited attention and present bias, researchers have tested the use of low-touch nudges, such as goal setting, reward programs, text reminders, and efforts to increase parents' engagement with their young children to improve literacy (Mayer et al., 2019; York, Loeb, & Doss, 2019). These nudges can serve as commitment devices and reminders of the importance of these activities for parents when they are faced with more immediate work and family obligations.

Moreover, even with the best of intentions, parents often have inaccurate beliefs about their children's education. For instance, they may have limited information about the number of days their child is absent or have an inaccurate understanding of an appropriate number of absences for a child. To overcome these limitations, one recent light-touch nudge in Philadelphia showed that a letter sent home to parents informing them of their child's absences increased daily attendance and decreased chronic absenteeism (Rogers & Feller, 2018).

Adolescents also have a particularly strong present bias, which can lead them to make suboptimal choices about their education. In this situation, too, parents may not be aware of their children's choices or the significance of those choices in the long term. One recent study in Wisconsin found that sending brochures to parents informing them of the benefits of science, technology, engineering, and mathematics (STEM) classes, along with a newly created website, increased STEM high school coursework completion (Harackiewicz et al., 2012). These researchers provided information to the parents, rather than the students, understanding that parents will communicate their preferences to their children and will often make more beneficial decisions that focus on children's long-term welfare rather than their short-term preferences.

ACCESS TO POSTSECONDARY EDUCATION

An area that has received significant research attention is the application of behavioral economic ideas for increasing college applications, applications for financial aid, and college enrollment for students who have completed high school. The benefits to both individuals and society when students complete high school and obtain postsecondary degrees are significant. However, low-income students and those from historically underserved groups tend to fall out of the education pipeline more easily than do their more advantaged peers (with similar performance metrics): they are less likely both to attend college and to opt for more selective institutions (Hoxby & Avery, 2013; Wilbur & Roscigno, 2016). Factors that may impede lower-income students include behavioral biases (status quo, debt aversion, and present bias), the administrative burden of the admissions process, and their uncertainty about how to obtain financial aid (Dynarski & Scott-Clayton, 2006; Hoxby & Turner, 2015; Dynarski et al., 2021). The process of learning about college, applying for admission, and applying for financial aid poses a significant administrative burden (see Chapter 13) that is daunting for any student but especially so for historically disadvantaged students.

One promising approach has been to address students' inaccurate beliefs about their prospects at key points in the education life cycle, such as the transition from middle school to high school coursework. Interventions have been designed to foster students' belief in their intellectual capacity, affirm their perception of the value of school, and challenge negative stereotypes (e.g., Yeager et al., 2016). Work conducted in the United Kingdom suggests that interventions designed to influence parents' expectations about the benefits of a university degree are promising (Delavande & Fumagalli, 2019).

A number of studies have addressed the fact that students may be unaware of financial aid opportunities available to them and frequently underestimate their likelihood of receiving aid and admission—that is, they have inaccurate beliefs (Hoxby & Turner, 2015). For example, two states have run large-scale programs to increase college attendance among low-income students to counter such beliefs. Michigan informed a cohort of low-income students of an available benefit: any low-income state resident admitted to the University of Michigan was guaranteed four years of free tuition and fees (Dynarski et al., 2021). Researchers found that the students who received the distinctive mailing that explained the benefits were nearly 2.5 times more likely to apply than those who did not receive it (68% and 26%, respectively). They also reported that approximately one-fourth of the students who applied in response to the mailing were students who otherwise would not have applied to college at all.

Researchers in California sought to increase financial aid applications among low-income students who were qualified to receive aid by altering the content of letters sent to high school seniors (Linos, Reddy, & Rothstein, 2021). They found that the revised letters, which informed students of scholarship opportunities and offered social-belonging messages (conveying that all students would be welcome), generated more applications than the original letter; however, the revised letters did not ultimately increase scholarship use. In a second field experiment, they also included cost information for the schools in which the students indicated interest, obtained from their Free Application for Federal Student Aid (FAFSA) applications. The cost information increased the likelihood that students enrolled in their lowest-cost alternative, which was frequently a community college, shifting them away from four-year public and private California schools.

These studies suggest that relatively simple changes in the way information is provided can overcome inaccurate beliefs and thus increase postsecondary applications and enrollments. Furthermore, these studies show that potential students tend to acquire information about college access and funding gradually, so it is important that interventions are repeated multiple times and aligned with the issues that potential students confront. For example, many students begin to think about paying for the actual costs of higher education only after they are admitted; thus, it may be useful to provide information about actual costs and financial assistance at an earlier stage in the process so that students do not rule out the possibility of college because they lack information about possibilities for aid.

Default settings have also been tested as a way of lowering administrative burden in the education context. When Maine passed legislation that required all public high school juniors to take the SAT in 2006, the proportion of students who took the test increased by 43 percent and enrollment in four-year colleges rose 4 to 6 percent among public high school seniors (Hurwitz et al., 2015).

Researchers have also studied nudges designed to increase completion of the FAFSA form, which requires a considerable amount of time and knowledge. The goal of the nudges is to overcome limited attention and present bias. For example, in one innovative field experiment, several low-income families were offered free assistance filling out the FAFSA as a component of tax services at H&R Block (Bettinger et al., 2012). Families included in the treatment group were also given cost information for local colleges. This combination of services increased FAFSA completion, receipt of financial aid, college attendance, and college persistence.

FAFSA completion is also one of the few areas in which researchers have attempted to use nudges to expand a program that was successful at a smaller scale. In one study, the Common Application, a vehicle through which many prospective college students apply to multiple colleges simultaneously, was used to convey reminders to students to complete the FAFSA early (Bird et al., 2021). These messages incorporated personalization, were from organizations with which the students would be familiar, and highlighted deadlines. In a second portion of the study, researchers used messaging through a portal that allows state residents to use one application for all of the state's public four-year colleges, several private colleges, and community colleges.

However, the authors reported that these interventions did little to increase either enrollment or financial aid receipt, and they offered three possible explanations that may be relevant for other domains. First, the interventions were done on a large scale through impersonal state- or national-level institutions. Students may place less trust in these more distant entities, so similar interventions offered by local ones could be more successful. Second, because these large-scale interventions included a large set of potential students, the messages were necessarily less customized to specific student recipients. Finally, the authors also noted that students are likely more informed about FAFSA now than in the past, which would reduce possible treatment effects. Such nudges as emails and texts have been unsuccessful (Bergman, Denning, & Manoli, 2019).

Looking across the available work, the interventions designed to encourage students to pursue further educational attainment either make the tasks involved easier or simply provide information and reminders about what needs to be done and thus aim to overcome inaccurate beliefs.[3] Those that actually simplify the tasks, such as providing help with FAFSA forms, changing policy defaults, and providing consistent advising, show consistent positive results (e.g., Hurwitz et al., 2015; Barr & Castleman, 2021). Reminders and enhanced information have been less successful (e.g., Avery et al., 2021; Barr & Castleman, 2021; Bird et al., 2021). These results suggest that further study in several areas would be beneficial: using defaults and offering small incentives for key decisions, such as registering for courses that will count toward a degree or other objective, and developing ways to strengthen engagement with advisors and mentors.

It is also important to note that although matriculating in college is a vital step, many young people who do so fail to earn a degree: just over

---

[3]The committee benefited from a presentation by Ben Castleman of the University of Virginia at a workshop in July 2022.

one-half of students who enroll in a four-year degree program earn the degree within six years, and approximately one-third of those who enroll in a two-year program complete it (Oreopoulos & Petronijevic, 2019). It is likely that behavioral factors contribute to the reasons some students fail to thrive academically in college or drop out, but studies of approaches based on behavioral economics, such as nudging students to improve study habits or set goals, have not yet borne fruit (Oreopoulos & Petronijevic, 2019; Clark et al., 2020).

TEACHER PERFORMANCE

Behavioral economics approaches have also been applied to influence teachers' performance, as measured by the test results of their students. Financial incentives have been used to motivate teachers to take actions to improve their students' performance.[4] This may sound like a straightforward economic incentive, but behaviorally informed approaches to this incentive are designed to take advantage of understanding people's responses to incentives framed in specific ways. In one example, community college instructors were offered a $50 bonus for every student who passed an exam (Brownback & Sadoff, 2020). They were given part of the cash bonus in advance but would lose some of the bonus if fewer than half of their students passed and earn more if more than half passed. The researchers found that this loss-framed incentive increased student performance and also reduced course dropout rates, although teachers prefer contracts with a gain frame.[5]

A similar study in the K–8 setting compared the efficacy of versions of a teacher incentive program that used either a gain- or loss-frame bonus system to target student performance on a math test; it showed significant positive effects for the loss-framed bonus and insignificant results for the gain-framed bonus (Fryer et al., 2022). Researchers who have looked at financial rewards for teachers without the loss frame have found limited or no benefits (e.g., Allan & Fryer, 2011; Springer et al., 2012; Dee & Wyckoff, 2015; Imberman, 2015; Loyalka et al., 2019).

It is worth noting a few critiques of this approach. For example, an examination of the effects of such incentives on Black–White test score gaps found that they were actually exacerbated by a teacher bonus program (Hill & Jones, 2021). Critics have also questioned the theoretical basis for this type of incentive: the assumption that teachers may know how to use more

---

[4]Researchers have also examined the use of financial incentives offered directly to students, but evidence for this approach is mixed (see, e.g., Fryer, 2011; Levitt et al., 2016).

[5]Researchers have found that the possibility of losing a prospective benefit is more highly motivating to people than the prospect of gaining a similar benefit (see, e.g., Romanowich & Lamb, 2013; Czibor et al., 2022).

effective practices but choose not to make the additional effort required until motivated to do so by external incentives (McArdle, 2010; Kozlowski & Lee Lauen, 2019). In addition, teacher performance is the product of decisions and other factors that play out daily over months, which involve complex incentives and other behavioral principles.

FINDINGS

Education is a central influence in children's and adolescents' lives, and efforts to improve educational performance can create large social returns. Researchers have produced research on ways to influence parent–child interactions, boost college attendance and applications for financial aid, and boost test scores through influencing teacher practice. This body of work points to several areas as particularly promising:

- The use of low-touch nudges to affect parent–child interactions can directly address issues with limited attention and present bias, which limit the effectiveness of those interactions with respect to education challenges.
- Steps to directly reduce the administrative burden of applying to college and applying for financial aid, as well as providing support to students for these tasks, have increased college applications and applications for financial aid.
- Creating default choices for high school students, such as automatic registration for college admissions tests, encourages them to take steps to pursue postsecondary education.
- For teacher performance, providing loss-frame incentives for teacher compensation is a promising avenue, although the available research is quite limited, and teachers prefer gain-framed contracts.

There are many more questions than answers about how behavioral economics approaches can address challenges in education. For example, young children and adolescents are still developing cognitively, and it is possible that behaviorally based interventions could be most effective if tailored to key developmental stages. Another possibility is that designing interventions that are specifically targeted to males and females, taking into consideration their differing developmental trajectories, could enhance their effectiveness, but researchers have not yet shown how such tailoring might work. So far, the bulk of the available research focuses on postsecondary schooling, so much less is known about how behaviorally based interventions can improve performance for middle school students. Would a loss frame for teacher pay matter for young children? These are just a few of the unanswered questions.

There are reasons such research is especially difficult in education settings. Children are a protected class, so institutions rightly impose stringent safeguards for research with them. These necessary safeguards make it more complex to perform studies in schools. Future behavioral economics research will require patience to plan and implement, following researchers from other disciplines who have conducted research in schools ethically and responsibly. The behavioral economics work already conducted points to the potential for significant benefits in this important domain.

REFERENCES

Allan, B. M., & Fryer, R. G. (2011). *The power and pitfalls of education incentives.* Discussion Paper 2011-07. The Hamilton Project. https://scholar.harvard.edu/files/fryer/files/092011_incentives_fryer_allen_paper2.pdf

Avery, C., Castleman, B. L., Hurwitz, M., Long, B. T., & Page, L. C. (2021). Digital messaging to improve college enrollment and success. *Economics of Education Review, 84,* 102170. https://doi.org/10.1016/j.econedurev.2021.102170

Barr, A. C., & Castleman, B. L. (2021). *The bottom line on college advising: Large increases in degree attainment.* EdWorkingPaper 21-481. Annenberg Institute for School Reform at Brown University. https://doi.org/10.26300/xdsa-5e22

Bergman, P., Denning, J. T., & Manoli, D. (2019). Is information enough? The effect of information about education tax benefits on student outcomes. *Journal of Policy Analysis and Management, 38*(3), 706–731. https://doi.org/10.1002/pam.22131

Bettinger, E. P., Long, B. T., Oreopoulos, P., & Sanbonmatsu, L. (2012). The role of application assistance and information in college decisions: Results from the H&R Block FAFSA experiment. *The Quarterly Journal of Economics, 127*(3), 1205–1242. https://doi.org/10.1093/qje/qjs017

Bird, K. A., Castleman, B. L., Denning, J. T., Goodman, J., Lamberton, C., & Rosinger, K. O. (2021). Nudging at scale: Experimental evidence from FAFSA completion campaigns. *Journal of Economic Behavior & Organization, 183,* 105–128. https://doi.org/10.1016/j.jebo.2020.12.022

Brownback, A., & Sadoff, S. (2020). Improving college instruction through incentives. *Journal of Political Economy, 128*(8), 2925–2972. https://doi.org/10.1086/707025

Clark, D., Gill, D., Prowse, V., & Rush, M. (2020). Using goals to motivate college students: Theory and evidence from field experiments. *Review of Economics and Statistics, 102*(4), 648–663. https://doi.org/10.1162/rest_a_00864

Czibor, E., Hsu, D., Jimenez-Gomez, D., Neckermann, S., & Subasi, B. (2022). Loss-framed incentives and employee (mis-)behavior. *Management Science, 68*(10), 7065–7791. https://doi.org/10.1287/mnsc.2021.4280

Damgaard, M. T., & Nielsen, H. S. (2018). Nudging in education. *Economics of Education Review, 64,* 313–342. https://doi.org/10.1016/j.econedurev.2018.03.008

Dee, T. S., & Wyckoff, J. (2015). Incentives, selection, and teacher performance: Evidence from IMPACT. *Journal of Policy Analysis and Management, 34*(2), 267–297. https://doi.org/10.1002/pam.21818

Delavande, A., & Fumagalli, L. (2019). *Information, expectations and transition to higher education.* Nuffield Foundation. https://www.nuffieldfoundation.org/wp-content/uploads/2019/02/information-expectations-transition-higher-education-1.pdf

Dynarski, S., Libassi, C. J., Michelmore, K., & Owen, S. (2021). Closing the gap: The effect of reducing complexity and uncertainty in college pricing on the choices of low-income students. *American Economic Review, 111*(6), 1721–1756. https://doi.org/10.1257/aer.20200451

Dynarski, S. M., & Scott-Clayton, J. E. (2006). The cost of complexity in federal student aid: Lessons from optimal tax theory and behavioral economics. *National Tax Journal, 59*(2), 319–356. https://doi.org/10.17310/ntj.2006.2.07

Fryer, R. G. (2011). Financial incentives and student achievement: Evidence from randomized trials. *The Quarterly Journal of Economics, 126*(4), 1755–1798. https://doi.org/10.1093/qje/qjr045

Fryer, R. G., Levitt, S. D., List, J., & Sadoff, S. (2022). Enhancing the efficacy of teacher incentives through framing: A field experiment. *American Economic Journal: Economic Policy, 14*(4), 269–299. https://doi.org/10.1257/pol.20190287

Harackiewicz, J. M., Rozek, C. S., Hulleman, C. S., & Hyde, J. S. (2012). Helping parents to motivate adolescents in mathematics and science: An experimental test of a utility-value intervention. *Psychological Science, 23*(8), 899–906. https://doi.org/10.1177/0956797611435530

Hill, A. J., & Jones, D. B. (2021). Paying for whose performance? Teacher incentive pay and the black–white test score gap. *Educational Evaluation and Policy Analysis, 43*(3), 445–471. https://doi.org/10.3102/01623737211001421

Hoxby, C. M., & Avery, C. (2013). *Low-income high-achieving students miss out on attending selective colleges*. Brookings Papers on Economic Activity. Brookings Institution.

Hoxby, C. M., & Turner, S. (2015). What high-achieving low-income students know about college. *American Economic Review, 105*(5), 514–517. https://doi.org/10.1257/aer.p20151027

Hurwitz, M., Smith, J., Niu, S., & Howell, J. (2015). The Maine question: How is 4-year college enrollment affected by mandatory college entrance exams? *Educational Evaluation and Policy Analysis, 37*(1), 138–159. https://doi.org/10.3102/0162373714521866

Imberman, S. A. (2015). *How effective are financial incentives for teachers?* IZA World of Labor. https://doi.org/10.15185/izawol.158

Kozlowski, K. P., & Lee Lauen, D. (2019). Understanding teacher pay for performance: Flawed assumptions and disappointing results. *Teachers College Record, 121*(2), 1–38. https://doi.org/10.1177/016146811912100206

Kuhfeld, M., Soland, J., & Lewis, K. (2022). *Test score patterns across three COVID-19-impacted school years*. EdWorkingPaper 22-521. Brown University. https://edworkingpapers.com/sites/default/files/ai22-521.pdf

Lavecchia, A. M., Liu, H., & Oreopoulos, P. (2016). Behavioral economics of education: Progress and possibilities. *Handbook of the economics of education, 5*, 1–74. Elsevier. https://doi.org/10.1016/B978-0-444-63459-7.00001-4

Levitt, S. D., List, J. A., Neckermann, S., & Sadoff, S. (2016). The behavioralist goes to school: Leveraging behavioral economics to improve educational performance. *American Economic Journal: Economic Policy, 8*(4), 183–219. https://doi.org/10.1257/pol.20130358

Linos, E., Reddy, V., & Rothstein, J. (2021). Demystifying college costs: How nudges can and can't help. *Behavioural Public Policy*, 1–22. https://doi.org/10.1017/bpp.2022.1

Loyalka, P., Sylvia, S., Liu, C., Chu, J., & Shi, Y. (2019). Pay by design: Teacher performance pay design and the distribution of student achievement. *Journal of Labor Economics, 37*(3), 621–662. https://doi.org/10.1086/702625

Mayer, S. E., Kalil, A., Oreopoulos, P., & Gallegos, S. (2019). Using behavioral insights to increase parental engagement: The parents and children together intervention. *Journal of Human Resources, 54*(4), 900–925. https://doi.org/10.3368/jhr.54.4.0617.8835R

McArdle, F. (2010). Preparing quality teachers: Making learning visible. *Australian Journal of Teacher Education*, 35(8), 60–78. https://doi.org/10.14221/ajte.2010v35n8.5

Office for Civil Rights. (2022). *Education in a pandemic: The disparate impacts of COVID-19 on America's students*. U.S. Department of Education. https://www2.ed.gov/about/offices/list/ocr/docs/20210608-impacts-of-covid19.pdf

Oreopoulos, P., & Petronijevic, U. (2019). *The remarkable unresponsiveness of college students to nudging and what we can learn from it*. NBER Working Paper 26059. National Bureau of Economic Research. https://doi.org/10.3386/w26059

Rogers, T., & Feller, A. (2018). Reducing student absences at scale by targeting parents' misbeliefs. *Nature Human Behaviour*, 2(5), 335–342. https://doi.org/10.1038/s41562-018-0328-1

Romanowich, P., & Lamb, R. J. (2013). The effect of framing incentives as either losses or gains with contingency management for smoking cessation. *Addictive Behaviors*, 38(4), 2084–2088. https://www.ncbi.nlm.nih.gov/pmc/articles/PMC3575603

Springer, M. G., Pane, J. F., Le, V. N., McCaffrey, D. F., Burns, S. F., Hamilton, L. S., & Stecher, B. (2012). *No evidence that incentive pay for teacher teams improves student outcomes: Results from a randomized trial*. RAND Corporation. https://doi.org/10.7249/RB9649

Wilbur, T. G., & Roscigno, V. J. (2016). First-generation disadvantage and college enrollment/completion. *Socius*, 2, 2378023116664351. https://doi.org/10.1177/2378023116664351

Yeager, D. S., Romero, C., Paunesku, D., Hulleman, C. S., Schneider, B., Hinojosa, C., Lee, H. Y., O'Brien, J., Flint, K., Roberts, A., Trott, J., Greene, D., Walton, G. M., & Dweck, C. S. (2016). Using design thinking to improve psychological interventions: The case of the growth mindset during the transition to high school. *Journal of Educational Psychology*, 108(3), 374–391. https://doi.org/10.1037/edu0000098

York, B. N., Loeb, S., & Doss, C. (2019). One step at a time: The effects of an early literacy text-messaging program for parents of preschoolers. *Journal of Human Resources*, 54(3), 537–566. https://doi.org/10.3368/jhr.54.3.0517-8756R

10

Criminal Justice System

Problems in the U.S. criminal justice system have been well documented. A 2014 report on incarceration rates described a system in a state of crisis that compares unfavorably with those in other industrialized nations (National Research Council, 2014). Estimates of the total number of people currently imprisoned in the United States vary, but according to data collected by the Department of Justice, 1,215,800 people were in state or federal prisons at the end of 2020 (Carson et al., 2021). Other estimates also include people in local jails and those incarcerated prior to trial, as well as those incarcerated in Indian territories. For example, the World Prison Brief (n.d.) estimated that 1,675,400 people were incarcerated in the United States in 2020.[1] The trend of incarceration was upward for decades: the number of people incarcerated in state and federal prisons grew from 200,000 in 1973 to 1.5 million in 2009 (National Research Council, 2014). More recently, the trend has been downward; there are varied explanations for this trend. The United States still has the highest per capita incarceration rate in the world (664 per 100,000), and, by one calculation, every state in the country also has a higher incarceration rate than nearly all democratic nations (Widra & Herring, 2021).

Those in prisons and jails are disproportionately Black, Hispanic, and Native American (Carson, 2021). The prison population reflects persistent sources of disadvantage in U.S. society: large percentages of inmates have

---

[1]The Prison Policy Initiative's estimate for 2020 was 1,797,000, and they offer separate estimates for people imprisoned in U.S. territories and immigration detention (Sawyer & Wagner, 2022).

not completed high school, were first arrested before age 19, have a parent who has been incarcerated, or come from families who have received public assistance (Wang et al., 2022). Approximately one-tenth of this population had been homeless during childhood. A substantial proportion have histories of substance use disorder.

Apart from the high cost of incarcerating this many people—$80 billion a year, by one estimate—researchers have documented long-term harm to those who are imprisoned, even those convicted of minor offenses, and to the communities in which they live (see, e.g., Western & Pettit, 2010). Many analysts and policy makers argue that the current system exacerbates economic inequality, the effects of institutional racism, and problems with violence and family instability that particularly affect high-poverty communities (National Research Council, 2014). Incarceration itself, however, is only the final step in a long series of events and processes in the criminal justice system.[2] The process begins with the alleged commission of a crime and is followed by arrest and court processes. The court process involves charging, bail, plea bargaining, conviction, and sentencing. Sentencing has the most direct impact on the high incarceration rate. Many of the people in the system repeat the process in what is essentially a revolving door: criminal behavior eventually resulting in incarceration, which is followed by further criminal behavior, which starts the process anew. Every step in this process—including those that support the revolving door, particularly the difficulty that individuals released from prison face in establishing themselves in the labor market and civil society—involves a complex set of actors, social and legal processes and norms, policing practices, and sentencing guidelines.

INFLUENCE OF BEHAVIORAL FACTORS

The behavioral aspects of the steps in these processes have been well documented in a long and extensive literature from sociology, psychology, and economics that explores the causes of criminal behavior. For example, an influential 1968 study used traditional economic analysis to characterize the first step (criminal behavior) as the action of a rational individual accurately perceiving the short- and long-run benefits and costs of committing a crime (Becker, 1968). Becker's theory built on very old analyses of the benefits and costs of criminal behavior, including the work of Beccaria (1872) and Bentham (1907), as well as the broader literature on deterrence

---

[2]The committee benefited from a workshop presentation by Aurélie Ouss of the University of Pennsylvania that provided background for this section. See https://www.nationalacademies.org/event/07-18-2022/workshop-on-behavioral-economics-exploring-applications-and-research-methods

theory. But Becker was the first to use all the elements of the traditional economic model, portraying an individual who commits a crime as rationally weighing the gains from committing the crime against the costs of doing so, taking into account an accurate assessment of the probability of arrest and the probability of incarceration if arrested. That person may have strong rational reasons for choosing the risk associated with the criminal behavior; in Becker's view, the "person commits an offense if the expected utility to him exceeds the utility he could get by using his time and resources at other activities" (Becker, 1968, p. 176). Thus, Becker argued that criminal justice policy should be aimed at raising the costs of crime by increasing the penalties (e.g., increased police presence, longer prison sentences).[3]

In contrast to this theory, empirical studies of people who commit crimes suggest that they do not accurately perceive either the benefits or the costs of their actions, in the short run or the long run; that they often act on impulse; and that they commit acts that they later regret. While people usually have a rough sense of what types of crimes have greater penalties than others, they only imperfectly perceive the specific sanctions for criminal behavior, and their perceptions are heavily influenced by situational factors and context (Apel, 2022). Perceptions of the probability of apprehension following a crime are highly individual and based on particular experiences (including whether they have committed crimes or have been apprehended previously, which increases knowledge), not on full rational calculations. In short, people who may be considering criminal activity estimate sanction risk in ways that are influenced by a variety of personality characteristics and behavioral factors, not just rational calculation (Pickett & Bushway, 2015; Miceli, Segerson, & Earnhart, 2022). One researcher (Pogarsky, 2002) distinguishes between potential offenders who are "incorrigible," on whom sanctions for criminal behavior have no impact, and those who are "deterrable" and might be deterred by sanctions; he regards the differences between the two as inherently behavioral. This body of work points to the behavioral influences identified in Chapter 3 as among the key building blocks of behavioral economics: limited attention, cognitive barriers, reference dependence, and inaccurate beliefs.

Police officers are also influenced by behavioral forces when carrying out arrests and in other encounters with the public, and these influences have been well documented (Owens et al., 2018). The same holds true for judges and other court officers, who, while necessarily following the

---

[3]Many elements of Becker's theory appear in the criminology literature in different forms. That literature has long considered the power of deterrence in models of deterrence theory, and there is also a rational choice model in that literature that is related to Becker's theory (see Cullen, Agnew, & Wilcox, 2018, for a review of criminological theory). However, these other theories did not build so directly on the traditional economic model and do not always have the same implications for policy.

law, have discretion in court proceedings and sentencing that can reflect behavioral biases. Studies of judicial decisions have highlighted the potential for those decisions to be subjective, to be based on erroneous understandings, and to reflect ad hoc assessments of the circumstances (Bibas, 2004; Danziger, Levav, & Avnaim-Pesso, 2011; Bushway & Owens, 2013; Stevenson, 2018).

APPLICATION OF BEHAVIORAL IDEAS

Despite the widespread recognition of these behavioral issues in the criminal justice system and their importance to policies designed to prevent crime, relatively little research in this field has used the specific lens of behavioral economics (Loughran, 2019, p. 738). We review a few of the available studies to illustrate the types of topics that have been addressed, including many not conducted by economists but which have elements similar to those emphasized in behavioral economics.

Some work that has directly addressed criminal behavior itself is discussed in a review of studies that used behavioral economics to examine decision making by offenders. This review describes valuable findings from the last two decades (Pogarsky, Roche, & Pickett, 2018). For example, studies show that there are biases in how people who commit crimes assess the probabilities of arrest and detection. Biases in assessing probabilities are a central component of prospect theory (see Chapter 1), which argues that individuals' assessments of probabilities systematically depart from true (objective) probabilities because they are affected by extraneous characteristics.

Other studies show that people are inconsistent in their estimates of those probabilities for different situations and tend to be affected by the salience and framing of the risk rather than the objective probabilities, an example of reference dependence. For example, a person considering stealing a purse from a parked car at night is much more likely to be deterred if they think the purse might have a trackable iPhone in it, even if the probability that it does is very small: this is an example of giving a small probability event excessive weight because it is salient. People also have inconsistent scales of response: they estimate probabilities of arrest very differently depending on the exact numeric scale they are offered. Pickett (2018) has suggested that more effective communication about probabilities of arrest and the use of framing effects in how those probabilities are publicly communicated could lead to specific policies that might reduce crime.

The review (Pogarsky, Roche, & Pickett, 2018) also covers studies of behavioral factors in crime deterrence, and the authors highlight key findings; for example, people who may be considering criminal behavior assess probabilities in a nonlinear fashion, using perceived thresholds, or "tipping points," in those probabilities to make decisions, and they do not respond to variations in probabilities below the tipping point. This behavior involves cognitive errors and inaccurate beliefs, as well as reference dependence if those tipping points are taken from some perceived, but possibly mistaken, reference point. The research showed that the tipping point changed depending on the "starting point" for the probability of arrest.

Other work covered in the review (Pogarsky, Roche, & Pickett, 2018) showed that at-risk individuals tend to be averse to ambiguity, a common finding in behavioral science: that is, people act not on the basis of the probabilities of their arrest (whether objective or subjective) but on the basis of how certain they are of those probabilities. "Ambiguity aversion," the tendency to favor the known over the unknown, was first formalized in economics by Camerer & Weber (1992). They showed that people are more comfortable with decisions when they believe they know more about the probabilities of events even if their subjective beliefs are held fixed. This phenomenon has been shown to affect the impact of police crackdowns. For example, the deterrent effects of such crackdowns are initially small because at-risk individuals initially have not learned what the probabilities of arrest are going to be and hence do not commit crimes because of the ambiguity; however, after learning those probabilities, people are more likely to commit crimes because the ambiguity is reduced (Sherman, 1990).

One study examined whether youth at risk of being involved in criminal activity in Chicago rationally calculated benefits and costs, applying a form of cognitive-behavioral theory (Heller et al., 2017). The therapy was based on the hypothesis that youth from violent neighborhoods learn to automatically respond aggressively to any situation in which they are challenged and that such automatic responses lead to aggressive responses in situations in which they are not needed or appropriate. The study required young men to undergo training sessions where they were taught to slow down, think for a moment, and consider a response rather than automatically responding. This type of behavior modification is typical of approaches developed in the context of cognitive psychology, and it is related to the concept of heuristics that behavioral economists use (see Chapter 2). This seemingly modest behavioral intervention had a major impact and at a relatively low cost: total arrests were reduced by 28–35 percent, and violent crime arrests were reduced by 45–50 percent.[4]

In the area of policing, it is standard practice for officers to make their own judgments in each situation about whether to be aggressive in

---

[4]We note that researchers in criminology have long debated the role of "human agency" in individual decisions to engage in crime, where that term refers to portraying individuals contemplating crime as purposeful and reflecting deliberate choice rather than just reflecting outside social influences (Paternoster & Bushway, 2009; see also Paternoster et al., 2015; Paternoster, 2017). Cullen (2017) proposes a balanced approach with both human agency and social influences considered.

confronting suspects or to emphasize the appearance of fairness in those decisions. In many cases, officers do not accurately perceive the views of suspects, who may interpret police behavior as unfair and violating their expectations for just interactions with law enforcement. In a study with some similarities to the Chicago study of at-risk youth described above, researchers tested an intervention that trained police officers in moderate risk areas to slow down their thought processes during citizen encounters: the training resulted in officers being less likely to resolve encounters by arrests (Owens et al., 2018).

In another intervention with both police and a community's relationship to police, researchers tested the hypothesis that neighborhood residents' perception of police officers in their area was affected by whether they had any personal knowledge of the local officers (Shah & LaForest, 2022). The study was carried out in low-income neighborhoods. One intervention involved providing neighborhood residents with mundane information about officers' favorite food, their hobbies, or why they became an officer; another intervention involved officers handing out "outreach" cards to residents. The intervention reduced crime rates in the first three months after the intervention.

Researchers have also examined court practices and behaviors, including the frequent problem of people who have been charged with a crime failing to appear in court. The most common financial incentive to appear is the setting of bail that will be forfeited if the accused does not appear, but some evidence suggests that bail does not, in fact, have much effect on the probability of appearance (Ouss & Stevenson, 2022). A study in New York City showed that 40 percent of those issued summons to appear failed to do so, leading to warrants for their arrest, which further worsened the accused's situation (Fishbane, Ouss, & Shah, 2020). The authors hypothesized that many people simply forgot about the need to appear or did not understand the complicated summons they had received, an example of limited attention and cognition. The authors tested an intervention that included use of summons documents redesigned to prominently display the designated court appearance date and also highlight the consequences of not appearing (i.e., arrest warrant) as well as text message reminders. The intervention significantly reduced failures to appear, resulting in 30,000 fewer arrest warrants. The effect was strongest in neighborhoods with low levels of income and high proportions of Black and Hispanic residents. This evidence that many people who fail to appear in court did not intend to do so contradicted the view of many lay people interviewed by the authors, who said that failures to appear are intentional.

A significant body of work has examined the effect of sentencing length on criminal behavior and identified the importance of behavioral concepts. For example, a study of recidivism by those who have been convicted and incarcerated showed that recidivism was affected by whether the convicted people framed their sentences as a loss or gain relative to their expectations, an example of reference dependence (Bushway & Owens, 2013). Specifically, people who were given sentences shorter than those recommended in sentencing guidelines were more likely to re-offend than those given sentences that were in line with the guidelines. The authors recommended aligning actual sentences with guidelines.

More broadly, researchers have found that making long sentences longer has little impact on crime rates (National Research Council, 2014). There is also evidence that certain types of proactive policing, if carefully designed to target areas and types of offenders with the highest rates of crime, can have a deterrent effect (National Academies of Sciences, Engineering, and Medicine, 2018). These findings are consistent with the behavioral economics concept of present bias (that individuals are more responsive to immediate costs and benefits and less responsive to important long-run factors).[5] However, much about deterrence is not well understood, and the National Research Council (2012) has called for more research into how perceptions of the risks of capital punishment, for example, are formed.

Several studies have also examined behavioral effects on plea bargaining. The standard model of plea bargaining is that a defendant bases a decision about whether to accept a plea bargain on the probability of conviction if the case goes to trial, the expected length of the sentence if convicted, and the characteristics of the plea bargain itself.[6] Yet one study showed that bargaining outcomes are also affected by attorney competence, compensation, and workloads; resources; and sentencing and bail rules, all of which are consistent with the traditional economic model. But outcomes were also found to be affected by lack of information about the probability of conviction, opening the door to biased perceptions that are based on salience, framing, and other behavioral factors (Bibas, 2004).

A randomized controlled trial in which students were told to assume that they were innocent or guilty and then were offered plea deals offers additional evidence (Garnier-Dykstra & Wilson, 2021). When the plea deals were framed as a gain (i.e., a greater-than-expected reduction in the seriousness of the charge), the innocent students were more likely to accept the deal (and plead guilty), while the guilty were less likely to do so. This is another example of reference dependence, where the decision is based in

---

[5]Becker (1968) also noted that individuals may respond more to the probability of arrest than to the expected sentence but interpreted this as an indication that individuals prefer risk; in contrast, in behavioral economics this phenomenon is interpreted as present bias. The finding that immediate punishment appears to have more impact than long-run, or delayed, punishment is an old finding in the literature (see, e.g., Perry, Erev, & Haruvy, 2002).

[6]There are a number of models of rational plea bargaining, including by Landes (1971), which frame the issue in terms of a rational economic bargaining model.

part on perceived comparisons with other possible outcomes: in general, innocent defendants are less likely to accept deals than guilty defendants—as traditional theory would predict, since innocence should be positively correlated with the probability of an acquittal at trial. Some innocent defendants were influenced to accept the deal if it was framed as a particularly strong gain. In contrast, however, a randomized trial that used actual probabilities of conviction and sentence length showed that prosecutors and defense attorneys generally acted as would be predicted by the traditional economic model (Bushway, Redlich, & Norris, 2014).

FINDINGS

Behavioral factors that are not generally considered in traditional economic models have an influence at all points in the criminal justice system: they influence the determinants of criminal behavior, policing practices, court proceedings, judicial decision making, and the effects of incarceration. Key findings from the research include:

- People who are considering committing crimes are heavily affected by inaccurate perceptions of the probabilities of arrest. They are also affected by reference dependence and framing when assessing the subjective probabilities of arrest.
- Police officers have inaccurate beliefs about community residents' perceptions of their actions, which lead them to engage in suboptimal behavior in situations that require decisions about apprehension and arrest.
- Courts do not accurately assess the perceptions of defendants regarding bail penalties, use of sentencing guidelines, and the role of information in the trial process. The reactions of defendants are not what courts assume, and the result can be poorer outcomes for defendants and society.

Despite these findings, the evidence for the effects of behavioral interventions at various steps of the criminal justice system is too scant so far to support definite conclusions on their effectiveness and potential. More research is needed on the role of behavioral factors in the criminal justice system and on the most effective interventions to reduce criminal behavior and to improve policing and judicial processes. Research is needed in several key areas:

- how to directly address the behavioral biases that people have when choosing to commit a crime, including their biased assessments of the consequences of criminal behavior;

- how to more effectively engage police and their communities to reduce the biased perceptions each has of the other; and
- how to improve court processes to provide defendants with accurate information and to reduce their biased perceptions of the outcomes, as well as to provide judges and attorneys with more knowledge and understanding of the behavioral biases of defendants.

REFERENCES

Apel, R. (2022). Sanctions, perceptions, and crime. *Annual Review of Criminology, 5*(1), 205–227. https://doi.org/10.1146/annurev-criminol-030920-112932

Beccaria, C. B. (1872). *An essay on crimes and punishment.* W.C. Little & Co.

Becker, G. S. (1968). Crime and punishment: An economic approach. *Journal of Political Economy, 76*(2), 169–217. https://doi.org/10.1007/978-1-349-62853-7_2

Bentham, J. (1907). *An instruction to the principles of morals and legislation.* Clarendon Press.

Bibas, S. (2004). Plea bargaining outside the shadow of trial. *Harvard Law Review, 117*(8), 2463–2547. https://doi.org/10.2307/4093404

Bushway, S. D., & Owens, E. G. (2013). Framing punishment: Incarceration, recommended sentences, and recidivism. *The Journal of Law and Economics, 56*(2), 301–331. https://doi.org/10.1086/669715

Bushway, S. D., Redlich, A. D., & Norris, R. J. (2014). An explicit test of plea bargaining in the "Shadow of the Trial." *Criminology, 52*(4), 723–754. https://doi.org/10.1111/1745-9125.12054

Camerer, C., & Weber, M. (1992). Recent developments in modeling preferences: Uncertainty and ambiguity. *Journal of Risk and Uncertainty, 5*, 325–370. https://doi.org/10.1007/BF00122575

Carson, E. A. (2021). *Prisoners in 2021—Statistical tables.* NCJ 302776. U.S. Department of Justice, Office of Justice Programs, Bureau of Justice Statistics. https://bjs.ojp.gov/sites/g/files/xyckuh236/files/media/document/p21st.pdf

Carson, E. A., Sandler, D. H., Bhaskar, R., Fernandez, L. E., & Porter, S. R. (2021). *Employment of persons released from federal prison in 2010.* U.S. Department of Justice, Office of Justice Programs, Bureau of Justice Statistics. https://bjs.ojp.gov/sites/g/files/xyckuh236/files/media/document/eprfp10.pdf

Cullen, F. T. (2017). Choosing our criminological future: Reservations about human agency as an organizing concept. *Journal of Developmental and Life-Course Criminology, 3*, 373–379. https://doi.org/10.1007/s40865-017-0070-9

Cullen, F. T., Agnew, R., & Wilcox, P. (2018). *Criminological theory: Past to present.* (6th ed.). Oxford University Press.

Danziger, S., Levav, J., & Avnaim-Pesso, L. (2011). Extraneous factors in judicial decisions. *Proceedings of the National Academy of Sciences, 108*(17), 6889–6892. https://doi.org/10.1073/pnas.1018033108

Fishbane, A., Ouss, A., & Shah, A. K. (2020). Behavioral nudges reduce failure to appear for court. *Science, 370*(6517), eabb6591. https://doi.org/10.1126/science.abb6591

Garnier-Dykstra, L. M., & Wilson, T. (2021). Behavioral economics and framing effects in guilty pleas: A defendant decision making experiment. *Justice Quarterly, 38*(2), 224–248. https://doi.org/10.1080/07418825.2019.1614208

Heller, S. B., Shah, A. K., Guryan, J., Ludwig, J., Mullainathan, S., & Pollack, H. A. (2017). Thinking, fast and slow? Some field experiments to reduce crime and dropout in Chicago. *The Quarterly Journal of Economics, 132*(1), 1–54. https://doi.org/10.1093/qje/qjw033

Landes, W. M. (1971). An economic analysis of the courts. *Journal of Law and Economics*, *14*(1), 61107.
Loughran, T. A. (2019). Behavioral criminology and public policy. *Criminology & Public Policy*, *18*(4), 737–758. https://doi.org/10.1111/1745-9133.12465
Miceli, T. J., Segerson, K., & Earnhart, D. (2022). The role of experience in deterring crime: A theory of specific versus general deterrence. *Economic Inquiry*, *60*(4), 1833–1853. https://doi.org/10.1111/ecin.13083
National Academies of Sciences, Engineering, and Medicine. (2018). *Proactive policing: Effects on crime and communities*. The National Academies Press. https://doi.org/10.17226/24928
National Research Council. (2012). *Deterrence and the death penalty*. The National Academies Press. https://doi.org/10.17226/13363
———. (2014). *The growth of incarceration in the United States: Exploring causes and consequences*. The National Academies Press. https://doi.org/10.17226/18613
Ouss, A., & Stevenson, M. (2022). Does cash bail deter misconduct? *American Economic Journal: Applied Economics*. https://www.aeaweb.org/articles?id=10.1257/app.20210349&&from=f
Owens, E., Weisburd, D., Amendola, K. L., & Alpert, G. P. (2018). Can you build a better cop? *Criminology & Public Policy*, *17*(1), 41–87. https://doi.org/10.1111/1745-9133.12337
Paternoster, R. (2017). Happenings, acts, and actions: Articulating the meaning and implications of human agency for criminology. *Journal of Developmental and Life-Course Criminology*, *3*, 350–372. https://doi.org/10.1007/s40865-017-0069-2
Paternoster, R., & Bushway, S. (2009). Desistance and the "feared self": Toward an identity theory of criminal desistance. *The Journal of Criminal Law and Criminology*, *99*(4), 1103–1156. https://www.jstor.org/stable/20685067
Paternoster, R., Bachman, R., Bushway, S., Kerrison, E., & O'Connell, D. (2015). Human agency and explanations of criminal desistance: Arguments for a rational choice theory. *Journal of Developmental and Life-Course Criminology*, *1*, 209–235. https://doi.org/10.1007/s40865-015-0013-2
Perry, O., Erev, I., & Haruvy, E. (2002). Frequent probabilistic punishment in law enforcement. *Economics of Governance* 3, 71–86.
Pickett, J., & Bushway, S. (2015). Dispositional sources of sanction perceptions: Emotionality, cognitive style, intolerance of ambiguity, and self-efficacy. *Law and Human Behavior*, *39*(6), 624–640. https://doi.org/10.1037/lhb0000150
Pickett, J. T. (2018). Using behavioral economics to advance deterrence research and improve crime policy: Some illustrative experiments. *Crime & Delinquency*, *64*(12), 1636–1659. https://doi.org/10.1177/0011128718763136
Pogarsky, G. (2002). Identifying "deterrable" offenders: Implications for research on deterrence. *Justice Quarterly*, *19*(3), 431–452.
Pogarsky, G., Roche, S. P., & Pickett, J. T. (2018). Offender decision-making in criminology: Contributions from behavioral economics. *Annual Review of Criminology*, *1*(1), 379–400. https://doi.org/10.1146/annurev-criminol-032317-092036
Sawyer, W., & Wagner, P. (2022, March 14). *Mass incarceration: The whole pie 2022*. Prison Policy Initiative. https://www.prisonpolicy.org/reports/pie2022.html
Shah, A. K., & LaForest, M. (2022). Knowledge about others reduces one's own sense of anonymity. *Nature*, *603*(7900), 297–301. https://doi.org/10.1038/s41586-022-04452-3
Sherman, L. W. (1990). Police crackdowns: initial and residual deterrence. *Crime Justice*, *12*, 1–48.
Stevenson, M. T. (2018). Distortion of justice: How the inability to pay bail affects case outcomes. *The Journal of Law, Economics, and Organization*, *34*(4), 511–542. https://doi.org/10.1093/jleo/ewy019

Wang, L., Sawyer, W., Herring, T., & Widra, E. (2022). *Beyond the count: A deep dive into state prison populations.* Prison Policy Initiative. https://www.prisonpolicy.org/reports/beyondthecount.html#childhood

Western, B., & Pettit, B. (2010). Incarceration & social inequality. *Daedalus, 139*(3), 8–19. https://doi.org/10.1162/DAED_a_00019

Widra, E., & Herring, T. (2021). *States of incarceration: The global context 2021.* Princeton University Library. http://arks.princeton.edu/ark:/88435/dsp013x816q83m

World Prison Brief. (n.d.). *United States of America.* https://www.prisonstudies.org/country/united-states-america

11

Findings Across the Policy Domains

The committee's review of research from the six selected domains allowed us to look for themes, commonalities, lessons, and unexpected connections in the evidence. As our charge directed, we hoped to learn about evidence that certain intervention strategies or approaches are effective across multiple contexts, domains, or circumstances, as well as what might be learned from approaches that so far have not been widely effective. We looked for evidence about how the core principles described in Chapter 3 affect decision making in the context of specific real-world applications and how the intervention strategies described in Chapter 4 operate in varied domains, contexts, and populations.

The domains we selected cover important public policy areas, but these are by no means the only domains in which behavioral economics interventions have been studied. Even for the areas discussed in this report we did not have sufficient resources for a comprehensive review: rather, we undertook a broad overview of what has been learned. Other domains, such as voting behavior and charitable giving, have been studied in similar ways in the United States, and evidence from other countries—work on compliance with tax policies and regulations in the United Kingdom is an example—would also contribute valuable evidence. Nevertheless, review of these six domains provided evidence about application of behavioral economics ideas across quite varied settings.

FINDINGS

Our investigation revealed clear specific findings as well as several consistent themes, both of which highlighted the need for further research. It is important to note that some of the domains we examined have been the subject of more thorough research than others. While we had no systematic way to compare coverage, it was clear that, for example, a much larger volume of research has been produced in the domain of health than in any others we studied. Table 11-1 provides an overview of the findings from each of the domains for which the strongest evidence is available.

Overall, behavioral economics research has produced significant and growing evidence in five of the domains; the domain of criminal justice has not yet been extensively studied. The strength and volume of the evidence—and the degree to which it has been generalized, replicated, and applied at a broad scale—varies. The importance of the five core principles is demonstrated by this work, although not all principles have been used in interventions in all the domains. For example, in the criminal justice domain, the work has not included interventions to explicitly address or appeal to social norms. In the domains of social safety net benefits and retirement benefits, reference dependence and framing have not been extensively addressed. These gaps may reflect omissions in our necessarily brief overview of the work in each domain; they may be the result of publication bias (i.e., studies with null findings have not been published); or they may be an indication that some of the principles may be more or less relevant in different contexts. More important is that this body of work has confirmed in real-life policy settings that people's actions and decisions are strongly affected by behavioral factors discussed in Chapter 3. This result may not be surprising, but it is a strong and necessary foundation for further progress in designing interventions that address the complex factors involved in human behavior.

Looking at interventions, four strategies have strong empirical evidence of effectiveness: defaults, simplification or removal of hassle factors, immediacy, and framing of choice sets. Two other strategies have shown mixed or less robust evidence: behaviorally informed incentives and implementation prompts.

The interventions that show the strongest effects all have fairly precisely targeted specific behavioral issues that are relevant to the problem the intervention addresses. The intervention strategies for which the evidence is mixed highlight the importance of applying human-centered design and related approaches to the selection and refinement of behavioral interventions in specific contexts discussed in Chapter 4. That is, these interventions appear to show effectiveness when tailored precisely to specific circumstances and populations: this effectiveness is clearly shown in the studies discussed in Chapters 5–10. Thus, evaluations of behavioral interventions

TABLE 11-1 Overview of Findings on Behavioral Economics from Six Domains

Domain	Primary Findings
Health	Medication adherence: structural approaches to lowering barriers (such as forgetfulness, inattention, and inaccurate or incomplete information) are the most promising interventions. Physical activity: behaviorally informed incentives using loss framing have shown promise for increasing physical activity. Colorectal cancer screening: default or opt-out interventions are the most successful among interventions tried for increasing rates of screening. HIV prevention and adherence to treatment: behaviorally informed financial incentives, promotion of testing and treatment services, and provision of information about HIV risk and treatment effectiveness are all promising interventions for increasing HIV prevention and adherence to treatment. Vaccination: three strategies show the most promising behavioral evidence for increasing vaccination rates—making information about vaccines more salient, offering incentives, and changing defaults. Medical provider behavior: changing default settings and providing comparative information on the performance of peers are the most promising interventions to influence provider behavior to be more in line with guidelines.
Retirement Savings	Strong influence of core principles: in making decisions about retirement saving benefits, people are strongly influenced by the core principles—limited attention and cognition; incorrect beliefs; present bias; and, to a slightly lesser degree, reference dependence. Use of default designs by employers and firms: default interventions have a major impact on saving for retirement, with little evidence of significant downsides for employees. These positive effects have been demonstrated across a wide variety of settings, making them one of the behavioral designs with the largest generalizability. Other characteristics of retirement plans, including framing, wording, and visuals, have also been shown to affect choice of plan and have the potential to at least modestly increase retirement assets.
Social Safety Net Benefits	The evidence on the effectiveness of low-cost nudges to encourage participation in social safety net programs is mixed, with some interventions showing modest effects on take-up but others showing no significant effect or any effect at all unless the study population includes households that have previously participated in the program. A few more costly large-scale interventions, particularly those implemented by the U.S. Department of Agriculture for the Supplemental Nutrition Assistance Program, have shown positive effects on take-up by providing additional information and by simplifying application forms and otherwise reducing the administrative burden.

continued

TABLE 11-1 Continued

Domain	Primary Findings
Climate Change	Providing information to consumers to address present bias and limited attention and cognition and using nudges related to social norms and preferences have been shown to encourage energy conservation, climate-friendly transportation decisions, and engagement in land use conservation programs if carefully targeted to the concerns of the target population.
Education	Parent–child interactions: the use of low-touch nudges, such as goal setting, reward programs, text reminders, and efforts to increase parents' engagement with their young children to improve literacy, can directly address issues with limited attention and present bias to increase the effectiveness of those interactions. Postsecondary education: several interventions have increased college application and applications for financial aid—reducing the administrative burden of the applications; providing support to students for these tasks; and setting up default choices for high school students, such as automatic registration for college admissions tests. Teacher performance: loss-frame incentives for teacher compensation could be a promising avenue to improve teacher performance, although the research is in its infancy.
Criminal Justice	Behavioral factors influence all points in the criminal justice system: determinants of criminal behavior, policing practices, court proceedings, judicial decision making, and incarceration. Although the evidence is limited, enough research has been conducted to suggest considerable potential for their effectiveness.

are most valuable when they incorporate rigorous examination of specific group treatment effects.

More specifically, several findings stand out:

- Retirement savings: The strongest result in our review of the six domains is that making retirement savings a default choice for employees is consistently effective. A substantial body of research has confirmed this finding and tested variations in how it can be done. That evidence has been so strong that it has influenced federal legislation.
- Health: Evidence demonstrates the value of modest, low-cost interventions that target very specific challenges. The evidence also shows the cumulative value of small-scale, low-cost interventions.
- Climate change: Across a range of efforts, the evidence demonstrates the high value of targeting specific concerns, as well as the cumulative value of multiple small-scale, low-cost interventions.
- Social safety net programs: Broad-scale interventions to reduce the administrative burden and better reach the neediest populations who can benefit from social safety net programs can be effective when carefully targeted.

It is important to note that most of the available evidence that demonstrates positive effects is for interventions that bring about short-term or one-time effects. Although some one-time changes can have lasting effects, ways of bringing about persistent or sustained change have not often been examined; achieving longer-lasting effects is likely to prove much more challenging. It is difficult to change habits with a single light-touch or nudge intervention; multiple, repeated interventions are likely necessary. It is also challenging to change behaviors when the costs or outcomes of a decision are removed from the point at which it is made. For example, in the context of daily decisions about energy usage, the effect on a person's electric bill—or on climate change—is quite far removed from an instance of forgetting to turn off a light. In this case, making the desired behavior change salient and making rewards or benefits of the behavior change immediate are promising strategies, although they may require repeated interventions.

In general, much more is known about promising interventions than about ways to translate, adapt, and implement them in varied contexts and at a broad scale. Many individual studies of interventions have been carried out across the six domains, but there has been far less work to follow up promising results with replication studies and with rigorous research on implementation and scaling (discussed in Chapter 12). Implementation and scaling studies are a crucial next step for identifying the intervention strategies that successfully scale and the contextual, institutional, or policy factors that predict successful implementation.

At the same time, methodological innovations are needed to uncover ways to tailor interventions to their targets and develop more robust and systematic approaches to understanding behavioral barriers—both of which have important implications for intervention design. Continued basic science, such as controlled laboratory studies that identify a promising mechanism of behavior change, is an important and needed input to the intervention design process.

Finally, it is worth noting that although there is a substantial body of work to consider, there are stones that remain unturned: it is important to distinguish between having evidence of no effects from an intervention and not having evidence of effects one way or the other because the intervention has not been adequately tested. A complicating factor is that research that demonstrates no effects is less likely to be published and accessible (discussed in Chapter 12). One possible factor in the variation in research attention across the six domains may be professional incentives. For example, funders may be more willing to support research in the health domain than in other domains, particularly replication and generalizability studies, and there are more journals and other media for studies in this domain.

In sum, a striking takeaway from our review of the impact of behavioral economics on policy is that real policy impact will happen only when interventions that show effectiveness in a laboratory setting are translated for real-world application, carefully designed for the intended context, accepted by policy makers, and implemented at scale (discussed in Chapter 13). An excellent example of interventions for which such work has been done is the work on increasing usage of Supplemental Nutrition Assistance Program benefits (see Chapter 7); more such work is needed.

CONCLUSIONS

The committee's findings from across the six domains led the committee to several conclusions about policy design.

Conclusion 11-1: Core principles of behavioral economics have been tested repeatedly across six domains—health, retirement benefits, social safety net benefits, climate change, education, and (to a lesser extent) criminal justice—and the evidence for their importance and value in the design of policy interventions is well established.

Occasionally, it is possible to achieve headline effects—those that are large and enduring, such as the impact of default settings on retirement savings. However, such results are rare: more often, effect sizes are smaller, but it is important to keep this point in context. The objectives policy makers pursue can be both grand (improving the nation's cardiovascular health, improving student achievement and attainment, mitigating the effects of climate change) and precise (encouraging customers to conserve energy, boosting 4th-grade reading scores). Interventions that are effective, albeit on a modest scale, are a vital component in an array of strategies, particularly if they are low in cost. Indeed, as the research on interventions related to climate change demonstrates, pursuing grand policy objectives requires a variety of approaches. Small interventions are no substitute for structural changes or strong economic incentives, but that is no reason to ignore the accumulated benefits that small, low-cost interventions can contribute in addressing major problems.

Moreover, it is clear that knowledge about behavior is indispensable to the design of effective policies in any domain in which the objective is modifying human behavior and decision making.

Conclusion 11-2: The strong evidence that the five core principles play a significant role in human decisions means that the design of effective policies intended to influence decision making requires careful, expert attention to behavioral factors.

Experts trained in behaviorally based policy development are needed for the development of effective policies in part because there are no easy shortcuts in the design and application of behaviorally informed policies (discussed in Chapter 14).

Conclusion 11-3: There is clear and strong evidence that specific interventions based on behavioral economics principles have been effective at changing targeted behaviors, but matching the tool to the challenge, the circumstances, and the target population is critical to success and requires careful attention. To achieve policy goals, interventions that show effectiveness in laboratory or highly controlled settings need to be translated for real-world application, carefully adapted for the intended context, accepted by policy makers, and implemented at scale.

Part III discusses the implications of these conclusions for training, funding, policy making, and further research.

Part III

Looking to the Future

12

Conducting and Disseminating Behavioral Economics Research

Much progress has been made in establishing the theoretical foundations of behavioral economics and the fruitful application of this research in many policy domains. In this chapter, we step aside from the content of this work to consider how research in the field is conducted. Issues with the conduct and dissemination of research limit its impact, and we make recommendations about ways to strengthen the field, with a focus on three issues:

- Replicability: Can researchers replicate the results from a given study in a follow-up study, even using modestly different means of analyzing the data?
- Generalizability: Can the results from a study be generalized to other settings, populations, and groups, even when relatively minor changes are made in the nature of the intervention being tested?
- Publication bias: Does the scientific process by which research gets disseminated and published bias the conclusions that researchers and the policy community draw from research?

These issues are not unique to behavioral economics or other behavioral and social science fields. We focus on their particular relevance to behavioral economics because the results of interventions are usually nuanced and effects depend on precise wording, framing, and the definitions of the target population, which makes generalizing results especially important and challenging. Effect sizes are often small, which means that the results may be particularly subject to changes in the analytic method used and the generalizability of the results. Finally, these issues are important for both policy makers and academic researchers as they collaborate to identify the research that will be most useful for addressing specific issues, translating it for application in the design and development of interventions, and implementing those interventions at scale (discussed in Chapter 13).

REPLICABILITY

We look first at replicability in a narrow sense: whether the results of a particular study or intervention will be the same if retested in another study for the exact same policy or intervention, on the same population used in the original study, using the same data. The volume of behavioral economics research has grown dramatically over the last four decades, and because the demand increasingly is for evidence about policy applications (rather than theoretical exercises), the interest in replication has grown.

Publication in peer-reviewed journals is regarded as the best way to ensure that high-quality and reliable research becomes known. In the early 2000s, a paper published in the flagship journal of the American Economic Association, the *American Economic Review*, showed that results previously published in dozens of papers could not be replicated (McCollough & Vinod, 2003). In some cases, the authors had not kept the data or computer programs that had produced their results, but errors of computation were also identified. The *American Economic Review* subsequently began requiring authors to make their data and computer programs publicly available, and other journals in the field followed suit; since then, many studies have been successfully replicated. The *American Economic Review* has recently gone further, assigning a data editor to replicate, at least in primary substance, all papers accepted for publication. This process has not been adopted at most journals because it requires a major commitment of resources. However, some have suggested that journals should go even further and ask the reviewers of submitted articles to replicate analyses themselves, but this is regarded as infeasible or impractical in all but the simplest cases (e.g., of randomized controlled trials with small numbers of observations and few variables).

A somewhat broader issue with replicability is the robustness of research findings: whether seemingly minor changes in follow-up studies—such as in the exact sample used in the analysis, the covariates used, or other methods of handling the data—change the results. It is common for researchers conducting follow-up analyses to select a subsample of a larger, complete dataset used in the initial study, and that subsampling can result in changes in findings. In multivariate analyses, minor decisions in the estimation method used, computation of standard errors, and control variables can have significant effects on results. In addition, most researchers conduct what is known as specification searching, meaning that they search for results that accord with their a priori expectations. Reports produced on this basis will present only a selective set of results based on that searching.

The review process can reveal some of the effects of such a search process, as peer reviews ask authors to conduct robustness checking themselves in order to detect whether search choices affected the reported results. But such a check would require that the researchers who conducted the study provide not only the exact dataset and variables used in the published results but also the larger dataset from which the published data were drawn, as well as all variables used in the analysis. This requirement is not always met in economics journals today, which often require only the provision of data and variables used in the published results. Another possibility is for project proposals to include plans for an external group to replicate the authors' analysis, with funding and data sharing as needed.

Journals in other social sciences now often ask authors to post their programs and data, although this was not common until a few years ago, when attention to reliability and reproducibility gained significant public attention (see National Academies of Sciences, Engineering, and Medicine, 2019). In response, many journals began indicating whether the authors of each paper have posted their data and code and preregistered.[1] In psychology, there has been a dramatic increase in publication of replication papers. In one activity, a group of researchers chose 100 lab experiments published in psychology journals and attempted to reproduce the results originally published. The results showed that only 37 percent of the replication experiments had statistically significant results, and the effect sizes were less than half those in the published papers, suggesting that the original studies had overstated the magnitude of the findings (Open Science Collaboration, 2015).

A barrier to making the data used in published articles available to other researchers is that behavioral economics data (and, more generally, behavioral sciences data) often have restricted access to protect privacy or for other reasons. Many of the studies cited in Chapters 5–10 were based on confidential records from company pension plans, schools, health care providers, and welfare departments, none of which are available to other researchers without specific permission from those who provided the data. Researchers conducting randomized controlled trials are also governed by strict privacy and confidentiality rules that prohibit release of the data in any form that might reveal the identity of the people in the study.

In some cases, it may be possible to do indirect replicability analysis without the data from a particular study, if a near-exact duplicate study

---

[1]Preregistration is the practice of a researcher's publicly sharing the intended research and analysis plan for the work. In addition to letting other researchers know about ongoing work, it can help deal with the problem of a researcher simply not reporting the results or even provide confirmation that the research was carried out.

can be undertaken. In many lab experiments, for example, the nature of the study population is precisely defined, as are the instructions to the study treatment and control groups. When this has been done, a new study on the exact same population with the exact same instructions can be conducted.

GENERALIZABILITY

We have noted that few of the studies identified in the six domains we examined used data from large-scale natural experiments or from design-based interventions with broad samples of the population of interest. Many of the studies in our review were conducted in a single geographical area, and many covered populations that are not representative of the general population in terms of race, gender, or socioeconomic status. Without tests of interventions and programs in different settings and different groups, it is difficult to know whether a particular policy tested in one setting and on one group would have the same results in a different setting and a different group.[2]

A related but conceptually distinct issue is whether minor variations in the treatment itself generate significant differences in findings. This issue is particularly important in behavioral approaches, especially nudges, where the framing (including the language used, the imagery chosen, and representation of choices) is carefully chosen by the study researchers. But whether differences in those framing issues and other minor variations would lead to different results cannot be known without testing those alternatives. Understanding these variations is important, and so too is testing in different settings and with different groups, to determine whether any treatment variations are different in only some settings or for only some groups.

In an ideal world, researchers would provide a complete mapping of how findings differ for a large set of minor variations in a treatment and across a wide variety of settings and groups, but there are many barriers to such an ideal. One is that in academic research there are more professional incentives for testing new interventions than for testing old ones: novelty is often of more interest than replication of an existing treatment in a different area or on a different population. Funders of research are also often more interested in testing new interventions than simply learning about the generalizability of existing interventions. Another barrier is that most interventions require the cooperation of an institution (a school, a private company, a health care provider), and such institutions are naturally interested primarily in tailoring an intervention to benefit the populations for

---

[2]Polman & Maglio (2022) suggest that some gains in generalizability can be made in experimental settings by making the experimental settings more representative of the general population (e.g., not just students) and hence more realistic.

which they are responsible, not in replicating evidence about what may have worked for other institutions and in other settings.

These barriers can constrain learning about who will most benefit from an intervention. As we emphasize throughout this report, a long-run goal in behavioral research is to learn which people respond to an intervention and under what circumstances. Achieving this goal may be impeded by an emphasis on either narrow populations that are not representative or broad study populations that produce average effects that dilute the findings that may apply to specific groups.

PUBLICATION BIAS

Publication bias is the term for the situation in which the research studies published in professional journals or other research outlets, taken together, are not a reliable summary of all the findings in the field or are a selective reporting of them. While some degree of selectivity in publication is inevitable, it is a concern if the reporting favors only certain kinds of results. Publication bias is found in all social sciences, but its seriousness varies across disciplines and methods of study: the extent of publication bias is larger in sociology and political science than in economics, for example (Gerber & Malhotra, 2008a, 2008b; Brodeur et al., 2016; Camerer et al., 2016; Vivalt, 2019; Brodeur, Cook, & Heyes, 2020).

One kind of publication bias derives from conflict of interest: it occurs when an author interprets the evidence and reaches a particular conclusion because they will benefit financially. An example may occur if a company funds research the results of which may affect its business or profits. This type of conflict of interest has gained much attention in academic institutions in the last decade, though the issue is perhaps most acute in medical and engineering schools, where faculty have incentives to either own their own firms or do extensive consulting work. Most universities now require strict acknowledgment of funding sources for all academic research. Many professional journals also require acknowledgment of funding sources and other possible conflicts of interest. Nonacademic institutions that publish research also generally report funding sources because those institutions almost exclusively conduct sponsored research. For example, a substantial percentage of randomized controlled studies of nudge interventions are funded by sponsors, and this is usually acknowledged in the published report.

A second type of publication bias occurs when the result of a study is deemed by the researchers to be less likely to be published than other results. A finding that something did not work well or perform as expected—of null results or statistical insignificance, for example—is generally more difficult to publish than findings of significance (e.g., Andrews & Kasy, 2019). In some cases, null results may not even be submitted for publication.

A third type of publication bias results from specification searching, noted above in connection with replicability. Researchers may tend to seek findings that meet their a priori expectations, and the difficulty in publishing null results and unexpected findings in professional peer-reviewed outlets reinforces this tendency. However, even projects that do not involve specification searching will be less likely to be published if the initial specification yields a null finding. Peer review may uncover some of these instances, as reviewers ask authors to test alternative specifications, but allowing independent researchers access to the full dataset on which the search took place is another method of addressing the bias.

Tests for the existence of publication bias typically rely on the classical theory of hypothesis testing in statistics. It is assumed that a given intervention has a true effect, but that random samples from a population will provide a distribution of estimates that are centered on the true effect but are sometimes higher and sometimes lower. This assumption means that even if the true effect is, say, positive, a certain fraction of estimates will be zero or negative, though the study as published may not show the expected number of zero or negative effects: this would be one indicator of publication bias. This effect is evidence because applied researchers have commonly agreed to assume that the true effect is probably nonzero.[3] Thus, when the distribution of results from the study is substantially different from what would be expected, publication bias is a likely culprit (Andrews & Kasy, 2019).

RECOMMENDATION

Before offering possible solutions to these problems, we wish to emphasize that we do not suggest that the evidence reviewed in this report is unreliable. The results from some of the studies we analyzed have been replicated, and some of the interventions have been tested in multiple settings and found to have similar effects, as detailed in Chapters 5–10. In other cases, the evidence supports the robustness of the results, so publication bias is unlikely. However, addressing issues with replicability, generalizability, and publication bias would significantly increase the overall usefulness of behavioral economics research evidence.

---

[3]The most common cutoff value is approximately two, implying that the probability (p) that the true effect is positive is 90 percent (sometimes 95 percent values are used). The phenomenon of "p-hacking," which has generated much discussion in recent years, is the research practice of conducting specification searching until the p-value (i.e., the probability that the true effect is nonzero) is at least 90 percent, equivalent to searching for specifications that have a t-statistic of at least two.

Replicability

The most promising solution to the problem of replicability is for behavioral science researchers to make the data used in their analyses available so that other researchers can try to replicate their results (Simonsohn, 2013). Although there are barriers to this objective, discussed above, much more could be done to address this problem. There are still many journals that do not ask authors to provide their data and computer code for published articles, even when the data are in the public domain. Many university and for-profit academic publishers could provide more financial support for the editorial staff of professional journals to check computer code themselves. Proposals have also been made to set up research data centers or other secure computing facilities where proprietary data can be reanalyzed by licensed researchers who are subject to penalties for disclosure of private information. Funders—including the National Science Foundation and the National Institutes of Health—have already taken steps in this direction but could go further.

Generalizability

To address challenges with generalizability, researchers could test their interventions in a wide variety of settings, populations, and groups and test alternative forms of their interventions in those different settings. Another possibility is the creation of a database of studies, including ones that had not been published in selective journals, that would be accessible to all, so that null results and other significant findings are not overlooked. However, the development and maintenance of such a database would be a significant and potentially expensive endeavor, and questions about who might do that work and oversee the inclusion of valid research would need to be addressed.

Publication Bias

One initial step toward the acknowledgment of potential publication bias would be for those who conduct meta-analyses and summaries of the literature to include tests of publication bias.[4] While there has been progress toward this goal, there are still meta-analyses that do not pay attention to such correction or do it only in a cursory way. Since there are different methods of correcting for publication bias, the authors of a meta-analysis can produce the results of the set of leading corrections in the same way

---

[4]Such tests include funnel plots and, ideally, imputations of the likely effect size, if it were possible to observe the null effect studies that are not published—for example, following the procedure in Andrews & Kasy (2019).

that researchers estimating event studies often present the point estimates for different leading estimators. Adopting such corrections is also critical to provide reasonable expectations about effect size to researchers, referees, and editors so that estimated effect sizes can be judged to be large or small relative to those expectations.

Other possible steps could counter publication bias. One is for editors to promote topics that are less subject to publication bias and establish a goal of publishing null findings. Researchers can contribute by conducting studies that predict the results from a future study, based on evidence to date and prior reasoning (DellaVigna, Pope, & Vivalt, 2019[5]). Comparing these forecasted results with the actual result can reveal when a null result contrasts with the prior beliefs of the research community. Yet another suggestion is to have researchers record the designs of their analyses in advance and delineate the exact specifications and statistical methods to be used in the analysis of the data, which will reduce the likelihood of specification searching. The American Economic Association has a registry of randomized controlled trials of this type. This suggestion could be taken further if studies could be accepted for publication on the basis of such preregistration, independent of the study's subsequent findings.

Another possibility would be to create a more complete database of studies (including those with no selective publication) to encourage the correct calculation of standard errors, and to support studies appropriate to small effects sizes. Such an effort would require substantial resources from sponsoring institutions, but government and nongovernment funders could suggest, or even require, that researchers report the results of all their analyses, including those with null results, and also post them on a database that is searchable by others. This approach would make a larger set of studies available for other researchers. It would also be possible to take advantage of situations in which a large set of unpublished reports that are not necessarily intended for formal publication can nevertheless be made available to researchers. This is possible for randomized controlled trials conducted by nudge units and in cases where peer-reviewed study designs have to be reported before being carried out.[6]

We note that many researchers do not take into account common features of data that can bias standard errors downward, such as autocorrelation, geographic correlation, and multiple testing of hypotheses. Journal editors could require that these calculations be provided to avoid low standard errors and upward biased findings of statistical significance.

---

[5] Also see their Social Science Prediction Platform at https://socialscienceprediction.org

[6] This was done for the Time Sharing Experiments in Social Science: see Franco, Malhotra, & Simonovits (2014).

In addition, many researchers do not select sample sizes large enough for their studies when the true effect size is relatively small, as is the case for many nudges. Encouraging researchers to design studies with appropriate sample sizes would lead to fewer chance findings.

As we acknowledge above, these issues are relevant across all social and behavioral science fields, but behavioral economics as a field is in a position to lead the way. By addressing these issues, behavioral economists and those who support their work can not only strengthen the field's research and reputation but also set an example that will benefit other fields.

> Recommendation 12-1: Researchers, funders of research, university leaders, and journal editors in behavioral economics should take steps to support the replicability and generalizability of behavioral economics research, more fully acknowledge publication bias and take steps to detect its presence, and counter publication bias using a variety of approaches.

Table 12-1 provides examples of the ways researchers, funders, journal editors, and university leaders could strengthen research in behavioral economics—and set an example for other fields in which similar problems arise.

TABLE 12-1 Examples of Ways to Strengthen Research

Goal	Researchers	Funders	Journal Editors	University Administrators
Encourage and reward the publication of null results		X	X	X
Encourage the use of sample sizes sufficient to detect small effects		X	X	
Conduct, encourage, and reward replication of results and research transparency	X	X	X	X
Commit to uncovering systematic use of p-hacking measures and funnel plots in meta-analyses and designs in order to enhance transparency	X	X	X	
Set standards for evidence gathering and evaluation		X	X	
Develop a shared, searchable platform of studies that is maintained in perpetuity as a resource for future researchers, whether or not the studies' results are published		X		X

REFERENCES

Andrews, I., & Kasy, M. (2019). Identification of and correction for publication bias. *American Economic Review*, *109*(8), 2766–2794. https://doi.org/10.1257/aer.20180310

Brodeur, A., Lé, M., Sangnier, M., & Zylberberg, Y. (2016). Star wars: The empirics strike back. *American Economic Journal: Applied Economics*, *8*(1), 1–32. https://doi.org/10.1257/app.20150044

Brodeur, A., Cook, N., & Heyes, A. (2020). Methods matter: P-hacking and publication bias in causal analysis in economics. *American Economic Review*, *110*(11), 3634–3660. https://doi.org/10.1257/aer.20190687

Camerer, C. F., Dreber, A., Forsell, E., Ho, T. H., Huber, J., Johannesson, M., Kirchler, M., Almenberg, J., Altmejd, A., Chan, T., & Heikensten, E. (2016). Evaluating replicability of laboratory experiments in economics. *Science*, *351*(6280), 1433–1436.

DellaVigna, S., Pope, D., & Vivalt, E. (2019). Predict science to improve science. *Science*, *366*(6464), 428–429. https://doi.org/10.1126/science.aaz1704

Franco, A., Malhotra, N., & Simonovits, G. (2014). Publication bias in the social sciences: Unlocking the file drawer. *Science*, *345*(6203), 1502–1505. https://doi.org/10.1126/science.1255484

Gerber, A. S., & Malhotra, N. (2008a). Publication bias in empirical sociological research: Do arbitrary significance levels distort published results? *Sociological Methods & Research*, *37*(1), 3–30. https://doi.org/10.1177/0049124108318973

———. (2008b). Do statistical reporting standards affect what is published? Publication bias in two leading political science journals. *Quarterly Journal of Political Science*, *3*(3), 313–326. https://doi.org/10.1177/1532673X09350979

McCollough, B. D., & Vinod, H. D. (2003). Verifying the solution from a nonlinear solver: A case study. *American Economic Review*, *93*(3), 873–892.

National Academies of Sciences, Engineering, and Medicine. (2019). *Reproducibility and replicability in science*. The National Academies Press.

Open Science Collaboration. (2015). Estimating the reproducibility of psychological science. *Science*, *349*(6251), aac4716. https://doi.org/10.1126/science.aac4716

Polman, E., & Maglio, S. J. (2022). Improving the generalizability of behavioral science by using reality checks: A tool for assessing heterogeneity in participants' consumership of study stimuli. *Perspectives on Psychological Science*. https://doi.org/10.1177/17456916221134575

Simonsohn, U. (2013). Just post it: The lesson from two cases of fabricated data detected by statistics alone. *Psychological Science*, *24*(10), 1875–1888. https://doi.org/10.1177/0956797613480366

Vivalt, E. (2019). Specification searching and significance inflation across time, methods and disciplines. *Oxford Bulletin of Economics and Statistics*, *81*(4), 797–816. https://doi.org/10.1111/obes.12289

13

Implementing Behavioral Economics Approaches

Despite strong evidence from across domains and contexts that strategies based on behavioral economics can contribute significantly to important policy objectives, there is also evidence of how challenging it is to apply this academic evidence beyond the scale and setting of the research studies (e.g., Haines & Donald, 1998; Bogenschneider & Corbett, 2010; Kajermo et al., 2010).[1] These challenges are in no way unique to the application of ideas from behavioral economics to policy—generalizable insights that work in the real world are elusive in nearly all social science fields (National Research Council, 2012).

A study of the adoption of the results of randomized controlled trials in behavioral economics research, funded by the U.S. Agency for International Development, estimated that less than one-third of the ideas tested were implemented at scales that could yield significant policy results (Kremer, Rao, & Schilbach, 2019). Others have estimated that the so-called voltage drop—the decline in effect sizes that can be expected when an evidence-based program is implemented at a broad scale—may range between 50 and 90 percent (List, 2022). It is reasonable to expect that a significant percentage of ideas tested will not bear fruit, and it is likely that the percentage will vary across domains and types of research. Nevertheless, trying to understand why promising ideas sometimes do not succeed when broadly implemented is clearly important.

---

[1] This section draws on the paper by Elizabeth Linos commissioned for this study, available at https://nap.nationalacademies.org/resource/26874/NASEM_Commissioned_Report_Linos.pdf

This chapter provides an overview of the challenges that confront policy makers and practitioners when they attempt to use behavioral economics strategies to address policy issues, and ways of addressing those challenges. The process of translating research findings to effective, broad-scale, real-world applications is complex and, ideally, involves an interactive feedback loop that links theory, experimentation, design, evaluation, and implementation. This chapter examines the circumstances that affect whether research intended for policy applications succeeds, focusing on the goals of researchers and policy makers, administrative issues, the accessibility of research, and the challenges of translating the relevant findings into a new context and putting them to work at the necessary scale.

CONNECTING RESEARCH AND PRACTICE

Much of what is known about behavioral economics has been discovered by academic researchers using randomized controlled trials (e.g., Tversky & Kahneman, 1985). In this work, researchers often control the setting, which guarantees that the experimental conditions necessary to arrive at causal estimates are met. Such studies often involve the researchers' own students and are carried out in research labs: that is, they often rely on highly structured study conditions and narrow populations.[2] However, the testing of behavioral economics ideas in the public sector is also essential, despite the sometimes competing objectives of researchers and policy makers.

Researchers and Policy Makers: Different Goals

Researchers are primarily interested in testing hypotheses and expanding understanding of scientific ideas that are generalizable; thus, they design and test interventions under carefully controlled conditions. Policy makers and others in the public sphere are equally interested in evidence about interventions, but they are also focused primarily on finding solutions for social problems and achieving their policy objectives. Those agencies and actors value evidence of effectiveness, but their primary goal is not necessarily to generate knowledge for its own sake or to be concerned about findings that do not contribute to their policy objectives. They are concerned about the populations they serve, their political preferences, and other factors in

---

[2]This was the case for the seminal work of Tversky & Kahneman (1985) on human heuristics and cognitive biases, as well as the seminal work of Madrian & Shea (2001) on the importance of default opt-out retirement policies in a large U.S. corporation where the researchers were given extensive control of the experimental setting, and the Volpp et al. (2009) study of a smoking cessation program at General Electric.

their immediate contexts. Outside the public sphere, behavioral economics research is also conducted by private, for-profit entities, who use behavioral economics ideas for managing personnel policies at their firms, as well as for marketing and other purposes. They generate findings in response to the questions that arise in their businesses and are not necessarily focused on sharing those results or actively engaging with the research community.

Behavioral Principles in Policy Practice

Research in the settings of public-sector agencies has focused attention on the choices that the public administrator makes, in addition to the decisions made by the people whom the intervention is designed to influence (e.g., Thaler & Sunstein, 2009; Sanders, Snijders, & Hallsworth, 2018). This work has pointed to notable differences in how behavioral economics principles work in the administration of public policy—as opposed to the context of individual decision making.

One key idea from this work is that the cost-benefit model of traditional economics is inadequate to explain the choices that people make when interacting with government administrators and agencies (Moynihan, Herd, & Harvey, 2015; Herd & Moynihan, 2019). People face administrative burden (see Chapter 3) when they participate in a program: that is, the combination of requirements, procedures, and policies developed by policy makers and administrators to regulate the program. But those regulations may reduce the likelihood that people will actually use services and programs. Although this issue is acknowledged by traditional economists, behavioral economics research shows that people's responses to the presence or removal of administrative burdens significantly exceed what would be predicted by traditional economics.

Navigating complicated paperwork and government websites, as well as challenges in communicating with government agencies, are examples of administrative burden. Individuals experience learning costs when they interact with government agencies and have to become familiar with the benefits and entry requirements for different social programs. Individuals may also experience psychological costs, such as stigma associated with program participation or dissonance between their self-image and their stereotype of who needs assistance. Program recipients also may face compliance costs, the burdens of maintaining their eligibility to receive benefits, such as recertification and follow-up interviews.

It has been suggested that public administrators may use these administrative burdens to adjust the flow of cases and the disbursement of expensive benefits and that the origins of the burdens in the policy and the political processes deserve further study (Herd & Moynihan, 2019). The example of the Free Application for Federal Student Aid (FAFSA; see Chapter

9) illustrates the importance of this issue: simplifying FAFSA forms is not the most efficacious way to connect families to financial aid, and certain groups may be disproportionately affected by the status quo and would be better able to participate if the system was redesigned.

Another claim is that the perceived manipulation that occurs with choice architecture in the public sector can lead to reactance (De Jonge, Zeelenberg, & Verlegh, 2018), that people will respond negatively when they perceive that others, particularly government agencies, are attempting to limit their freedom of choice (Brehm, 1966). Reactance often causes people to make choices that are not consistent with their preferences but allow them to feel in control of the situation (Jachimowicz et al., 2017). The result is people making suboptimal choices, choices they would not have made in the absence of the intervention (Jung & Mellers, 2016).

An example from the Netherlands illustrates reactance (Krijnen, Tannenbaum, & Fox, 2017). In 2016, the Netherlands passed a law that presumed a person's consent for organ donation rather than using opt-in consent. The goal of the legislation was to increase organ donation; it was based on overwhelming evidence showing that opt-out defaults increased participation. In this case, however, the policy choice created reactance, and the number of people opting out rose dramatically, including among those who had previously elected to donate. While the number opting out eventually declined and the policy ultimately increased organ donation, the negative reactance had long-term effects. Thus, it has been argued that, to avoid reactance, nudges should preserve freedom of choice and provide alternatives (Sunstein, 2017).

The conclusion from this and similar work is that the conditions that are possible in designing research to be carried out with a public-sector partner in the real world are actually quite different from the ideal research design (Fels, 2022). In public administration settings, the public partner frequently controls access to the data; the research environment; and, ultimately, the authority to permit the research. This necessary control leads to conflicting goals for the intervention. Academic researchers seek generalizable knowledge, and therefore they place the highest priority on a strong causal research design. In contrast, a public administrator's primary goal is to understand the success of their particular intervention in a specific context (Sanders, Snijders, & Hallsworth, 2018). Following a study design closely is not generally a top priority for a public administrator, who may be uncomfortable with the need to withhold an intervention from people they perceive to be in need, even if it is done through randomized selection. Additionally, they may be comfortable with less firmly supported claims as a basis for action than researchers look for. Moreover, many public administrators have decided that the intervention being studied is effective before agreeing to use it, so some of the study requirements may conflict with their public service motivation (Glennerster & Takavarasha, 2013).

Another way in which research in a public-sector context may differ from academic studies has to do with novelty. Findings about applications that produce novel results, such as the importance of social norms regarding utility use, appeal to academic audiences: they are easier to publish and gain attention from academic peers. This phenomenon is illustrated in a study of the social norming principle, which also illustrates the differing motivations of researchers and administrators. The study showed that people who received notices suggesting they used more energy than their neighbors reduced their own consumption by two percent (Allcott, 2011). The public administrator was eager to apply this finding on a wide scale. However, the researchers suspected that the novelty of this intervention, which attracted the public's attention and thus had salient motivation, was driving the results. If that were the case, repeated exposure would likely reduce the efficacy of the treatment over time and ultimately mean that it was less valuable for the administrator's goals than it had seemed (Sanders, Snijders, & Hallsworth, 2018).

ACCESSIBILITY OF RESEARCH

To benefit from evidence, policy makers and others in the public sector need to know it exists, understand what it means, and value its potential to help with the problem they want to solve (Linos, 2022).[3] Few policy makers have ample time to follow academic research in depth, and most want to be made aware of new research that is relevant to their work as efficiently as possible.[4] Several factors influence the ease with which policy makers can identify and gain access to research findings that are reliable and relevant to their work.

Persistent problems with publication bias (see Chapter 12) can distort impressions of the state of a field even for trained experts. If the evidence most likely to be shared widely reports surprising success stories (that may or may not ultimately be replicated), a policy maker's ability to understand what evidence to implement is severely limited. Policy makers vary in the training and experience they have had in understanding and applying academic research and in the value and importance they believe it has for their own policy work. Moreover, the same behavioral biases that may affect how any person interprets new information (e.g., present bias, limited

---

[3]This and the following section draw in part on ideas in Linos (2022), commissioned for the project.

[4]For a detailed discussion of this problem, see National Academies of Sciences, Engineering, and Medicine (2022).

attention; see Chapter 3) also apply to policy makers and practitioners (e.g., Moynihan & Lavertu, 2012; Bellé, Cantarelli, & Belardinelli, 2017; Battaglio et al., 2019).

Intermediary institutions, such as think tanks and clearinghouses, explicitly attempt to bridge the gaps between academic researchers and policy makers. By translating research findings into everyday language, such institutions support policy makers in understanding what has been learned in several ways, particularly by weighing more rigorous studies more heavily and by synthesizing results; in these ways, they make it easier to digest the main findings in large bodies of work. For example, the What Works Centre, funded by the government of the United Kingdom, is designed to help public-sector organizations "create, share, and use high-quality evidence in decision-making" (What Works Network, 2013, Introduction). Another example from the United Kingdom is the independent nonprofit Education Endowment Foundation (EEF), which not only funds education research but also collects and disseminates policy-relevant evidence related to the relationship between family income and educational achievement in ways that are easy to digest.[5] The EEF categorizes different types of educational interventions on the basis of their cost, the likely effect size, and how rigorous the evidence base is.

With respect to publication bias, improving research transparency would be a substantial benefit (see Chapter 12). The work of intermediary organizations and efforts to improve research transparency are valuable, but research is needed to improve understanding of the challenges policy makers and practitioners face in learning about and understanding new evidence. For example, it would be helpful to know who in a government agency needs to know and understand the evidence for it to be adopted. Some theories of change emphasize the role of political leaders as central to evidence adoption (e.g., Damanpour & Schneider, 2009), but others focus more on individual knowledge brokers in more mid-level roles (e.g., Ward, House, & Hamer, 2009; Smits et al., 2018; Meza et al., 2021). Others argue that innovation depends on distributed innovators across teams and more comprehensive interventions across multiple policy positions (e.g., Grol & Grimshaw, 2003; Meijer, 2014). Research on how training, peer networks, and communities of practice help to spread knowledge would be valuable, as would research on the effects of the materials and dissemination efforts of intermediate organizations on policy makers.

---

[5]See https://educationendowmentfoundation.org.uk/

TRANSLATING EVIDENCE FOR USE

Once a policy maker identifies an evidence-based intervention that targets a specified policy objective, the next challenge is to translate the intervention for a particular context: there will never be an "off-the-shelf" intervention that has been tested that can be applied in a new context without modification. Researchers themselves face challenges in replicating studies in different environments, and the challenges for policy makers are greater. Policy makers need to identify the components of an intervention that are essential to its effectiveness, understanding the mechanism through which it brings about change and how that mechanism will function in the policy context in which it is to be used. Ideally, policy makers would rely on evidence produced in a wide set of contexts to evaluate the relevance of research findings, including settings that are not primarily WEIRD (western, educated, industrialized, rich, and democratic) when evaluating the relevance of research findings, but this is not always possible.

Because the needed work requires skills, authority, and resources, there has been a growing recognition of the need for full-time employees who focus on data, research, and evaluation in government agencies. Increasingly, agencies have created evidence teams and fellowship programs to help develop the infrastructure needed to translate research into a policy context. Local governments may supplement their resources with hired experts. At the federal level, the Office of Management and Budget has focused on ensuring that all agencies have the capacity to use evidence in decision making.

A separate challenge is adopting an approach at scale. As noted above, effect sizes are generally lower when interventions are taken to scale; reduction in effects is likely partly a product of site selection bias. That is, the sites selected to first test a new behavioral intervention may be correlated with the likelihood of impact (Allcott, 2015). Sites for study are likely selected precisely because the population may be especially amenable to the approach, and study samples may not be representative of the population at large.

There is no substitute for testing new behavioral insights that are candidates for translation from research to practice. The Office of Evaluation Sciences (OES), a part of the federal General Services Administration, supports and conducts randomized controlled trials of research-based ideas that are brought to the public sector. It is worth noting that, as providers of technical assistance to federal agencies, the OES staff focus on making progress with policy objectives rather than on seeking opportunities to test theories or behavioral insights. When designing experiments, OES draws on both the academic literature and previous experiments by the government. By testing similar behavioral concepts in many settings, OES is not only creating empirical evidence of which behavioral insights translate but also actively measuring effect sizes at scale, providing estimates of average effects that internalize any voltage drop.[6]

The OES example is very useful, but more work on the details of translating intervention mechanisms to new contexts will be valuable. Replicating findings in more diverse contexts is a logical goal, but other approaches could include involving representatives of the population the intervention is intended to help in designing adaptations, as well as the frontline workers who will deliver it.

The OES example is an illustration of a successful unit at the federal level in the United States. Many other successful examples, such as the Behavioral Insights Team (a nudge unit) in the United Kingdom, are also at the central government level. Creating design, evaluation, and implementation units at the state and local levels is much more challenging because public agencies at those levels have many fewer resources and expert personnel. Some cities have successfully established such units, generally in the form of nudge units. An example is The Lab @ DC, operated by the office of the mayor of the District of Columbia, but city-level units are not common.[7] State and local governments are more likely to need the help of external organizations, either intermediary institutions like those discussed above or consulting organizations that can replace the need for in-house government staff.

ADOPTING INTERVENTIONS AT A BROAD SCALE

Even when a solid body of evidence exists and needed changes for the context have been carefully addressed, there is no guarantee that an intervention will perform as expected when implemented on a broad scale, whether in the public or private sector (Athey & Luca, 2019; DellaVigna, Kim, & Linos, 2022; List, 2022). This is true for virtually all interventions, not just behavioral ones. One study of 73 randomized controlled trials conducted in U.S. cities showed that only one-third of the tested behavioral treatments were ultimately adopted (DellaVigna, Kim, & Linos, 2022).

Researchers have investigated why some organizations are better able to implement interventions based on solid evidence. They suggest that larger entities that have greater resources and larger staffs are in a better position to set up routines and practices for transferring knowledge and for learning as an organization—and are therefore better equipped to act effectively on new evidence (e.g., Besley & Persson, 2009; Moynihan & Landuyt, 2009; Argote & Miron-Spektor, 2011; Bekkers, Tummers, & de Vries, 2015). Two

---

[6]Recently, OES has also committed to publishing all preanalysis plans (Linos, 2022).
[7]See https://thelabprojects.dc.gov

other factors are important in policy settings. A change in political leadership may create obstacles to knowledge transfer and may also introduce political calculations about efforts associated with a previous administration. Such political transitions also often entail employee turnover, particularly of career civil servants who may have played a critical role in innovation. The review of 73 randomized controlled trials noted above also suggests that incremental improvements to existing infrastructure are much more likely to be adopted than completely new programs (DellaVigna, Kim, & Linos, 2022).

CONCLUSION AND RECOMMENDATIONS

What would make it easier for policy makers and practitioners to implement the evidence-based approaches they know about and value that are readily applicable to their contexts? We see two avenues for strengthening this capacity: (1) increased attention to collaboration among those trained in behavioral economics and those trained in implementation science or public management, and (2) improved training in behavioral economics to help prepare policy makers and staff to collaborate in translating research ideas for real-world policy development and design. A new subfield of public administration scholarship dedicated to using evidence from behavioral economics has also started to gain steam, but in the committee's view, behavioral economics or another field that directly addresses behavior should be a core element of the curriculum for students preparing for careers in public administration (e.g., Grimmelikhuijsen et al., 2017).

Conclusion 13-1: Collaboration among researchers and policy makers is invaluable both for the continued development of knowledge about the application of behavioral economics to policy and for the development of effective policies. The development of strong intermediary institutions that can function to bring the two groups together and to assist in the translation between different languages could contribute to such collaborations.

Recommendation 13-1: Government units should consider adopting the example of the Office of Evaluation Sciences, in the General Services Administration, to support and fund in-house capabilities for integrating behavioral specialists into policy development, such as through institutional structures that facilitate learning and collaboration among policy makers and researchers in the design, implementation, and evaluation of behavioral economics–based policies in all relevant domains. The use of temporary research appointments and consulting organizations could bring expertise and assistance to state and local government entities that cannot afford permanent in-house staff.

Recommendation 13-2: University leaders should ensure that training in the principles of behavioral economics and critical thinking about their translation and application to policy making is a core component of training for students pursuing degrees in public administration.

REFERENCES

Allcott, H. (2011). Social norms and energy conservation. *Journal of Public Economics*, 95(9–10), 1082–1095. https://doi.org/10.1016/j.jpubeco.2011.03.003

———. (2015). Site selection bias in program evaluation. *The Quarterly Journal of Economics*, 130(3), 1117–1165. https://doi.org/10.1093/qje/qjv015

Argote, L., & Miron-Spektor, E. (2011). Organizational learning: From experience to knowledge. *Organization Science*, 22(5), 1123–1137. https://doi.org/10.1287/orsc.1100.0621

Athey, S., & Luca, M. (2019). Economists (and economics) in tech companies. *Journal of Economic Perspectives*, 33(1), 209–230. https://doi.org/10.1257/jep.33.1.209

Battaglio Jr., R. P., Belardinelli, P., Bellé, N., & Cantarelli, P. (2019). Behavioral public administration ad fontes: A synthesis of research on bounded rationality, cognitive biases, and nudging in public organizations. *Public Administration Review*, 79(3), 304–320. https://doi.org/10.1111/puar.12994

Bekkers, V. J. J. M., Tummers, L., & de Vries, H. (2015). Innovation in the public sector: A systematic review and future research agenda. *Public Administration*, 94(1), 146–166. https://doi.org/10.1111/padm.12209

Bellé, N., Cantarelli, P., & Belardinelli, P. (2017). Cognitive biases in performance appraisal: Experimental evidence on anchoring and halo effects with public sector managers and employees. *Review of Public Personnel Administration*, 37(3), 275–294. https://doi.org/10.1177/0734371X17704891

Besley, T., & Persson, T. (2009). The origins of state capacity: Property rights, taxation, and politics. *American Economic Review*, 99(4), 1218–1244. https://doi.org/10.1257/aer.99.4.1218

Bogenschneider, K., & Corbett, T. J. (2010). *Evidence-based policymaking: Insights from policy-minded researchers and research-minded policymakers*. Routledge.

Brehm, J. W. (1966). *A theory of psychological reactance*. Academic Press.

Damanpour, F., & Schneider, M. (2009). Characteristics of innovation and innovation adoption in public organizations: Assessing the role of managers. *Journal of Public Administration Research and Theory*, 19(3), 495–522. https://doi.org/10.1093/jopart/mun021

De Jonge, P., Zeelenberg, M., & Verlegh, P. W. (2018). Putting the public back in behavioral public policy. *Behavioural Public Policy*, 2(2), 218–226. https://doi.org/10.1017/bpp.2018.23

DellaVigna, S., Kim, W., & Linos, E. (2022). *Bottlenecks for evidence adoption*. NBER Working Paper 30144. National Bureau of Economic Research. https://doi.org/10.3386/w30144

Fels, K. M. (2022). Who nudges whom? Expert opinions on behavioural field experiments with public partners. *Behavioural Public Policy*, 1–37. https://doi.org/10.1017/bpp.2022.14

Glennerster, R., & Takavarasha, K. (2013). *Running randomized evaluations: A practical guide*. Princeton University Press. https://doi.org/10.1515/9781400848447

Grimmelikhuijsen, S., Jilke, S., Olsen, A. L., & Tummers, L. (2017). Behavioral public administration: Combining insights from public administration and psychology. *Public Administration Review*, 77(1), 45–56. https://doi.org/10.1111/puar.12609

Grol, R., & Grimshaw, J. (2003). From best evidence to best practice: Effective implementation of change in patients' care. *The Lancet, 362*(9391), 1225–1230. https://doi.org/10.1016/S0140-6736(03)14546-1

Haines, A., & Donald, A. (1998). Making better use of research findings. *British Medical Journal, 317*(7150), 72–75. https://doi.org/10.1136/bmj.317.7150.72

Herd, P., & Moynihan, D. P. (2019). *Administrative burden: Policymaking by other means.* Russell Sage Foundation.

Jachimowicz, J. M., Chafik, S., Munrat, S., Prabhu, J. C., & Weber, E. U. (2017). Community trust reduces myopic decisions of low-income individuals. *Proceedings of the National Academy of Sciences, 114*(21), 5401–5406. https://doi.org/10.1073/pnas.1617395114

Jung, J. Y., & Mellers, B. A. (2016). American attitudes toward nudges. *Judgment & Decision Making, 11*(1). https://journal.sjdm.org/15/15824a/jdm15824a.pdf

Kajermo, K. N., Boström, A. M., Thompson, D. S., Hutchinson, A. M., Estabrooks, C. A., & Wallin, L. (2010). The BARRIERS scale—The barriers to research utilization scale: A systematic review. *Implementation Science, 5*(1), 1–22.

Kremer, M., Rao, G., & Schilbach, F. (2019). Behavioral development economics. *Handbook of behavioral economics: Applications and foundations 1, 2*, 345–458. North-Holland. https://doi.org/10.1016/bs.hesbe.2018.12.002

Krijnen, J. M., Tannenbaum, D., & Fox, C. R. (2017). Choice architecture 2.0: Behavioral policy as an implicit social interaction. *Behavioral Science & Policy, 3*(2), i–18. https://doi.org/10.1353/bsp.2017.0010

Linos, E. (2022). *Translating behavioral economics evidence into policy and practice.* Commissioned paper prepared for the Committee on Future Directions for Applying Behavioral Economics to Policy, National Academies of Sciences, Engineering, and Medicine. https://nap.nationalacademies.org/resource/26874/NASEM_Commissioned_Report_Linos.pdf

List, J. A. (2022). *The voltage effect: How to make good ideas great and great ideas scale.* Currency.

Madrian, B. C., & Shea, D. F. (2001). The power of suggestion: Inertia in 401(k) participation and savings behavior. *The Quarterly Journal of Economics, 116*(4), 1149–1187. https://doi.org/10.1162/003355301753265543

Meijer, A. J. (2014). From hero-innovators to distributed heroism: An in-depth analysis of the role of individuals in public sector innovation. *Public Management Review, 16*(2), 199–216. https://doi.org/10.1080/14719037.2013.806575

Meza, R. D., Triplett, N. S., Woodard, G. S., Martin, P., Khairuzzaman, A. N., Jamora, G., & Dorsey, S. (2021). The relationship between first-level leadership and inner-context and implementation outcomes in behavioral health: A scoping review. *Implementation Science, 16*(1), 69. https://doi.org/10.1186/s13012-021-01104-4

Moynihan, D. P., & Landuyt, N. (2009). How do public organizations learn? Bridging cultural and structural perspectives. *Public Administration Review, 69*(6), 1097–1105. https://doi.org/10.1111/j.1540-6210.2009.02067.x

Moynihan, D. P., & Lavertu, S. (2012). Does involvement in performance management routines encourage performance information use? Evaluating GPRA and PART. *Public Administration Review, 72*(4), 592–602. https://doi.org/10.1111/j.1540-6210.2011.02539.x

Moynihan, D., Herd, P., & Harvey, H. (2015). Administrative burden: Learning, psychological, and compliance costs in citizen-state interactions. *Journal of Public Administration Research and Theory, 25*(1), 43–69. https://doi.org/10.1093/jopart/muu009

National Academies of Sciences, Engineering, and Medicine. (2022). *Ontologies in the behavioral sciences: Accelerating research and the spread of knowledge.* The National Academies Press. https://nap.nationalacademies.org/login.php?record_id=26464

National Research Council. (2012). *Using science as evidence in public policy.* The National Academies Press. https://nap.nationalacademies.org/login.php?record_id=13460

Sanders, M., Snijders, V., & Hallsworth, M. (2018). Behavioural science and policy: Where are we now and where are we going? *Behavioural Public Policy*, 2(2), 144–167. https://doi.org/10.1017/bpp.2018.17

Smits, P., Denis, J.-L., Préval, J., Lindquist, E., & Aguirre, M. (2018). Getting evidence to travel inside public systems: What organisational brokering capacities exist for evidence-based policy? *Health Research Policy and Systems*, 16(1), 122. https://doi.org/10.1186/s12961-018-0393-y

Sunstein, C. R. (2017). *Human agency and behavioral economics: Nudging fast and slow*. Springer.

Thaler, R. H., & Sunstein, C. R. (2009). *Nudge: Improving decisions about health, wealth, and happiness*. Penguin Books.

Tversky, A., & Kahneman, D. (1985). The framing of decisions and the psychology of choice. *Behavioral decision making*, 25–41. Springer. https://doi.org/10.1007/978-1-4613-2391-4_2

Volpp, K. G., Troxel, A. B., Pauly, M. V., Glick, H. A., Puig, A., Asch, D. A., Galvin, R., Zhu, J., Wan, F., DeGuzman, J., & Corbett, E. (2009). A randomized, controlled trial of financial incentives for smoking cessation. *New England Journal of Medicine*, 360, 699–709. https://doi.org/10.1056/NEJMsa0806819

Ward, V., House, A., & Hamer, S. (2009). Knowledge brokering: The missing link in the evidence to action chain? *Evidence & Policy*, 5(3), 267–279. https://doi.org/10.1332/174426409X463811

What Works Network. (2013). *What Works Network*. Last updated January 17, 2023. https://www.gov.uk/guidance/what-works-network

14

Advancing the Field of Behavioral Economics

Behavioral economics has grown steadily as a field over the last several decades. Journals and academic departments devoted to it have established themselves, and behavioral economists have studied the application of their ideas to numerous policy challenges, as detailed throughout this report. Returning to the charge that guided this study, we close with our review of the development of the field and its theoretical foundations, as well as our findings about the primary behavioral economics strategies and how they have been applied. In this chapter we synthesize key conclusions from the research to date and offer recommendations to guide the future development of the field and capitalize fully on its potential to help meet critical societal goals, including directions for the research that is needed to support continued growth.

CONCLUSIONS

We draw two primary conclusions from our review: that behavioral knowledge is indispensable to the development of effective policy interventions and that work is needed to support intervention design and broad-scale implementation.

Developing Effective Policy Interventions

Foundational theoretical work that has integrated understanding of cognitive and psychosocial processes with economic analysis has pointed to five core principles that help to explain human decision making: limited attention and cognition, inaccurate beliefs, present bias, reference dependence and framing, and social preferences and social norms (see Chapter 3). Empirical research has provided strong evidence that these behavioral factors play a major role in human decisions and are therefore key factors to consider in assessing the impact of public policy programs and in designing interventions to modify human behavior.

We acknowledge that our review of the available evidence was not comprehensive and that, for reasons discussed throughout the report, positive findings of effects may be more likely to garner attention than null or negative findings. We hope the field will continue to produce studies that can provide the most robust evidence of effectiveness—or lack of it—such as large-scale studies and meta-analyses.

Nevertheless, the accumulated evidence across the six domains is significant: it shows that decision processes are dynamic, malleable, and context dependent and that understanding these factors helps to explain how and why people behave in ways that appear to be counter to rational calculations. That evidence from research in behavioral economics demonstrates that those behavioral decision processes recur repeatedly and have significant impact on policy-relevant behavior, which in turn has strong implications for policies that differ from those that are suggested by traditional economics.

This report examines this impact in six important domains, but behavioral economics concepts are also being applied in many other contexts, including contexts not generally considered for behavioral economics input. For example, recent reports of the National Academies of Sciences, Engineering, and Medicine that addressed improving fuel economy (2021), reducing consumer food waste (2020), and reducing alcohol-impaired fatalities (2018) all discuss behavioral economics approaches among varied other interventions. Behavioral economics has also had a profound influence in commercial contexts, as we note below. In the future, understanding of behavior has the potential to play a key role in other urgent societal issues we have not addressed, such as combating misinformation; see Box 14-1.

Conclusion 14-1: The very strong evidence that complex cognitive, social, behavioral, and contextual factors influence judgment and decision making means that behavioral economics concepts are indispensable for advancing scientific understanding of policy-relevant human behavior and for designing public policies. Behavioral economics has produced invaluable evidence about why people act in seemingly irrational ways, how they respond to interventions, and how public policy and practice interventions can be designed to modify the habitual and unconscious ways that people act and make decisions.

> **BOX 14-1**
> **Using Behavioral Knowledge to Combat**
> **False and Misleading Information**
>
> False and misleading information—whether it is false information spread deliberately to cause harm or out of ignorance, or hate speech—is proliferating. It is not an easy phenomenon to measure, but a 2019 report showed that 89 percent of U.S. adults reported seeing false or misleading news (Mitchell et al., 2019). False and misleading information causes harm in multiple ways and in many public policy domains, and people's receptivity to it is clearly related to key behavioral concepts, such as limited attention and social norms, as well as other cognitive factors, such as a lack of reasoning (Pennycook & Rand, 2021).
> Efforts to combat misinformation using artificial intelligence and fact checking have had mixed results (see, e.g., Woolley, 2020; Pennycook & Rand, 2021). Behaviorally based interventions offer intriguing possibilities in this arena, but they need to be robust to the rapidly changing nature of the Internet and responsive to the contexts and identities that strongly influence people's susceptibility to misinformation. Generalized interventions, such as accuracy prompts, show promise, as do educational approaches that "inoculate" people against misinformation (Compton, 2013; Kozyreva, Lewandowsky, & Hertwig, 2020; Roozenbeek et al., 2022; van der Linden, 2022). The application of specific behavioral approaches to these issues is an area for further study.

Supporting Design and Implementation

The evidence for the importance of behavioral ideas is strong, but the refinement of strategies for applying these principles in a systematic way to the design of policies and interventions remains a frontier challenge. There is clear and strong evidence that specific interventions based on these principles have been effective at changing certain targeted behaviors, and it is also clear that behavioral economics research has contributed to a large and expanding set of policy interventions that includes strategies with excellent empirical evidence of effectiveness (e.g., defaults, framing). For other intervention approaches commonly studied, such as behaviorally informed incentives and social proof interventions, the evidence is mixed, nuanced, or still emerging.

Some types of decisions appear to be more amenable to behaviorally informed interventions than others. It is comparatively easy to influence a one-time, up-or-down decision, such as whether or not to opt in to a retirement savings plan, or to make it easier and more likely for a target population to complete a specific action, such as filling out an application form. Interventions that have targeted more complex behaviors, such as programs to reward teachers for increasing their students' test scores, or approaches to changing how clinicians approach complex diagnosis and treatment decisions, have not yielded such clear-cut or consistent results.

It is important to acknowledge that research demonstrating positive effects for behavioral economics interventions typically shows modest effect sizes. This is not necessarily a surprising finding, particularly because many of the intervention studies are comparatively low in cost and easy to administer. However, as we emphasize clearly in the work on climate change—a challenge of unmeasurable magnitude—the application of combinations of individually modest interventions can cumulatively bring important changes and benefits for relatively little cost.

Throughout the report we also identify additional persistent challenges in the application of behavioral economics for policy: it is not easy or straightforward to generalize findings from specific contexts, and implementing successful interventions at scale remains elusive. Moreover, deeper understanding of why and when observed effects occur would be valuable. Even when intervention or policy studies demonstrate a positive effect on behavior, there is insufficient knowledge about mechanisms of action and about differential responses to the intervention or policy by different groups. For example, in the context of inaccurate beliefs, understanding of the relevant mechanisms would be enhanced if data on both beliefs and behavior were collected and analyzed. For example, testing whether beliefs held by participants before the intervention were inaccurate and whether the intervention was effective in changing them would be valuable. Our review of six policy domains (in Part II) also suggests that behavioral economists have yet to fully embrace the concept of behavioral design—the systematic process by which interventions and strategies to change human behavior are designed. That is, specific interventions are often tested without sufficient attention to behavioral design principles.

Conclusion 14-2: The field of behavioral economics has made significant advances over the past 20 years, producing evidence about both general principles and specific intervention approaches that address policy challenges in many domains. However, the field has not yet produced generalizable and implementable practice guidance and intervention design strategies for determining what works, when, and for whom. Whether the goal of providing such specific guidance can be achieved, given the importance of context and the unique characteristics of many targets of behavior change, is not clear.

RECOMMENDATIONS

As noted above, behavioral economics research has generated a large volume of promising results. But there is also much more to learn, and there are contributions to be made in new policy domains. The committee recommends strategies for funders, research and professional organizations, and universities to support future development in the field of behavioral economics; such support would certainly be appropriate in other research fields, but our focus is on work in behavioral economics. We also recommend priorities for research.

Recommendation 14-1: Researchers and funders of research should balance attention and funding across:
- basic research in intervention design, interdisciplinary investigation, and development of methods;
- research to support applications of behavioral economics concepts in practice, including implementation and scale-up and evaluation; and
- research to explore and support the positive contributions of behavioral economics to society, including attention to equity of impact and attitudes about behavioral interventions.

Recommendation 14-2: Funders and university leaders should prioritize investments in interdisciplinary research collaborations.

Behavioral economics is rooted in the integration of ideas from diverse academic domains, and its future progress will depend on continued interdisciplinary collaboration. Such interaction is not easy and faces well-known obstacles: differences in theoretical perspectives, terminology, research methods and tools, and standards of evidence all bring challenges. Nevertheless, interdisciplinary work, involving researchers from many domains, including cognitive and social psychology and neuroeconomics, can help to pinpoint how the human brain processes and responds to information.

Practical strategies, such as setting up (and funding) multidisciplinary labs or working groups in which teams of researchers can regularly collaborate and identifying funders for methodologies and projects that do not fit established research contexts, can help to address the challenges of implementation (see Chapter 13). Examples include the Behavioral Economics Design Initiative at the University of Pittsburgh, which focuses on behavioral economics and mechanism design, and the Nudge4 Lab at the University of Virginia.[1] In general, establishing stronger incentives (e.g., in the contexts of research support, journal publication, academic advancement) for interdisciplinary research and training for students and younger scholars in interdisciplinary work will yield long-term benefits for the field.

---

[1] See https://sites.google.com/view/bedi-university-of-pittsburgh/home and https://nudge4.org

Recommendation 14-3: Researchers and funders of research should prioritize research related to methods and ways of understanding the mechanisms of behavior and behavior change. Specifically, research is needed to:
- advance behavioral design and intervention design methods to better link behavioral principles and insights to specific intervention and policy goals;
- advance methods for conducting pilot and rapid-cycle studies;
- accumulate more evidence on how findings from one setting can be applied to other settings or at broader scales;
- realize the potential for artificial intelligence and machine learning approaches to improve tailoring and targeting;
- bring cutting-edge adaptive trial design approaches to behavioral economics studies; and
- incorporate empirical methods from other disciplines and fields that can enrich behavioral economics research.

Recommendation 14-4: Researchers, funders of research, and entities that support or sponsor behavioral units in organizations should prioritize research and practice initiatives that increase the impact of behavioral economics findings through implementation, scale-up, and evaluation of potentially successful interventions and policies.

As evidence that an intervention has been effective in a particular context accumulates (in any research field), it is important that larger studies, with larger samples and more variants, be conducted to replicate the findings and test how well the intervention works in practice, across contexts and populations. In some cases, the results will be confirmed; in others, they will not; and others will point to a redesign or a refinement. This phase of the research—scaling studies that involve patience and resources—is essential for behavioral tools to bring meaningful societal benefits.

Many social science disciplines and policy domains emphasize the importance of systems of ongoing evaluation, in which research, design and development, testing of ideas, and evaluation each contribute to a continuous cycle of learning and refinement and improvement of policy interventions (see, e.g., Patton, Sawicki, & Clark, 2012). In the context of behavioral economics interventions, ongoing data collection, pilot testing, and long-term surveillance are of particular importance because of the need to assess the durability and sustainability of effects, as well as differential response to policies by different populations. The committee examined many policy interventions that were designed with behavioral principles in mind but was not able to look systematically, from the perspective of policy makers, at how regularly behavioral factors are currently considered in the design of policy. It seems likely, however, that the majority of policy recommendations still rely primarily or exclusively on traditional economic modeling.

> **Recommendation 14-5:** Researchers, funders of research, and entities that support or sponsor behavioral units in organizations should prioritize ongoing investigations into the role of behavioral economics in society, with specific attention to the equity implications of behavioral economics policies and interventions; the implications of public attitudes toward the ethics of behavioral economics research and practice, as well as their acceptance by the general public; and possible public policy interest in commercial applications of behavioral economics findings.

It was not part of our charge to identify priorities for the specific policy goals that should be addressed using behavioral economics approaches, but three issues in policy implementation raise broad questions: equity of impact, attitudes about interventions, and commercial application of behaviorally based findings.

Equity of Impact

It is reasonable to ask whether behavioral interventions are reaching those most in need, and whether such interventions in some cases may have the negative unintended consequence of increasing inequalities (Blumenthal-Barby & Burrough, 2012; Lunze & Paasche-Orlow, 2013; Lin, Osman, & Ashcroft, 2017). These are empirical questions and, as far as the committee is aware, there is limited evidence on them.

Attitudes About Behavioral Interventions

The use of behavioral interventions, such as nudges, can be perceived as paternalistic (as can many government interventions). That is, behavioral economics reveals that people's behaviors and actions cannot be assumed to accurately reveal their preferences or reflect their conscious thinking about a decision. Thus, policy makers using behaviorally informed interventions are making decisions for people about what would be optimal for them. Thus, it is important to give close scrutiny to how the target of change is chosen and how certain policy makers are that the change will actually benefit the people who are induced to make it.

It is also important to consider how researchers and policy makers know that a particular outcome, which may appear to be desirable from a societal perspective, can be construed as beneficial to an individual, and that, in effect, manipulating a person to change their behavior is an unmitigated good (Liscow & Markovits, 2022). Another important question is whether people's attitudes about interventions affect their responses to them—that is, whether the perception that nudges and other behaviorally based interventions may be paternalistic might influence the way people respond when they recognize that they are the target of one. These issues may arise with any sort of incentive, but the possibility that some people may respond when they recognize behaviorally based strategies—such as an energy bill that compares one's energy use with that of one's neighbors—by determining to resist the desired behavior merits investigation.

Commercial Application of Behavioral Economics Knowledge

Ideas grounded in behavioral research are used in commercial contexts, usually to induce people to buy things. While it is not the job of behavioral economics researchers to police the applications of their ideas, they might profitably explore such understudied questions as how behavioral ideas are being used, how consumer responses may vary across business and policy domains, and when marketing that takes advantage of knowledge of biases crosses an ethical line.

All human decision making is influenced by the context in which those decisions are made. The influence of context on decisions often occurs in ways that consumers are aware of, through design, detectable nudges, and so on. But many factors have been shown to influence people's decisions in ways that they are often unaware of and cannot control; moreover, even hypothetical questions can influence people's subsequent decisions (Fitzsimons & Shiv, 2001).

Advertising, of course, is a hugely profitable and effective means of shaping preferences, often in ways consumers are unaware of and unable to avoid. In a study offering loans to low-income borrowers, various features of the offer letter that had no economic implications were found to have a large effect on take-up. There is compelling evidence that television advertising influences children's food and beverage preferences, requests, and consumption habits. One study found that a majority of Australian children ages 9–10 believed that Ronald McDonald knew best what children should eat (Olfman, 2005). Another study found that the number of hours of television watched by children ages 3–8 correlated with their caloric intake and their requests for—and their parents' subsequent purchases of—foods they see on television (Taras et al., 1989). These peripheral and undetected effects on people's decision behavior have been observed among novices and experts, in situations of intentional manipulation, in cases where people are not aware of the manipulation, and sometimes when the manipulating factors are altered without any human involvement.

Although researchers in the field of behavioral industrial organization, in particular, have examined some of these questions, there are no straightforward rules or answers (for a review, see, e.g., Heidhues & Kőszegi, 2018). It is important that researchers and those who apply and use research keep these questions in mind when making decisions, including in the design of research studies and selection of study populations. Empirical investigation of how behavioral economics findings are used by both public and private entities to influence consumer attitudes and behaviors could contribute to public policy thinking about the possibility of using regulatory mechanisms to limit actions that cross ethical boundaries.

Recommendation 14-6: Funders and university leaders should foster the development and application of behavioral economics by supporting training opportunities for public policy professionals. They should also support learning about practices for research transparency.

The successful development and implementation of policies that incorporate knowledge from behavioral economics depend in part on people who have been trained in behavioral principles and understand their application in policy making. Many policy schools are now including coursework on behavioral public policy; further progress in this area will be valuable for the field and for policy makers.

CONCLUDING OBSERVATION

We close with a few reflections on the future of behavioral economics. As ongoing questions about whether research discussed in this report is more properly regarded as a domain of economics or a domain of behavioral science suggest, the field's boundaries are not precise. From the committee's perspective, this was less important than the benefits behaviorally based approaches can bring in the development of policy. It is also perhaps a reason to think about future aspirations for application of these ideas, however they are categorized.

Most of the research we identified investigated ways in which behavioral biases interfere with a desired policy outcome and how behaviorally based interventions counteract those biases. This analysis can be applied beyond the context of the individual behaviors that are the focus of most behavioral economics research to help explain nonrational responses to complex regulatory structures, for example. That is, there may be behavioral solutions to problems that are not primarily the result of individual behavioral biases, such as the externalities that are such important considerations in combating climate change.

Thus, it is important not only to consider a broader range of solutions to behavioral biases but also to consider applying behavioral solutions even when there is no clear problem of cognitive bias. It is likely that ideas not explicitly identified as coming from behavioral economics research, but that nevertheless take advantage of behavioral insights, have already influenced the development of policy. All of these are reasons to be optimistic about the future contributions of the field.

REFERENCES

Blumenthal-Barby, J. S., & Burroughs, H. (2012). Seeking better health care outcomes: The ethics of using the "nudge." *The American Journal of Bioethics*, 12(2), 1–10. https://doi.org/10.1080/15265161.2011.634481

Compton, J. (2013). Inoculation theory. *The SAGE handbook of persuasion: Developments in theory and practice*, 2, 220–237. Sage.

Fitzsimons, G. J., & Shiv, B. (2001). Nonconscious and contaminative effects of hypothetical questions on subsequent decision making. *Journal of Consumer Research*, 28(2), 224–238.

Heidhues, P., & Kőszegi, B. (2018). Behavioral industrial organization. *Handbook of behavioral economics: Applications and foundations*, 1, 517–612. Elsevier. https://doi.org/10.1016/bs.hesbe.2018.07.006

Kozyreva, A., Lewandowsky, S., & Hertwig, R. (2020). Citizens versus the internet: Confronting digital challenges with cognitive tools. *Psychological Science in the Public Interest*, 21(3), 103–156. https://doi.org/10.1177/1529100620946707

Lin, Y., Osman, M., & Ashcroft, R. (2017). Nudge: Concept, effectiveness, and ethics. *Basic and Applied Social Psychology*, 39(6), 293–306. https://doi.org/10.1080/01973533.2017.1356304

Liscow, Z. D., & Markovits, D. (2022). Democratizing behavioral economics. *Yale Journal on Regulation*. SSRN. https://dx.doi.org/10.2139/ssrn.4012996

Lunze, K., & Paasche-Orlow, M. K. (2013). Financial incentives for healthy behavior: Ethical safeguards for behavioral economics. *American Journal of Preventive Medicine*, 44(6), 659–665. https://doi.org/10.1016/j.amepre.2013.01.035

Mitchell, A., Gottfried, J., Stocking, G., Walker, M., & Fedeli, S. (2019). *Many Americans say made-up news is a critical problem that needs to be fixed*. Pew Research Center. https://policycommons.net/artifacts/616783/many-americans-say-made-up-news-is-a-critical-problem-that-needs-to-be-fixed/1597473/

National Academies of Sciences, Engineering, and Medicine. (2018). *Getting to zero alcohol-impaired driving fatalities: A comprehensive approach to a persistent problem*. The National Academies Press. https://doi.org/10.17226/24951

———. (2020). *A national strategy to reduce food waste at the consumer level*. The National Academies Press. https://nap.nationalacademies.org/read/25876/chapter/13#262

———. (2021). *Assessment of technologies for improving light-duty vehicle fuel economy—2025-2035*. The National Academies Press. https://nap.nationalacademies.org/read/26092/chapter/13#312

Olfman, S. (2005). *Childhood lost: How American culture is failing our kids*. Greenwood Publishing Group.

Patton, C. V., Sawicki, D. S., & Clark, J. J. (2012). *Basic methods of policy analysis and planning*. Routledge. https://doi.org/10.4324/9781315664736

Pennycook, G., & Rand, D. G. (2021). The psychology of fake news. *Trends in Cognitive Sciences*, *25*(5), 388–402. https://doi.org/10.1016/j.tics.2021.02.007

Roozenbeek, J., Van Der Linden, S., Goldberg, B., Rathje, S., & Lewandowsky, S. (2022). Psychological inoculation improves resilience against misinformation on social media. *Science Advances*, *8*(34), eabo6254. https://doi.org/10.1126/sciadv.abo6254

Taras, H. L., Sallis, J. F., Patterson, T. L., Nader, P. R., & Nelson, J. A. (1989). Television's influence on children's diet and physical activity. *Journal of Developmental & Behavioral Pediatrics*, *10*(4), 176–180.

van der Linden, S. (2022). Misinformation: Susceptibility, spread, and interventions to immunize the public. *Nature Medicine*, *28*(3), 460–467. https://doi.org/10.1038/s41591-022-01713-6

Woolley, S. C. (2020). Bots and computational propaganda: Automation for communication and control. Social media and democracy. *The state of the field, prospects for reform* 89–110. Cambridge University Press.

Appendix

Biographical Sketches of Committee Members

ALISON M. BUTTENHEIM (*Co-Chair*) is a professor of nursing and health policy at the University of Pennsylvania. She is also the scientific director of the University of Pennsylvania's Center for Health Incentives and Behavioral Economics, as well as the behavioral design lead for Indlela, an HIV-focused nudge unit based in South Africa. As a leading expert in the application of behavioral economics to disease prevention, her research agenda has focused on vaccine acceptance and vaccine exemption policy in the United States, zoonotic disease prevention in Peru, and HIV prevention. She received her Ph.D. in public health from the University of California, Los Angeles.

ROBERT A. MOFFITT (NAS, *Co-Chair*) is the Krieger-Eisenhower Professor of Economics at Johns Hopkins University and holds a joint appointment with the Johns Hopkins Bloomberg School of Public Health. He is a fellow of the Econometric Society, a fellow of the Society of Labor Economists, a member of the National Academy of Sciences, a recipient of a MERIT Award from the National Institutes of Health, a recipient of a Guggenheim Fellowship, and a fellow of the American Academy of Arts and Sciences. He is known for his research on social policy, welfare programs, poverty, family structure, labor markets, income volatility, and applied statistical methods. He is a former president of the Population Association of America and president of the Society of Labor Economists. He was chief editor of the *American Economic Review*, coeditor of the *Review of Economics and Statistics*, and chief editor of the *Journal of Human Resources*. He received his Ph.D. in economics from Brown University.

STEFANO DELLAVIGNA is the Daniel E. Koshland, Sr. Distinguished Professor of Economics and professor of business administration at the University of California, Berkeley. He is a fellow of the American Academy of Arts and Sciences and of the Econometric Society, an Alfred P. Sloan fellow, and a Distinguished Teaching Award winner. He specializes in behavioral economics and has published in international journals such as the *American Economic Review*, the *Journal of Political Economy*, and the *Quarterly Journal of Economics*. He has been a co-editor of the *American Economic Review* since 2017. His recent work has focused on the ability of experts to forecast research results, the analysis of gender differences in editorial choices and academic honors, and the impact of nudges and bottlenecks in behavioral policy experiments. He received his Ph.D. in economics from Harvard University.

CATHERINE C. ECKEL is Sara and John Lindsey Professor and university distinguished professor in the Department of Economics at Texas A&M University, where she directs the behavioral economics and policy program. She is past president of the Economic Science Association and Southern Economic Association. She served as a National Science Foundation program director, was co-editor of the *Journal of Economic Behavior and Organization*, and served on the editorial boards of 12 journals. She received the Carolyn Shaw Bell Award, given by the American Economic Association, Committee on the Status of Women in the Economics Profession, for developing and participating in mentoring programs for women faculty. As an economist specializing in behavioral and experimental research, her contributions span many topics, including financial decision making; altruism and charitable fundraising; preferences and behavior of the urban poor; coordination of counter-terrorism policy; gender differences; racial/ethnic identity; and academic achievement. She received her Ph.D. in economics from the University of Virginia.

ANGELA FONTES is an independent consultant focused on household finance and investor decision-making research, with a specific focus on the financial well-being of African American and Hispanic/Latino families. She is the current president of the American Council on Consumer Interests, and on the Board of Directors at the Northwest Center. She is the principal investigator on several projects, including work with the Securities and Exchange Commission to conduct investor protection research and NORC's ongoing collaboration with the FINRA Investor Education Foundation. Her research can be found in journals such as the *Hispanic Journal of Behavioral Sciences*, the *Journal of the American Medical Association*, the *Journal of Family and Economic Issues*, the *Journal of Women, Politics, and Policy*, and *Financial Counseling and Planning*. Formerly, she was vice president of the Behavioral and Economic Analysis and Decision-making practice area at NORC at the University of Chicago and worked in business and market research consulting with Chamberlain Research Consultants and Leo Burnett. She is adjunct faculty at Northwestern University where she teaches graduate courses in behavioral economics and public policy, policy analysis, predictive analytics, and research writing. She received her Ph.D. in consumer behavior and family economics with a minor in sociology from the University of Wisconsin-Madison.

JOSHUA S. GRAFF ZIVIN is a professor of economics at the University of California, San Diego (UCSD), where he holds faculty positions in the School of Global Policy & Strategy and the Department of Economics. He is also the director of the Center on Global Transformation and a research associate at the National Bureau of Economic Research. Prior to joining UCSD, he was an associate professor of economics in the Mailman School of Public Health and the School of International and Public Affairs at Columbia University, where he served as the director of the Ph.D. program in sustainable development. He has published numerous articles on a wide range of topics in top economic, policy, and medical journals. His research interests are broad and include the areas of environmental, health, development, and innovation economics. Policy relevance serves as a guiding force behind all of this work. He received his Ph.D. in agricultural and resource economics from the University of California, Berkeley.

RACHEL E. KRANTON (NAS) is the James B. Duke Professor of Economics at Duke University and is currently serving as dean of social sciences in Duke's Trinity College of Arts & Sciences. She studies how institutions and the social setting affect economic outcomes. She develops theories of networks and has introduced identity into economic thinking. Her research contributes to many fields including microeconomics, economic development, and industrial organization. She is a member of the National Academy of Sciences, the American Academy of Arts and Sciences, a fellow of the Econometric Society, and was awarded a Chaire Blaise Pascal. She is launching, along with collaborators, a new research network, Economic Research on Identity, Norms, and Narratives. She received her Ph.D. in economics at the University of California, Berkeley.

LEONARD M. LOPOO is the Paul Volcker Chair in Behavioral Economics at the Maxwell School of Citizenship and Public Affairs at Syracuse University. He is also the co-founder and director of the Maxwell X Lab, a research lab that collaborates with public sector partners to develop and evaluate behavioral interventions. He has served on the Population Sciences Subcommittee of the Eunice Kennedy Shriver National Institute of Child

Health and Human Development and is an elected fellow of the National Academy of Public Administration. He studies the efficacy of behavioral interventions designed to increase program enrollment and reduce costs in public service delivery. His other primary branch of research asks if social policies, such as the Temporary Assistance for Needy Families program, the Supplemental Nutrition Assistance Program, and the Medicaid program, impact family formation decisions. He received his Ph.D. in public policy studies from the University of Chicago.

ELDAR SHAFIR is Class of 1987 Professor of Behavioral Science and Public Policy at Princeton University; director of Princeton's Kahneman-Treisman Center for Behavioral Science and Public Policy; scientific director at ideas42, a not-for-profit social science R&D lab; and visiting professor at Oxford University. His research focuses on cognitive science and behavioral economics, with a particular interest in the application of behavioral research to policy. He is past president of the Society for Judgment and Decision Making, a Guggenheim fellow, and an elected member of the American Academy of Arts and Sciences. He served as a member of President Barack Obama's Advisory Council on Financial Capability and was named one of Foreign Policy Magazine's 100 Leading Global Thinkers in 2013. He edited *The Behavioral Foundations of Public Policy* (2012), and co-authored *Scarcity: Why Having Too Little Means So Much* (2013). He received his Ph.D. from the Massachusetts Institute of Technology.

STACEY SINCLAIR[1] is a professor of psychology and public affairs at Princeton University. She has published numerous scholarly articles on the psychology of intergroup relations in outlets such as *Proceedings of the National Academy of Sciences of the United States of America*, *Journal of Personality and Social Psychology*, *Psychological Science*, and *Policy Insights from the Behavioral and Brain Sciences*. She is a fellow at the Society for the Psychological Study of Social Issues, the American Psychological Association, the Society for Personality and Social Psychology, and the Association for Psychological Science. Her research examines how inter-group and within-group interpersonal interactions serve as a vehicle by which prejudice and stereotypes are perpetuated, as well as how such interactions can reduce prejudice. Her lab is currently focused on how these factors shape the health and intellectual performance of members of stigmatized groups. She received her Ph.D. in social psychology from the University of California, Los Angeles.

---

[1] Committee Member until May 3, 2022

JENNIFER S. TRUEBLOOD is the Ruth N. Halls Professor of Psychological and Brain Sciences and Cognitive Science at Indiana University Bloomington and former president of the Society for Mathematical Psychology. Her research takes a joint experimental and computational modeling approach to study human judgment, decision making, and reasoning. She studies how people make decisions when faced with multiple, complex alternatives and options involving different risks and rewards. To address these questions, she develops probabilistic and dynamic models that can explain behavior and uses hierarchical Bayesian methods for data analysis and model-based inference. Her research contributions in decision making, psychology, and computational modeling have been recognized by the William K. Estes Early Career Award from the Society for Mathematical Psychology, the Early Career Award from the Psychonomic Society, an Alfred P. Sloan Foundation Research Fellowship for early-career researchers, the Early Investigator Award from the Society of Experimental Psychologists, and the Janet Taylor Spence Award from the Association for Psychological Science. She received her Ph.D. in cognitive science from Indiana University Bloomington.

PETER A. UBEL (NAM)[2] is the Madge and Dennis T. McLawhorn University Professor of Business, Public Policy, and Medicine at Duke University. A physician and a behavioral scientist, he uses the tools of decision psychology and behavioral economics to explore topics like informed consent, shared decision making, and health care cost containment. He has authored over 300 academic publications, the majority of which involve empirical explorations of decision psychology as it pertains to health care. He has also written for the *New York Times*, the *Los Angeles Times*, the *Atlantic*, and the *New Yorker*, and is a regular contributor at *Forbes*. His books include *Pricing Life* (MIT Press, 2000), *Free Market Madness* (Harvard Business Press, 2009) *Critical Decisions* (HarperCollins, 2012), and *Sick to Debt* (Yale University Press, 2019). He received his M.D. from the University of Minnesota, Rochester.

KEVIN G. VOLPP (NAM) is the Mark V. Pauly Presidential Distinguished Professor at the Perelman School of Medicine and the Wharton School, and director of Penn Center for Health Incentives and Behavioral Economics (CHIBE) at the University of Pennsylvania. At CHIBE, he leads many important experimental tests of new applications to behavioral economics to improve health and health care. He has published more than 300 papers and has expertise in secondary data and experimental measures as well as

---

[2]Committee Member until May 31, 2022

extensive experience working with public and private sector organizations on the creation and evaluation of new programs. Programs based on his team's research have led to health-promoting programs in place that affect tens of millions of Americans. He has won career achievement awards from the National Institutes of Health for his work in social and behavioral sciences, from the Society of General Internal Medicine, and from the Association for Translational Research. He is a member of the National Academy of Medicine. He received his Ph.D. in health economics and M.D from the University of Pennsylvania.